With Rifle and Shovel:
The 51st Pioneer Infantry Regiment in WWI

Margaret M. McMahon, Ph.D.

Other Books by Margaret M, McMahon, Ph.D.:

A Week of Genealogy: Things to Know and Do Online and Offline

A Weekend of Genealogy: Things to Know and Do Online and Offline

Researching Your U.S. WWI Army Ancestors

For information contact: 51stPioneers.com

On the cover: 51st Pioneer Infantry Regiment Flag, courtesy of COL Michael J. Stenzel, Bn Cdr 210th Armor March 1992 - September 1993, Historian 210th Armor Association.

ISBN-13: 978-1984347909
ISBN-10: 198434790X

Dedicated to the Men of the 51st Pioneer Infantry Regiment
Especially PVT 1CL Joseph Francis McMahon, Company B
May their service in the Great War always be remembered

Contents

INTRODUCTION

My Paternal Grandfather died when my Dad was a young boy. We had no stories, no pictures, and no history of his service. I began this effort to find out what he did in the Great War. What I ended up doing was being able to learn about a whole year of his life, getting to know where he traveled, what he did, what he saw. All this was done with military records, official histories, diaries, letters and images from the time.

The starting place for this journey was the New York State Archives website, which offered brief abstracts of New Yorkers' WWI military service (series B0808: Abstracts of World War I military service, 1917-1919). At that time, the abstracts were not available on Ancestry.com, but for a minimal fee I could order a photocopy of a Service Summary Abstract. I used the New York State Archives War Service Records Search Request form on their website to order photocopies of the WWI summary service cards for both of my Grandfathers. Now these records are available online at Ancestry.com, and the scanned digital images are in color. New York and other states had created these abstracts from the federal records of the soldiers' service. Since many of those original records were destroyed in the 1973 fire at the National Personnel Records Center (NPRC), these abstracts are invaluable for researching a soldier. That abstract was the basis for a timeline about my Grandfather's war service.

Next, I contacted the NPRC. I received a phone call from an archivist, to confirm that I received the record for the correct soldier. The archivist gave me an address, and it was where my Father was born. Although my Grandfather's records had been burned in the fire of 1973, the NPRC was able to provide a substitute record for him to verify his service: his Final Pay Voucher.

The U.S. Army Heritage and Education Center (USAHEC) offered a lecture about researching at their facility. One Saturday morning, I packed up my family and we drove to the lecture. Even my young son was captured by the lecture topic and the lecturer. He also enjoyed going through the exhibits on the Army Heritage Trail. Armed with the papers I had collected about my Grandfather, including the knowledge that he was in the "51 Pion Inf", I stopped at the research facility after the lecture. The person on duty did not recognize this military organization, so my next mission was to figure out what a "Pion Inf" was. It was, of course, an abbreviation for "Pioneer Infantry". That knowledge began to unlock the history of the remarkable men in these regiments.

I conducted a good deal of online research about the pioneer infantry. The Camp Wadsworth website was very informative (http://www.schistory.net/campwadsworth).

The New York State Military Museum and Veterans Research Center was also very helpful. Due to staff limitations, all requests needed to be mailed to them. In my research request, I clearly listed what I had already amassed about my Grandfather's service. They recommended the book "Three Quarters of a Century with the Tenth Infantry New York Guard, 1860-1935" by Clarence S. Martin. Chapter X covers World War I. That chapter gave me more information to add to the timeline I had made for my Grandfather, by including events from the history of the 51st Pioneer Infantry, which was formed from the NY Tenth Regiment Infantry. This chapter provided more information to add to the timeline for the whole 51st Pioneer Infantry, and more specifically, for my Grandfather's company.

Another book about the general history of the Pioneer Infantry that was recommended to me was "Pershing's Pioneers" by Moses N. Thisted. This book gives a good background about the Pioneer Infantry, and the history of the 1st Pioneer Infantry.

The research trips to NARA II in College Park over the past years have proved extremely productive. Record Groups (RG) 120 and 165 provided much helpful information. On those trips, I handled papers from a century ago, typed by the soldiers I was researching. At the end of each day, it was interesting to think the dirt on my hands was the same dirt that fell on their typewriters and paper as they made their way through the war and back again. That dirt connected me to them across a century.

The staff at the USAHEC was very helpful in checking my search methodology and use of their finding aids, offering suggestions and helping me to arrange a visit. There is tutorial on my website that shows the steps to finding material that the USAHEC holds about the 51st Pioneer Infantry (https://aweekofgenealogy.com/tutorials). There was a diary from SGT John Mansfield, who was the First Sergeant of Company B, the same company in which my Grandfather had served. There were also several of the newspapers that the 51st Pioneer Infantry Regiment published during the Army of Occupation.

My whole family made another working trip to the USAHEC to view the diary and the newspapers. The newspapers were full of news items about their time in Germany, included small items about events and company news about individuals. There were many articles focusing on when the soldiers would be returning home. Although I examined them all, my Grandfather did not make the news. The same History of the of the 51st Pioneer Infantry that was found in RG165 was serialized in the newspapers. SGT Mansfield's diary told a personal and amazing story. It would be the closest thing to hearing what my Grandfather did during the conflict. It contained the sights he saw and the experiences he had.

Last summer, our family made a longer working trip. We went to St. Louis, MO, for a visit to the NPRC over several days. The whole family was part of viewing and recording the Morning Reports for the 51st Pioneer Infantry, and the rosters for Company B. As we advanced the filmstrips and watched the screen, the story of the war from the perspective of each company unfolded. The manpower, the movements and the rations told the details of moving troops across an ocean and through France and Germany. Photographing from a screen proved a bit challenging, and a huge stack of photocopies accompanied us for the rest of our trip.

We continued west to the World War I Museum in Kansas City, MO. An admission to the Museum is for two days, so that you have time to see it all. We were educated by the interpretative exhibits, and inspired by the old and new parts of the Museum. We learned so much! We enjoyed authentic doughboy foods at the Over There Café, and spent time with an archivist downstairs in the Edward Jones Research Center.

Visiting with the Maryland WWI Centennial Commission folks and attending one of their meetings was energizing. Communicating with other WWI historians and family researchers has made this project exciting and relevant.

We made one more trip to the USAHEC to see the other diaries, photos and ephemera collections from other members of the 51st Pioneer Infantry. Our trip plans were complicated by a government shutdown, but the archivists were very flexible in rescheduling our visit.

This book is the result of many trips to archives and museums around the U.S. and countless hours piecing together the story of the 51st Pioneer Infantry Regiment (PIR). During all these research trips, and all the hours more spent in books, and more books, on the internet, and communicating with World War I historians, the story emerged of a group of men who physically worked their way through the war, even while shells and bullets rained down on them. Along the way, I wrote "Researching Your U.S. WWI Army Ancestors", based on the methodology I used and the sources I found in my research. That book was a resource to me while I was working on this one.

As with all my books, my goal was to write the book that I wish had been available when I wanted to learn about the 51st PIR. It contains background about all the Pioneer Infantry Regiments. The book tells the story of the 51st Pioneers from training to France and its battlefields, then back home. A timeline of the 51st Pioneers in training and service in France has been constructed from available official memos. There are brief biographical notes about some notable members of the 51st Pioneer Infantry. There is a list of the fallen members of the regiment, and information about the causes of their death and whether or not their remains were brought home to the United States. There is an alphabetic roster of the whole regiment, combined from multiple sources. Finally, some of the more personal histories from the men of the 51st Pioneers is given.

The men of the 51st Pioneer Infantry were mostly draftees. They did not ask to become members of the Pioneer Infantry. While other soldiers fought with rifles, they used shovels. They also saw combat. As shells went off around them, the pioneers filled the holes with rubble collected from destroyed villages. Those roads were the battlefield lifeline, allowing troops and supplies to move forward, while ambulances took the wounded back to hospitals. Personal records from Company G and Company H report that they were gassed, but there has been no mention of this in the historical records I have located to date.

They cleared the roads that had been booby-trapped by the retreating German Army. They marched long distances during the night to hide from the enemy. After the Armistice, they marched into Germany to be part of the Army of Occupation. The Pioneer Infantry provided labor where ever and when ever needed, including guarding railways and bridges, and burying the dead.

This book combines information found in numerous archives and a variety of other sources. The material has been blended into a whole new product that tells the story of the 51st Pioneer Infantry Regiment. It is intended to be both a narrative and a reference for those researching this Regiment.

Spelling and grammatical errors appear in the original documents. While some minor errors have been corrected in this book, some location names appear as they were spelled in the original documents.

THE PIONEER INFANTRY

The Pioneer Infantry were similar to regular army troops in that they were trained in infantry tactics, but they were also trained in combat engineering. There had been pioneer soldiers in the French, English and Indian armies. The word "pionnier" in French has been used for foot soldier.

The Pioneer Infantry Regiments were non-divisional, regimental troops. These troops were not to be permanently part of any division, but would be attached to armies or corps on an as-needed basis. They were designated as either Corps or Army troops.

Moses Thisted Collection, USAHEC.

An unknown Pioneer Infantry Officer described the Pioneer Infantry troops as: "They did everything the Infantry was too proud to do, and the Engineers too lazy to do."

COL Joseph L. Gilbreth described the Pioneer Infantry in the 51st Pioneer Infantry Regiment Newspaper. The following was transcribed by the author, with slight spelling errors corrected:

PIONEER INFANTRY DEFINED

The question of the Pioneer Infantry has been brought up for heated discussion on more than one occasion and there are many who are still in doubt as to the proper definitions of this branch of the service. For the benefit of those who have asked the question from time to time we decided to place it before an authority on the subject of military tactics. Colonel Gilbreth was chosen as the man who could best answer it. His reply to the question; "Who and what, are the Pioneer Infantry" is herewith published. The Colonel has covered the question very carefully in its entirety and his remarks are a source of great satisfaction.

1. The designation of Pioneer Infantry signifies the general scope of our arm of the service. In the first place Infantry is the backbone of the Army. The only reason for existence of any of the other armies is, that their relative importance depends entirely upon the degree, that they assist the Infantry to fulfil its missions.
2. The word Pioneer signifies path-finder or marker of the way. From this it would be easily inferred that Pioneer Infantry is that arm of the service that marks and prepares the way, so as to help the Infantry win battles.
3. How can it best do this work? First, by preparing roads, bridges, and supply routes for arms, ammunition, provisions and personnel, both to and from the front line of the battle. Second, they prepare the foreground for the attack and by accompanying the moppers-up to remove mines, and other obstacles.
4. They are not expected to be so highly trained for technical work as Engineers, but should be trained to do all the semi-technical work on the lines of communication, and up to and even beyond our most advanced elements of the fighting troops. They build temporary roads, railroads, bridges, trenches and all kinds of shelter both in active operations and in rest areas. They make demolitions and destroy enemy obstacles so as to prepare the ground for the advance of our attacking troops. Our best authorities do not place upon the Pioneer troops duties that can be done by unskilled labor, such as are done by carrying parties and simple fatigue duties.
5. Pioneer Infantry are not primarily fighting troops, but are trained as Infantry, simply in so far as to be able to protect their working parties. In general terms the Pioneer Infantry, is that arm of the service that smooths and paves the way, so that troops and supplies may reach the front-line trenches. They also open up the way for the advance of troops moving forward to the attack.
   J. L. Gilbreth
   Colonel, 51st Pioneer Inf

American Expeditionary Force Organization

The organization of the American Expeditionary Force had Armies at the top of the organization. Each Army was made up of several Corps. Each Corps was composed of multiple Divisions, which each contained several Regiments. A Regiment had a number of Battalions within it. Battalions held Companies, which in turn can be divided into several Platoons.

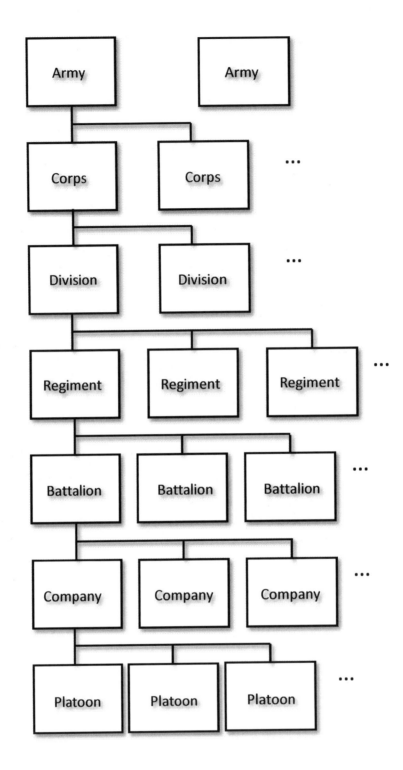

Organization of the American Expeditionary Forces.

The Pioneer Infantry Regiments were organized as non-divisional troops. They were designated as either Corps or Army troops. Army troops would be under the control of an Army, and Corps troops would be under the control of a Corps. The 51st Pioneer Infantry Regiment were designated as Corps Troops.

Pioneer Infantry Officers had collar insignia with the letter "P" superimposed over two crossed rifles, the number of the regiment above the "P" and the letter of the company below.

The Structure of the 51st Pioneer Infantry Regiment

The Regimental Headquarters of the 51st Pioneer Infantry Regiment consisted of the Colonel, Captains and a 1st Lieutenant. Colonel J. Guy Deming led the 51st Pioneer Infantry from the beginning of their organization until 13 December 1918. At that time, Lieutenant Colonel Saulpaugh was in command of the regiment. On 26 January 1919 Colonel Joseph L. Gilbreth took command.

There was a Headquarters Company, a Supply Company and a Medical Detachment. There were three Battalions, each with a major and a 1st LT, overseeing 4 companies. Each of the 12 Companies, identified by the letters A through M (excluding J), was led by a Captain. In each company, there were two or three 1st Lieutenants, and between one and three 2nd Lieutenants. Every company had a First Sergeant, who was the only one in the company to receive 2nd Class Accommodations on the larger ships traveling to and from France. Every Company also had a Supply Sergeant, a Mess Sergeant, Mechanics, Cooks, Sergeants, Corporals, Privates First-Class and Privates.

At maximum strength, the Headquarters Company of a Pioneer Infantry Regiment would have 253 troops: (1) Captain; (1) 1st Lieutenant; (3) 2nd Lieutenants; (5) Special Sergeants: (2) Color, (1) Mess, (1) Supply, (1) Stable; (13) Sergeants; (6) Specialists: (4) Cooks, (1) Horseshoer, (1) Mechanic; (48) Privates, 1st Class; (91) Privates; (49) Band members of all grades. For animals, there would be: (26) Horses for riding. For transportation, there would be: (16) Cycles: (14) Bicycles, (2) Motorcycles with sidecars. There would also be (1) Motor Car. For weapons the company would have: (66) Pistols and (187) Rifles.

Additionally, the Headquarters Company had the Regimental Sergeant Major. It also had the Band Leader, Assistant Band Leader, the Band Sergeant Major, Band Sergeant, Band Corporal, and First-, Second- and Third- Class Musicians. It had the Color Sergeant. It had an Orderly Sergeant and a Stable Sergeant.

The Supply Company had the Ordnance Sergeant, and Supply Sergeant for the Regiment. A Stable Sergeant, Wagoner, Horseshoer, and Saddler were among the ranks in the Supply company. The Supply Company would have carts, kitchens and wagons. The Mules would be used for draft and were part of the Supply Company.

Inspection of Mules. 1918, NARA, 165-WW-280A-027

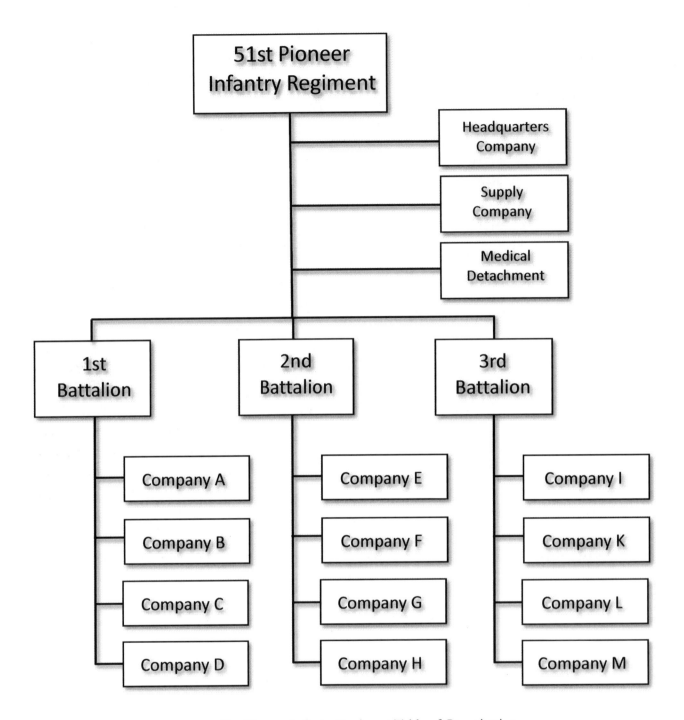

51st Pioneer Infantry Regiment Table of Organization.

Ranks

Enlisted men had ranks of Private and Private 1st Class (11th Grade). In 1920, after WWI, the Private First Class rank would become Lance Corporal.

Noncommissioned officers were Corporals and Sergeants: Corporal (10th Grade), Sergeant (9th Grade), Company Supply Sergeant (8th Grade), Stable Sergeant (7th Grade), Mess Sergeant (6th Grade), First Sergeant (5th Grade), Color

Sergeant (4th Grade), Battalion Sergeant Major (3rd Grade), Regimental Supply Sergeant (2nd Grade), and Regimental Sergeant Major(1st Grade).

Commissioned officer ranks are: Second Lieutenant, First Lieutenant, Captain, Major, Lieutenant Colonel, Colonel, Brigadier-General (1 star), Major-General (2 star), Lieutenant-General (3 star), General (4 star).

Pioneer Infantry Regiments

The following information about all of the Pioneer Infantry Regiments includes when and where each was organized, their service in the U.S. and overseas, and their demobilization.

1st Pioneer Infantry Regiment. Regiment was organized in January 1918 in Camp Wadsworth, SC, from the 1st NY Infantry. They left Camp Wadsworth on 1 July 1918 with 3483 officers and men. During July of 1918 they were stationed at Camp Mills, NY, and the Port of Embarkation at Hoboken, NJ. They trained for 6 months and served overseas for 12 months from July 1918 to July 1919. They were stationed at Camp Stuart, VA, in July 1919. They were demobilized in July 1919 at Camp Zachary Taylor, KY. They were Corps troops.

2nd Pioneer Infantry Regiment. Regiment was organized in January 1918 in Camp Wadsworth, SC, from the 14th NY Infantry. They left Camp Wadsworth on 25 June 1918 with 3479 officers and men. During July 1918 they were stationed at Camp Stuart, VA, and the Port of Embarkation at Newport News, VA. They trained for 5 months and served overseas for 16 months from July 1918 to October 1919. They were demobilized in November 1919 at Camp Dix, NJ. They were Army troops.

3rd Pioneer Infantry Regiment. Regiment was organized in February 1918 in Camp Greene, NC, from the 5th Massachusetts Infantry. They arrived at Camp Wadsworth from Camp Greene on February 8, 1918 and left Camp Wadsworth on August 17th with 3553 officers and men. During July 1918 they were stationed at Camp Stuart, VA, and the Port of Embarkation at Newport News, VA. They trained for 6 months and served overseas for 11 months from August 1918 to July 1919. They were station at Camp Merritt, NJ, in July 1919. They were demobilized in July 1919 at Camp Dodge, IA. They were Army troops.

4th Pioneer Infantry Regiment. Regiment was organized in February 1918 in Camp Greene, NC, from the 6th Massachusetts Infantry. They arrived at Camp Wadsworth from Camp Greene on February 9, 1918, and left Camp Wadsworth on September 17-18th with 3531 officers and men. During September 1918 they were stationed at Camp Stuart, VA, and the Port of Embarkation at Newport News, VA. They trained for 7 months and served overseas for 5 months from September 1918 to February 1919. They were demobilized in February 1919 at Camp Hill, VA. They were Corps troops.

5th Pioneer Infantry Regiment. Regiment was organized in February 1918 in Camp Greene, NC, from the 8th Massachusetts Infantry. They arrived at Camp Wadsworth from Camp Greene on February 7, 1918. They trained for 11 months and never went overseas. They were demobilized at Camp Wadsworth in January of 1919. They were Corps troops.

6th Pioneer Infantry Regiment. Regiment was organized in October 1918 in Camp Sherman. They trained for 4 months and never went overseas and were demobilized at Camp Sherman in February of 1919. This was an all African-American Regiment. They were Corps troops.

7th – 50th Pioneer Infantry Regiments. Regiments were never organized.

51st Pioneer Infantry Regiment. Regiment was organized in January 1918 in Camp Wadsworth, SC, from the 10th NY Infantry. They left Camp Wadsworth on 17 July 1918 with 3545 with officers and men. During July of 1918 they were stationed at Camp Merritt, NJ, and the Port of Embarkation at Hoboken, NJ. They trained for 6 months and served overseas for 12 months from July 1918 to July 1919. They were stationed at Camp Mills, NY, in July 1919. They were demobilized in July 1919 at Camp Upton, NY. They were Corps troops.

52nd Pioneer Infantry Regiment. Regiment was organized in January 1918 in Camp Wadsworth, SC, from the 12th NY Infantry. During July of 1918 they were stationed at Camp Upton, NY, and in August 1918 at the Port of Embarkation at Hoboken, NJ. They trained for 7 months and served overseas for 8 months from August 1918 to April 1919. They were demobilized in April 1919 at Camp Dix, NJ. They were Corps troops.

53rd Pioneer Infantry Regiment. Regiment was organized in January 1918 in Camp Wadsworth, SC, from the 47th NY Infantry. They left Camp Wadsworth on 30 July 1918 with 3549 officers and men. During July of 1918 they were stationed at Camp Upton, NY, and in August 1918 at the Port of Embarkation at Hoboken, NJ. They trained for 7 months and served overseas for 9 months from August 1918 to May 1919. They were stationed at Camp Stuart, VA, in May 1919. They were demobilized in May 1919 at Camp Upton, NY. They were Corps troops.

54th Pioneer Infantry Regiment. Regiment was organized in January 1918 in Camp Wadsworth, SC, from the 71st NY Infantry. They left Camp Wadsworth on 20 Aug 1918 with 3551 officers and men. During August 1918 they were stationed at Camp Stuart, VA, and the Port of Embarkation at Newport News, VA. They trained for 7 months and served overseas for 10 months from August 1918 to June 1919. They were stationed at Camp Stuart, VA in June 1919. They were demobilized in July 1919 at Camp Grant, IL. They were Army troops.

55th Pioneer Infantry Regiment. Regiment was organized in January 1918 in Camp Wadsworth, SC, from the 74th NY Infantry. They left Camp Wadsworth on 3 Sep 1918 with 3548 officers and men. During September 1918 they were stationed at Camp Stuart, VA, and the Port of Embarkation at Newport News, VA. They trained for 8 months and served overseas for 5 months from September 1918 to February 1919. They were demobilized in February 1919 at Camp Hill, VA. They were Army troops.

56th Pioneer Infantry Regiment. Regiment was organized in February 1918 in Camp Greene, NC, from the 1st Heavy Maine Field Artillery. They arrived at Camp Wadsworth from Camp Greene on February 18, 1918. They left Camp Wadsworth on August 30th with 3550 officers and men. During September of 1918 they were stationed at Camp Merritt, NJ, and in August 1918 at the Port of Embarkation at Hoboken, NJ. They trained for 7 months and served overseas for 9 months from September 1918 to June 1919. They were stationed at Camp Stuart, VA, in June 1919. They were demobilized in July 1919 at Camp Dix, NJ. They were Army troops.

57th Pioneer Infantry Regiment. Regiment was organized in February 1918 in Camp Greene, NC, from the 1st Vermont Infantry. They arrived at Camp Wadsworth from Camp Greene on February 10, 1918, left Camp Wadsworth on September 23rd with 3430 officers and men. They trained for 7 months and served overseas for 5 months from September 1918 to February 1919. They were demobilized in Camp Devens, MA, in January 1919. They were Army troops.

58th Pioneer Infantry Regiment. Regiment was organized in February 1918 in Camp Green, NC, from the 1st Connecticut Infantry. They arrived at Camp Wadsworth on February 20, 1918, with 28 officers and 169 enlisted men. They trained for 11 months and never served overseas. They were demobilized at Camp Wadsworth, SC, in January 1919. They were Army troops.

59th Pioneer Infantry Regiment. Regiment was organized in January 1918 in Camp Dix, NJ. They trained at Camp Dix, NJ. In August 1918 they were stationed at the Port of Embarkation at Hoboken, NJ. They trained for 7 months served overseas for 11 months from August 1918 to July 1919. They were stationed at Camp Mills, NY in July of 1919. They were demobilized at Camp Mills, NY in July of 1919. They were Army troops.

60th Pioneer Infantry Regiment. Regiment was organized in July 1918 in Camp Wadsworth, SC. The 8th Pennsylvania National Guard Band became part of this regiment. They trained for 6 months and never served overseas. They were demobilized in January 1919 at Camp Wadsworth, SC.

61st Pioneer Infantry Regiment. Regiment was organized in July 1918 in Camp Wadsworth, SC. The 13th Pennsylvania National Guard Band became part of this regiment. They trained for 6 months and never served overseas. They were demobilized in January 1919 at Camp Wadsworth, SC.

62nd Pioneer Infantry Regiment. Regiment was organized in July 1918 in Camp Wadsworth, SC. The 5th Missouri National Guard Band became part of this regiment. They trained for 6 months and never served overseas. They were demobilized in January 1919 at Camp Wadsworth, SC.

63rd Pioneer Infantry Regiment. Regiment was organized in October 1918 in Camp Dix, NJ. They trained for 3 months and never served overseas. They were demobilized in January 1919 at Camp Dix, NJ. This was an all African-American Regiment.

64th Pioneer Infantry Regiment. Regiment was organized in October 1918 in Camp Zachary Taylor, KY. They trained for 4 months and never served overseas. They were demobilized in January of 1919 at Camp Zachary Taylor, KY. This was an all African-American Regiment.

65th Pioneer Infantry Regiment. Regiment was organized in October 1918 in Camp Funston, KS. They trained for 2 months and never served overseas. They were demobilized in December 1918 at Camp Funston, KS. This was an all African-American Regiment.

66th – 74th Pioneer Infantry Regiments. Regiments were authorized, but never organized.

75th – 800th Pioneer Infantry Regiments. Regiments were never organized.

801st Pioneer Infantry Regiment. Regiment was organized in June 1918 in Camp Zachary Taylor, KY. During September of 1918 they were stationed at Camp Merritt, NJ, and at the Port of Embarkation at Hoboken, NJ. They trained for 3 months and served overseas for 9 months from September 1918 to June 1919. They were demobilized in June 1919 at Camp Zachary Taylor, KY. This was an all African-American Regiment. They were Corps troops. They served as non-combatants in France at the end of the war.

802nd Pioneer Infantry Regiment. Regiment was organized in July 1918 in Camp Sherman, OH. During August 1918 they were stationed at Camp Mills, NY, and at the Port of Embarkation at Hoboken, NJ. They trained for 1 month and served overseas for 11 months from August 1918 to July 1919. This was an all African-American Regiment. They were stationed at Camp Mills, NY in July 1919. They were discharged at Camp Gordon, GA, in July 1919. They were Army troops.

803rd Pioneer Infantry Regiment. Regiment was organized in July 1918 in Camp Grant, IL. During September 1918 they were stationed at Camp Upton, NY, and at the Port of Embarkation at Hoboken, NJ. They trained for 2 months and served overseas for 10 months from September 1918 to July 1919. They were stationed at Newport News, VA, in July 1919. They were discharged at Camp Grant, IL, in July 1919. This was an all African-American Regiment. They were Army troops.

803rd Pioneer Infantry Battalion on the U.S.S. Philippine (troop ship), Brest, France, July 18, 1919 LOC 2010651618

804th Pioneer Infantry Regiment. Regiment was organized in July 1918 in Camp Dodge, IA. During August 1918 they were stationed at Upton, NY, and in September 1918 at the Port of Embarkation at Hoboken, NJ. They trained for 2 months and served overseas for 10 months from September 1918 to July 1919. They were stationed at Camp Mills, NY, in July 1919. They were discharged at Camp Gordon, GA, in July 1919. This was an all African-American Regiment. They were Corps troops.

805th Pioneer Infantry Regiment. Regiment was organized in June 1918 in Camp Funston, KS. During August 1918 they were stationed at Camp Upton, NY, and in September 1918 at the Port of Embarkation at Quebec. They trained for 3 months and served overseas for 9 months from September 1918 to June 1919. They were discharged at Camp Shelby, MS, in July 1919. This was an all African-American Regiment. They were Army troops. Their nickname was the "Bear Cats" Regiment. They served in France, seeing 39 days of combat. They claimed to have the best Jazz band and best baseball team in France, and best vaudeville show in the AEF.

806th Pioneer Infantry Regiment. Regiment was organized in July 1918 in Camp Funston, KS. During September 1918 they were stationed at Camp Mills, NY, and at the Port of Embarkation at Hoboken, NJ. They trained for 2 months and served overseas for 9 months from September 1918 to June 1919. They were stationed at Camp Upton, NY, in June 1919. They were discharged at Camp Shelby, MS, in July 1919. This was an all African-American Regiment. They were Army troops.

807th Pioneer Infantry Regiment. Regiment was organized in July 1918 in Camp Dix, NJ. During September 1918 they were stationed at the Port of Embarkation at Hoboken, NJ. They trained for 2 months and served overseas for 10 months from September 1918 to July 1919. They were stationed at Newport News, VA, in July 1919. They were discharged at Camp Jackson, SC, in July 1919. This was an all African-American Regiment. They were Army troops.

808th Pioneer Infantry Regiment. Regiment was organized in July 1918 in Camp Meade, MD. During August 1918 they were stationed at the Port of Embarkation at Hoboken, NJ. They trained for 1 month and served overseas for 10 months from August 1918 to June 1919. They were stationed at Camp Alexander, in June 1919. They were discharged at Camp Lee, VA, in June 1919. This was an all African-American Regiment. They were Army Corps troops.

809 Pioneer Infantry Regiment. Regiment was organized in August 1918 in Camp Dodge, IA. During September 1918 they were stationed at Camp Upton, NY, and at the Port of Embarkation at Hoboken, NJ. They trained for 1 month and served overseas for 10 months from September 1918 to July 1919. They were stationed at Camp Mills, NY, in July 1919. They were discharged at Camp Sherman, OH, in July 1919. This was an all African-American Regiment. They were Corps troops. They served as non-combatants in France at the end of the war.

810 Pioneer Infantry Regiment. Regiment was organized in September 1918 in Camp Greene, NC. They trained for 3 months and never served overseas. They were discharged at Camp Greene, NC, in December 1918. This was an all African-American Regiment.

811 Pioneer Infantry Regiment. Regiment was organized in August 1918 in Camp Dix, NJ. During October 1918 they were stationed at the Port of Embarkation at Hoboken, NJ. They trained for 2 months and served overseas for 9 months from October 1918 to July 1919. They were stationed at Camp Mills, NY, in July 1919. They were discharged at Camp Dix, NJ, in July 1919. This was an all African-American Regiment. They were Corps troops. They served as non-combatants in France at the end of the war.

812 Pioneer Infantry Regiment. Regiment was organized in August 1918 in Camp Grant, IL. In September 1918 they were stationed at Camp Merritt, NJ. They trained for 5 months and never served overseas. They were discharged at Camp Grant, IL, in January 1919. This was an all African-American Regiment.

813 Pioneer Infantry Regiment. Regiment was organized in August 1918 in Camp Sherman, OH. During September 1918 they were stationed at Camp Mills, NY, and at the Port of Embarkation at Hoboken, NJ. They trained for 1 month and served overseas for 10 months from September 1918 to July 1919. They were stationed at Camp Alexander, VA, in July 1919. They were discharged at Camp Dix, NJ, in July 1919. This was an all African-American Regiment. They were Army troops.

814th Pioneer Infantry Regiment. Regiment was organized in August 1918 in Camp Zachary Taylor, KY. During October 1918 they were stationed at Camp Upton and at the Port of Embarkation at Hoboken, NJ. They trained for 2 months and served overseas for 2 months from October 1918 to December 1918. They were stationed at Camp Mills, NY, in December 1918. They were discharged at Camp Zachary Taylor, KY, in December 1918. This was an all African-American Regiment. They were Corps troops. They were known as the "Black Devils". Chaplain Hayes Farish officiated The Inaugural regimental services of the "Black Devils", on Sunday, Sept. 29th, 1918, at Camp Zachary Taylor, Louisville, KY.

Inaugural regimental services of the "Black Devils", 814th Pioneer Infantry, Chaplain Hayes Farish officiating, Sunday, Sept. 29th, 1918, LOC 2007664404

815th Pioneer Infantry Regiment. Regiment was organized in September 1918 in Camp Funston, KS. During September 1918 they were stationed at Camp Merritt, NJ, and in October 1918 at the Port of Embarkation at Hoboken, NJ. They trained for 1 month and served overseas for 9 months from October 1918 to July 1919. They were stationed at -, in July 1919. They were discharged at Camp Stuart, TX, in July 1919. This was an all African-American Regiment. They were Army troops. They served as non-combatants in France at the end of the war.

816th Pioneer Infantry Regiment. Regiment was organized in September 1918 in Camp Funston, KS. During October 1918 they were stationed at Camp Upton, NY, and at the Port of Embarkation at Hoboken, NJ. They trained for 1 month and served overseas for 10 months from October 1918 to August 1919. They were stationed at Camp Alexander, VA, in August 1919. They were discharged at Camp Shelby, MS, in August 1919. This was an all African-American Regiment. They were Army troops. They served as non-combatants in France at the end of the war.

817th Pioneer Infantry Regiment. Regiment was authorized, but never organized. Notes located in RG 165 suggest that this would have been organized at Camp Greene, NC.

Sources

Sweeney, William Allison. "History of the American Negro in the Great War: His Splendid Record in the Battle Zones of Europe", 1919.

51st Pioneer Infantry Regiment Records, U.S. National Archives and Records Administration II, RG 165, Box 438, College Park, MD.

805th Pioneer Infantry, http://en.wikipedia.org/wiki/805th_Pioneer_Infantry, accessed 10 Dec 2017.

Gilbreth, COL Joseph L. "Pioneer Infantry Defined", 51st Pioneers (Newspaper), No. 1, 19 APR 1919, Cochem, Germany.

Kilner, Walter G. Kilner and Andrew J. MacElroy. "The Cantonment Manual: Or, Facts for Every Soldier", https://books.google.com/books/about/The_Cantonment_Manual.html?id=DNkYisuPXzcC, accessed 4 Jan 2018.

Paulsen, Valdemar. Edited by Major Lucius A. Hine, "U.S. Army Facts and Insignia", Rand , McNally & Company, Chicago & New York, 1918.

Personnel Replacement in the U.S. Army, U.S. Army Center of Military History, CMH_Pub_104-9.

Tent and Trench website, www.schistory.net/campwadsworth accessed 10 Aug 2017.

Thisted, COL Moses. "Pershing's Pioneers", Alphabet Printers, Hemet, CA, 1980.

Wadsworth Gas Attach and The Rio Grande Rattler, "Getting the New Pioneers Ready", 19 Jan 1918.

TRAINING

One of the challenges that faced the United States at the beginning of the World War was that there was not a large standing army. Draftees needed to be trained quickly. Training camps were rapidly established in the United States, with the plan to continue training troops after their arrival in Europe.

Several of the camps that were established in World War I would become permanent forts. Of those, some would retain the same name. For example. Camp Meade became Fort Meade. Other camps would change the original name. Camp A. A. Humphries founded during WWI would change its name to Fort Belvoir, to recognize the Belvoir Plantation upon which it was founded.

There were sixteen temporary training camps constructed across the United States as National Guard Camps: Camp McClellan, AL; Camp Kearney, CA; Camp Cody, NM; Camp Fremont, CA; Camp Greene, NC; Camp Hancock, GA; Camp MacArthur, TX; Camp Wadsworth, SC; Camp Wheeler, GA; Camp Logan, TX; Camp Sevier, SC; Camp Sheridan, AL; Camp Doniphan, OK; Camp Beauregard, LA; Camp Shelby, Miss; and Camp Bowie, TX.

Cantonment were more permanent encampment for troops.

The cantonments for the National Army troops were: Camp Lewis, WA; Camp Funston, KS; Camp Custer, MI; Camp Devens, MA; Camp Dix, NJ; Camp Dodge, IA; Camp Gordon, GA; Camp Grant, IL; Camp Jackson, SC; Camp Lee, VA; Camp Meade, MD; Camp Pike, AR; Camp Sherman, OH; Camp Travis, TX; Camp Taylor, KY; Camp Upton, NY.

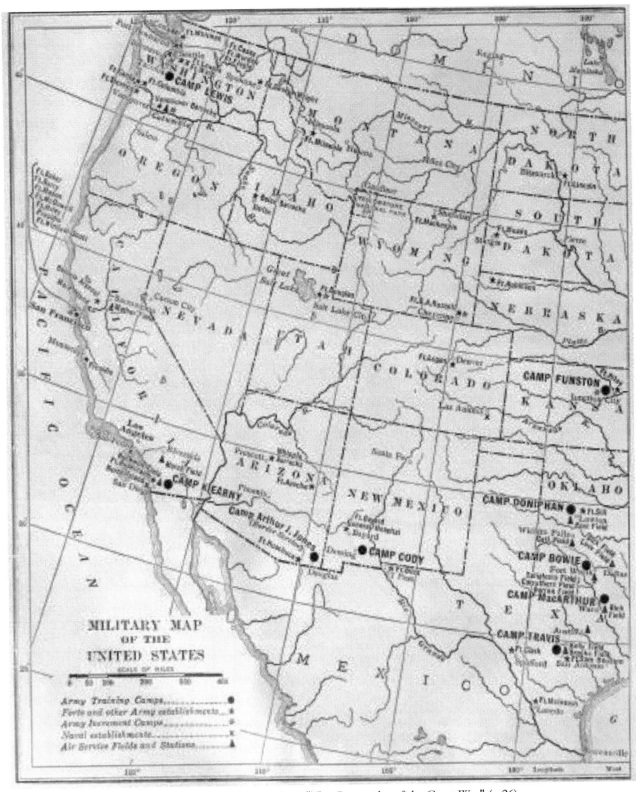

Military Map of United States from "The Geography of the Great War" (p 26).

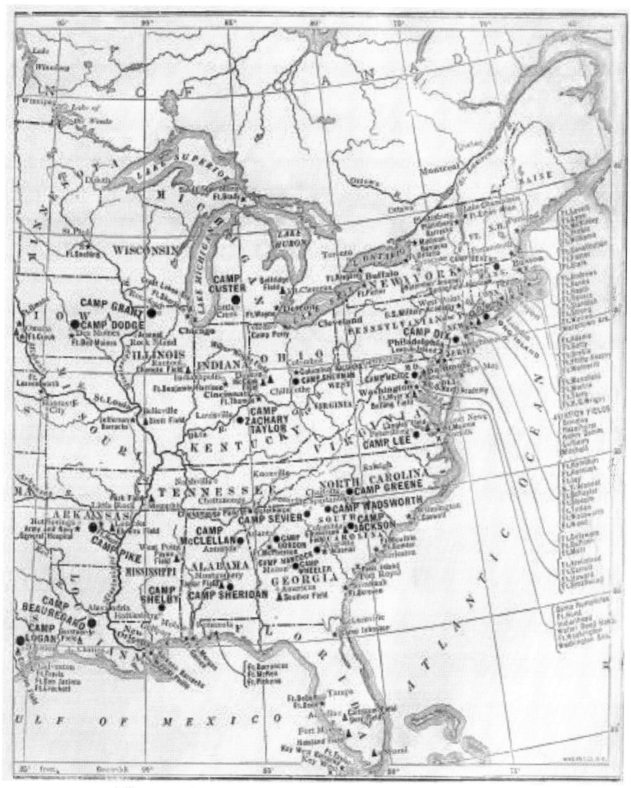

Military Map of United States, from "The Geography of the Great War" (p 27).

SITE	ORGANIZATION	TROOPS FROM—	CAMP	SITE	ORGANIZATION	TROOPS FROM—	CAMP
Ayer, Mass.	76th Division.	Maine, New Hampshire, Vermont, Massachusetts, Rhode Island, and Connecticut.	Devens	Spartanburg, S.C.	27th (old 6) Division.	New York.	Wadsworth
Yaphank, Long Island, N. Y.	77th Division.	Metropolitan portion of New York.	Upton	Augusta, Ga.	28th (old 7) Division.	Pennsylvania.	Hancock
Wrightstown, N.J.	78th Division.	Remainder of New York and Northern Pennsylvania.	Dix	Anniston, Ala.	29th (old 8) Division.	New Jersey, Virginia, Maryland, Delaware, and District of Columbia.	McClellan
Annapolis Junction, Md.	79th Division.	Southern Pennsylvania.	Meade	Greenville, S. C.	30th (old 9) Division.	Tennessee, North Carolina, and South Carolina.	Sevier
Petersburg, Va.	80th Division.	New Jersey, Virginia, Maryland, Delaware, and District of Columbia.	Lee	Macon, Ga.	31st (old 10) Division.	Georgia, Alabama, and Florida.	Wheeler
Columbia, S. C.	81st Division.	Tennessee, North Carolina, South Carolina, and Florida.	Jackson	Waco, Tex.	32d (old 11) Division.	Michigan and Wisconsin.	MacArthur
Atlanta, Ga.	82d Division.	Georgia and Alabama.	Gordon	Houston, Tex.	32d (old 12) Division.	Illinois.	Logan
Chillicothe, Ohio.	83d Division.	Ohio and West Virginia.	Sherman	Deming, N. Mex.	34th (old 13) Division.	Minnesota, Iowa, Nebraska, North Dakota, and South Dakota.	Cody
Louisville, Ky.	84th Division.	Indiana and Kentucky.	Taylor	Fort Sill, Okla.	35th (old 14) Division.	Missouri and Kansas.	Doniphan
Battle Creek, Mich.	85th Division.	Michigan and Wisconsin.	Custer	Fort Worth, Tex.	36th (old 15) Division.	Texas and Oklahoma.	Bowie
Rockford, Ill.	86th Division.	Illinois.	Grant	Montgomery, Ala.	37th (old 16) Division.	Ohio and West Virginia.	Sheridan.
Little Rock, Ark.	87th Division.	Arkansas, Louisiana, and Mississippi.	Pike	Hattiesburg, Miss.	38th (old 17) Division.	Indiana and Kentucky.	Shelby
Des Moines, Iowa.	88th Division.	Minnesota, Iowa, Nebraska, North Dakota, and South Dakota.	Dodge	Alexandria, La.	39th (old 18) Division	Louisiana, Mississippi, and Arkansas.	Beauregard
Fort Riley, Kan.	89th Division.	Kansas, Missouri, and Colorado.	Funston	Linda Vista, Cal.	40th (old 19) Division.	California, Nevada, Utah, Colorado, Arizona, and New Mexico.	Kearny
Fort Sam Houston, Tex.	90th Division.	Texas, Arizona, New Mexico, and Oklahoma.	Travis	Palo Alto, Cal.	41st (old 20) Division.	Washington, Oregon, Montana, Idaho, and Wyoming.	Fremont
American Lake, Wash.	91st Division.	Washington, Oregon, California, Nevada, Utah, Idaho, Montana, and Wyoming.	Lewis	Garden City, L. I., N. Y.	42d Division.	Most of the Middle and far Western States.	Mills
Charlotte, N. C.	26th (old 5) Division.	Maine, New Hampshire, Vermont, Massachusetts, Rhode Island, and Connecticut.	Greene				

National Army Cantonments from The United States in the Great War

Federalizing the State Guard Troops

The 51st Pioneer Infantry Regiment was formed from the 10th Infantry of the New York National Guard

All the companies of the 10th Infantry of the New York National Guard were mustered into federal service between 16 July and 22 July 1917. (SGT Mansfield recorded 15 July 1917 in his journal.) On 5 August 1917, the National Guard was officially drafted into the armed forces of the United States. The 10th New York National Guard, under the command of Colonel John F. Kline, was assembled at Camp Wadsworth, S. C.

Training at Camp Wadsworth

The 51st Pioneer Infantry Regiment trained at Camp Wadsworth, SC, until their departure in July 1919.

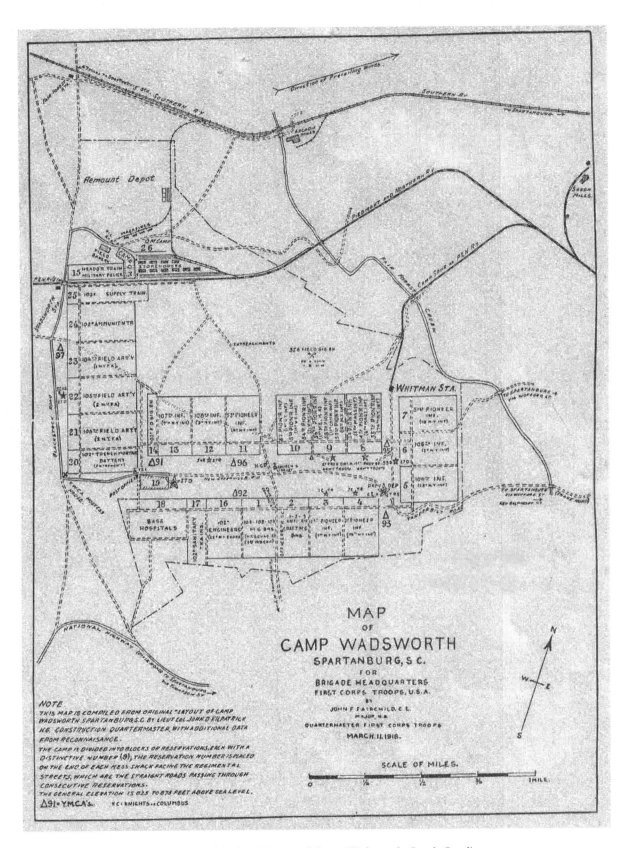

27th Division's 1918 map of Camp Wadsworth, South Carolina.

During their time at Camp Wadsworth they were training in both infantry and engineering subjects. This included marching and training in hand grenades and trench warfare. These photos show training and life at Camp Wadsworth.

An Army Messenger, Camp Wadsworth, SC, NARA, 165-WW-285A-011.

Infantry Drill, Camp Wadsworth, SC, NARA, 165-WW-147A-43.

Over the Top, Camp Wadsworth, Spartanburg, SC, NARA, 165-ww-146C-011.

Bridge Building, Camp Wadsworth, SC, NARA, 165-ww-144A-017.

Machine Gun Practice, Camp Wadsworth, SC, NARA, 165-WW-140F-012.

Troops on a Practice March. Camp Wadsworth, SC, NARA, 165-ww-152A-028.

Hand Grenade Practice, Camp Wadsworth, SC, NARA, 165-ww-149B-013.

Men and Horses Crawling Through Ditches and Tall Grass, Camp Wadsworth, SC, NARA, 165-WW-153B-10.

Hand Grenade Practice, Camp Wadsworth, SC, September 1917, NARA, 165-ww-149B-042.

Cleaning Up Camp, Camp Wadsworth, Spartanburg, SC, NARA, 165-WW-145A-2.

Hand Grenade Throwing, Camp Wadsworth, 1918, NARA, 165-ww-149B-026.

Scene at Camp Wadsworth, 1918, NARA, 165-WW-530B-050.

Trench Drill, Camp Wadsworth, S.C. 1918, NARA, 165-WW-151A-096.

New York Guardsmen Have Camouflaged Tank in Camp, 1918, NARA, 165-WW-70A-012.
"This camouflaged tank is one of the many instruments of war that are being used to help New York's Guardsmen at Camp Wadsworth train for the fighting "Over There"."

Sources

Abbot, Willis John. "The United States in the Great War". Leslie-Judge Co., New York, 1920.

American Unofficial Collection of World War I Photographs. U.S. National Archives and Records Administration II, RG 165: Records of the War Department General and Special Staffs, 1860 -1952, College Park, MD.

McMurry, Frank M. "The Geography of the Great War". The MacMillan Company, New York, 1918.

Lerwil, Leonard L. "The Personnel Replacement in the United States Army", CMH_Pub_104-9, August 1954.

TO FRANCE

During World War I, American Soldiers traveled overseas to Europe from ports in New York City, New Jersey, and Virginia. The U.S. Army used transport ships that were passenger liners, German ships seized at the beginning of the war, and ships borrowed from other Allied countries.

U.S. ships were painted with camouflage patterns in grey, black and blue. These were called dazzle ships. Since the targeting systems during the Great War were visual, the geometric shapes painted on the ships were effective at distorting a ship's silhouette and making it harder for the enemy to estimate a ship's type, size, speed, and heading.

On the morning of 29 June 1918, the 51st Pioneer Infantry left Camp Merritt, NJ, and marched to Alpine Landing to begin embarkation on the S. S. Kroonland at Pier #5 in Hoboken, NJ. From there, the soldiers were placed on ferries.

A ferry boat, New York, Library of Congress Prints and Photographs Division
LC-D4-13397

U.S.S. Kroonland

Photo courtesy of U.S. Navy, photo NH 52093, Source: Naval History & Heritage Command (NHHC).

Then they boarded the steamer U.S.S. Kroonland. The Kroonland brought troops to France six times. She also made postwar trips, then was returned to International Mercantile Marine Company.

The embarkation started at 10:00 A.M. and finished at 1:30 P.M. The ship sailed for Brest, France, at 3:30 P.M. There were 3245 troops on board, including all of the 51st Pioneer Infantry except Company A.

The journal of Gordon Van Kleeck, then a private in Company F of the U.S. 51st Pioneer Infantry, includes the story of their crossing. According to Gordon Van Kleeck, the Cincinnati was the ferry he boarded. During the passage, the soldiers wore overalls rather than uniforms, and sat in the lifeboats during the early morning until sunrise in case there was a submarine attack. Corp Van Kleeck's journal is included later in this book.

After leaving New York Harbor, the Kroonland traveled south until it met the other transports off the Norfolk Capes. The convoy of five transports, a cruiser and two destroyers then turned east.

On 8 Aug 1918 the U.S.S. Kroonland arrived in Brest, France, in the rain. While the Kroonland sailed past St. Mathieu lighthouse through LeGoulet Channel into Bay of Brest, French and British airplanes flew low looking for submarines. Several lighter-than-air blimp ships flew low in front of the convoy. Brest was the location of the American Naval Headquarters in France. More than 30 destroyers and multiple yachts escorted troop and supply convoys were based at Brest.

An airship escorts a convoy into Brest Harbor in 1918.
Photo courtesy of U.S. Navy photo NH 121616. Source: Naval History & Heritage Command (NHHC)

Landing at Brest, France, 8 August 1919.
Photo courtesy of U.S. Navy photo NH 965. Source: Naval History & Heritage Command (NHHC)

On 9 August 1918 Company A traveled to France on the S. S. Rochambeau. The S.S. Rochambeau was a French Transatlantic ocean liner, sailing regularly between Bordeaux and New York City. The boarding of all of the 537 troops, including Company A, began at 6:10 A.M. at Pier No. 57 in New York, NY, and finished at 9:10 A.M. The ship sailed at 2:05 P.M. Among the other troops traveling on the Rochambeau that trip was a detachment of cooking instructors from the Quarter Masters Corp.

Below, the S.S. Rochambeau is shown carrying troops from the 102nd Engineers (old 22nd N.Y.N.G.), of the 27th Division are shown returning to New York.

S.S. Rochambeau Photo courtesy of U.S. Navy photo NH 119248. Source: Naval History & Heritage Command (NHHC)

TIMELINE

This chapter contains a timeline that was compiled from organizational memos found at NARA II, and in the histories listed in the sources. The author transcribed, condensed and combined the material.

The National Defense Act of 1916 called for the Regular Army to be increased to 20 divisions (1 – 20), the 17 National Guard divisions to be brought up to strength and federalized (26 - 42), and that the National Army would have additional divisions (75 and up).

Like other men who boarded trains to travel to their training destination, the men drafted into 51st Pioneer Infantry men would have been given arm bands (brassards) by their local draft boards. The arm bands constituted a uniform and officially drafted them into service before they boarded the trains rather than draft them at a cantonment. This change was made to prevent issues with conduct on the trains.

Since the majority of troops going to Europe embarked at ports in New York Harbor, two embarkation camps to each hold 40,000 men were built in 1917. Camp Merritt in Tenafly, NJ, was one; the other was Camp Mills on Long Island, NY. Camp Upton, also on Long Island, would later support 20,000 men. Limited duty service men, who formed a subset of the 10.58% of those rejected by the draft board, would be trained there to fill administrative roles, allowing qualified men to be assigned to fighting units. Partially trained men from units that were already organized would be organized at the embarkation ports into casual companies of about 50 men, to serve as replacements. Due to a concern about the losses that might occur for specific communities, replacements for organizations with a local character, such as the 51st Pioneer Infantry, would not be drawn from the same region.

2.000 men were transferred from the 7th, 36th and 81st combat divisions to the First Army for the St. Mihiel Offensive. Some replacements found themselves in the front lines 5 or 6 days after their arrival at a French port. 24 hours after General Pershing's First Army launched the St. Mihiel Offensive, the salient that the Germans had fortified and occupied for four years had been pinched off.

The 51st Pioneer Infantry Regiment trained at Camp Wadsworth, in Spartanburg, SC. Overseas, traveled through France to participate in operations. They were assigned to Corps Engineers, 4th Army Corps, of the American Expeditionary Force. The 51st, as well as the 1st, Pioneer Infantry Regiments served as Corps Engineer support with the 4th Corps. They were initially under the tactical control of the 32nd French Corps. They served with the First Army Sep 1918, and served with IV and VI Army Corps Sep-Nov 1918. After the Armistice they worked on roads, as well as guarding trains and bridges. During the Army of Occupation, they would serve with the Third Army.

The story of the 51st Pioneer Infantry Regiment has its roots in the 10th Regiment Infantry, New York National Guard (NYNG), that was called up at the commencement of war in 1917. There were separate Companies of the old 10th New York Infantry Regiment throughout New York State.

The 10th NY Infantry guarded locations in New York State and Pennsylvania, before making their way to Camp Wadsworth Spartanburg, SC. They were ordered to mobilize and guard the water supply of New York. The regiment established its headquarters at New Paltz.

Squad of Men of 10th Regt Infantry, NYNG., guard roads and structures in NY State, April 1917, NARA, 165-WW-275D-026

Federalizing the 10th Infantry of the New York National Guard

The 51st Pioneer Infantry Regiment was formed from the 10th Infantry of the New York National Guard. All the companies of the 10th Infantry of the New York National Guard were mustered into federal service between 16 July and 22 July 1917. On 5 August 1917, the National Guard was officially drafted into the armed forces of the United States.

The regimental office was established in New Paltz, NY. The Regimental Headquarters Company, Supply Company and the First Battalion left Albany on 7 Feb 1917. The Regimental Headquarters Company, Supply Company and the Hospital Detachment were based at New Paltz, NY. On 15 July 1917, they were mustered into Federal Service. On 11 Aug 1917, they boarded a train for Washington, DC, but enroute they received orders to divert to Camp Meade, MD. In October, they were ordered to Camp Wadsworth, SC.

Company B was mustered into Federal Service on 15 July 1917. Company G was mustered into Federal service 21 July 1917 at Yonkers; it was drafted into Federal service on 5 August 1917. Company K was mustered into Federal service 20 July 1917, at Poughkeepsie, NY and was drafted into Federal service 5 August 1917. Company M. was mustered into Federal service 20 July 1917, at Kingston, and drafted into Federal service 5 August 1917. Company M was Demobilized 12 July 1919 at Camp Upton, New York.

The 28th Infantry Division Band Reorganized and on 14 August 1916 was redesignated as the Band Section, Provisional Headquarters Company, 13th Infantry Regiment. They mustered into Federal service 26 September 1916 at

Mount Gretna, PA. On 5 July 1918 they were redesignated as the Band Section, Headquarters Company, 51st Pioneer Infantry. They were Demobilized 8 January 1919 at Camp Wadsworth, SC.

During a harsh winter at Camp Wadsworth, the 10th NYNG was redesignated the 51st Pioneer Infantry. All but a skeleton of officers was stripped from the organization, and the numbers were built up in the Spring of 1918 with draftees.

Becoming the 51st Pioneer Infantry Regiment

On 4 Jan 1918 General Order (G.O.) 1 from Headquarters of the Provisional Depot for Corps and Army Troops at Camp Wadsworth, under the command of Brig. Gen. Guy V. Carleton issued this order:

> "In G. O. 1 emanating from its Headquarters Jan. 4th, 1918, and treating of certain transfers not of interest in this history, paragraph 2 contains the following statement:

> "2.   When these transfers have been effected, the infantry, regiments will be organized and trained as Pioneer Inf. The 1st N. Y. Inf. Will hereafter be designated as the 1st Pioneer Inf., the 14th N. Y. Inf. as the 2nd Pioneer Inf., the 10th N. Y. as the 51st Pioneer Inf.
>
> (c)   The 51st and 52nd Pioneer Infantry with the 3rd Anti-Aircraft Machine Gun Battalion attached will constitute a command designated as the 1st Provisional Brigade, Army Troops."

This marked the beginning of the 51st Pioneer Infantry.

6 April 1917. U.S. declares war on Germany.

5 June 1917. First Draft Registration.

9 July 1917. President Wilson formally drafts the National Guard into Federal service, with the draft to become effective on 5 August 1917.

20 July 1917. First lottery (drawing for the draft)

5 August 1917. The National Guard was officially drafted into the armed forces of the United States.

The 10th New York National Guard, under the command of Colonel John F. Kline was assembled at Camp Wadsworth, SC.

4 Jan 1918. The 10th Infantry NYNG was redesignated as 51st Pioneer. The 51st and 52nd Pioneer Infantry with the 3rd Anti-Aircraft Machine Gun Battalion attached will constitute a command designated as the 1st Provisional Brigade, Army Troops. The Pioneer Infantry Regiments were not part of any Division; they would be attached to an Army or a Corps. The 51st Pioneer Infantry Regiment was formed as a unit to be attached when needed to an American Corps.

14 Jan 1918. Col J Guy Deming from Ohio National Guard put in charge of 51st PIR. The 51st Pioneer Infantry was composed of 39 officers and 904 enlisted men after reorganization. It was filled to wartime strength with draftees.

17 May 1918. The first draft contingent arrived at Camp Wadsworth, SC. There were intense drills: digging trenches; road and bridge repair and building; infantry drill. They were busy from morning to late at night.

27 July 1918. The 51st PIR entrained for Camp Merritt, NJ, with 3545 officers and men.

29 July 1918. The 51st PIR left Camp Merritt, NJ, and marched to Alpine Landing. There jammed onto ferries, such as the Cincinnati, to Hoboken, NJ, then put aboard confiscated German steamer "Kroonland". All of the regiment except Company A sailed on the Kroonland. The 51st Pioneer Infantry traveled in C-208 2nd Phase. Crossing the Atlantic was uneventful.

In France

8 Aug 1918. U.S.S. Kroonland arrives Brest, France in the rain. (It rained the day they left 300/365 days in 1918.) British and French destroyers surrounded the troop ship as they approached the French coast, and several lighter-than-air blimp ships flew low in front of the convoy. French and British airplanes flew low looking for submarines. Their ship sailed past the St. Mathieu lighthouse through the LeGoulet Channel into Bay of Brest

9 Aug 1918. At noon they disembarked from the Kroonland, and marched from the docks to the city on a ramp-like roadway to a hearty welcome. They stayed at Pontanezan Barracks which were built by Napoleon when he was using Brest as his base for an attack on Britain. They marched from the docks to the city on a ramp-like roadway, and had a warm welcome.

11 Aug 1918. The approximate strength of the regiment was 88 officers and 2970 soldiers.

14 Aug 1918. The 51st Pioneer Infantry Regiment (U.S.) was under orders to move by rail from Brest to Toul and is placed at the disposal of the 32d French Army Corps for the time being. It was planned to arrive at Is-sur-Tille on 16th next and would be forwarded to its destination without delay.

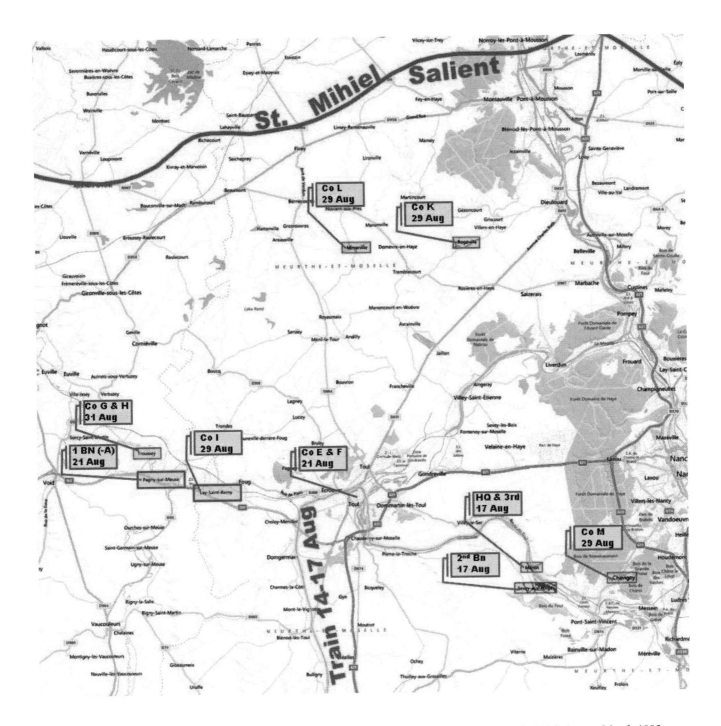

51st Pioneer Infantry Regiment Initial Stationing, courtesy of COL Michael J. Stenzel, Bn Cdr 210th Armor March 1992 - September 1993, Historian 210th Armor Association.

17 Aug 1918. The 51st PIR was due at about 4:00 A.M. They would detrain at MARON and billet at MARON and SEXCY-au-FORGES. The accommodations for billeting: Maron 50 officers; 1500 men; 125 animals; Sexcy 25 officers; 1200 men; 200 animals. Part of CHALIGNY was also available for overflow, if necessary, not to exceed 200 or 300 men.

19 Aug 1918. Regiment assigned to IV Army Corps. Placed under tactical control 32nd French Corps.

28 Aug 1918. The Headquarters of the Fourth Army directed that the Headquarters 2d Battalion and Companies "G" and "H" of the 51st Pioneer Infantry be moved from AUX FOURGES to TROUSSEY by night marches. All possible precautions would be taken while on the march and after arrival of troops at TROUSSEY to avoid hostile serial observation. Columns of troops can appear only between 8:00 P.M. and 4:30 A.M.

September Report from Regiment Headquarters: 2nd Bn [Battalion] detached and attached 6th Army Sept 12/18, Men wounded Sept 12 in woods near Beaumont St Mihiel Salient

8 Sep 1918. The following are the locations of the Organizations of this Regiment:

Bautzen Barracks (Toul) was the location of: Headquarters Co., Supply Co., Co. A, Co. B, Co. C, Co. G, Co. H, Co. I, Co. K , Co. L, and Co. M

Co. D was at Dongermain, France.

Co. E had 1 Platoon at Trondes, 1 Platoon at Ouvrage de la Cloche, 1 Platoon Ouvrage de la Bouvron, 1 Platoon Laneuveville, (Foug.).

Co. F had 1 Platoon Ouvrage de Franchville, ½ Platoon Ouvrage dur Ropage, ½ Platoon (west) de Vieux Canton, ½ Platoon (east) de Vieux Canton, ½ Platoon Ouvrage du Mordant

Company F and C each had ½ Platoon Villey St. Etienne.

("Ouvrage" is French for "work".)

8 -14 Sep 1918. At times during these dates, two companies from 51st Pion Infantry were attached to the 1st Division, preceding and during the St. Mihiel Operation.

12-16 Sep 1918. St. Mihiel Offensive, France.

The Place Des Halls (Market Square), St. Mihiel, LOC, 2016646031.

The town square of St. Mihiel, France, LOC, 2007663856.

Thiacourt, in the St. Mihiel Salient, which fell before American onslaught, Sept. 12-13, 1918, LOC, 2007663845.

Flirey, a front line town in the St. Mihiel Salient, where heavy fighting took place, LOC, 2007663866.

Limy, through which the American forces passed in cutting off the St. Mihiel Salient, 1918, LOC, 2007663841.

The town of Montsec, in the St. Mihiel Salient, LOC, 2007663877.

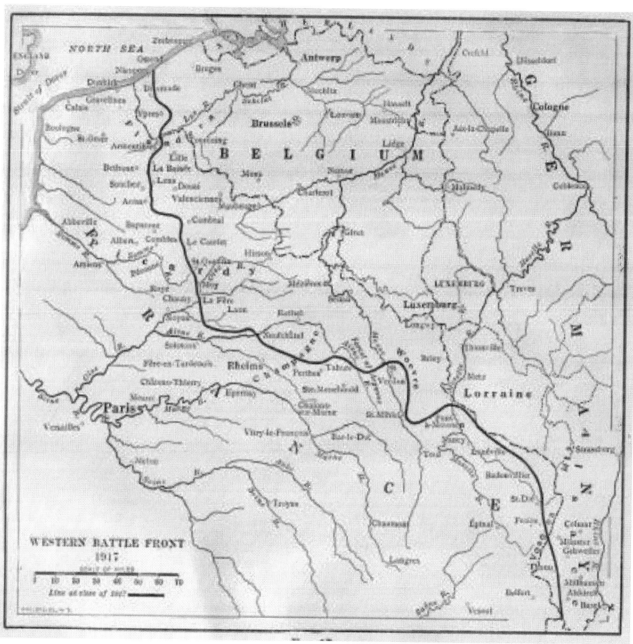

Map of Western Front from "The Geography of the Great War."

IV CORPS OPERATIONS 12 SEP 1918

51st Pioneer Infantry Regiment Initial Stationing, courtesy of COL Michael J. Stenzel, Bn Cdr 210th Armor March 1992 - September 1993, Historian 210th Armor Association

12 Sep 1918. Started to drive to St. Mihiel front.

12 Sep 1918. The 2nd Bn [Battalion] detached and attached 6th Army. Men were wounded in woods near Beaumont at St Mihiel Salient. They were between the advanced lines and artillery positions, tasked with repairing roads and bridges.

The Pioneers kept roads and bridges repaired and rebuilt. They were tasked with keeping the lines of communication open.

Trucks were filled with broken brick and stone from destroyed cities and villages. These trucks were prepositioned where enemy attacks were expected. As soon as a shell had exploded in a road, the crew came and repaired it.

14 Sep 1918. Companies B and D, under Captain Niles – ½ caught in barrage between Seicheprey and Richecourt – Corp. Slattery, Co. D, killed.

The History of the 301st Engineers included how part of the 51st Pioneer Infantry was used.

The 51st Pioneer Infantry, less two companies were 4th Army Corp troops used as engineers. They were made available to provide labor for engineering work. Two company were assigned to each of the three divisions in the line, and four companies to the corps.

One company of Engineers would be assisted by a company of Pioneer Infantry would be assigned to each of the three axial division roads. The three remaining companies and one company of Pioneer Infantry were assigned to work in the rear of the advancing Divisions. Their work was to improve communications, cut stakes, place materials, fill old trenches or road crossings, gather road materials from quarries, ruined villages and walls, and collect road planks from the dumps. There might be corduroying of roads and construction of bridges across trenches, gullies and streams. [Corduroying is make a road of logs that are laid down crosswise.]

The second battalion of the 51st Pioneers was attached to the 2nd Battalion, 315th Engineering, 90th Division, 6th Corps. Together they entered the ravine north of Faye-en-Haye, known as the "Valley of Death". The companies worked to make the Fey-en-Haye to Vilcey road wider so as to be capable of two-way traffic. The Pioneers were already at work when the 2nd Battalion arrived in the valley, keeping the roads from being unusable, during the time when it was under constant shell-fire and continued observation.

The 51st Pioneer were attached to the regiment with their 1st Battalion attached to the 1st Battalion of the 301st Engineers. The companies were located at Saint-Baussant, Xivray and Mont Sec. At all times their work was credible. Mont Sec was especially hard work, with the obstacles that the Germans had installed, such as barbed wire crossed back-and-forth across the road, the stakes used to hold it which destroyed the road, masonry and fallen trees. The road had also been damaged by shells and explosives.

17 Sep - 11 Nov, 1918. Toul Sector, France.

October Report from Regiment Headquarters: H.Q. changed from Bautzen Barracks Toul to Menil-le-Tour

10 Oct 1918. Headquarters Fourth Corps requested the names of 37 qualified soldiers from the regiment to attend Army Candidates School at LAVAL BONNE commencing 17 Oct 1918: for instruction in the Infantry section (by 12 Oct 1918)

13 Oct 1918. Company F of the 51st Pioneers was attached to the 2nd Battalion 301st Engineers and operated with those Companies D and F of the 301st Engineers, working on roads

14 Oct 1918. Headquarters Fourth Corps requests names eight Non-Commissioned Officers to attend Gas School 20 October 1918 (by 16 October)

21 Oct 1918. Company F of the 51st Pioneers accompanied the 2nd Battalion Companies D and F of the 301st Engineers to Puvenille Woods near Mamey. The 2nd Battalion was engaged in second-position wiring, and quartered in old French barracks. Each of the barracks held 60 men, and were cold and damp. The bunks were shared by rats that running around and squealing at night to protest that they had to share the barracks with soldiers.

23 Oct 1918. The Headquarters Fourth Army Corps sent a Memo to Commanding Officer, 51st Pioneer Infantry:

1. The Corps Commander directs me to inform you that this afternoon about four o'clock he observed working groups of the 51st Pioneer Infantry as follows: 1 group on the LIMEY-REMENAUVILLE road, just outside of REMENAUVILLE; one group in the town of REMENAUVILLE; 1 group on the road REMENAUVILLE-EUVEZIN, just outside of REMENAUVILLE.

2. Each of these groups was performing its work in a disinterested and lackadaisical manner.

3. A truck loaded with stone had stopped in the vicinity of the last mentioned group so near the center of the road as to block the road from traffic. The N.C.O. in charge of this group, when asked concerning the matter, stated that there was no room for the truck on the side and as a matter of fact there was at least 2 ½ feet of space on the right of the road that the truck might have utilized.

4. The Corps Commander directs that you give matters of this kind your attention, with a view of insuring competent supervision of working parties in order to produce the maximum result, impressing upon N.C.O.'s and men the necessity for maintaining a keener interest in the important labors that they are performing.

24 Oct 1918. After being delayed by road repair, Company F of the 51st Pioneers and the 2nd Battalion Companies D and F of the 301st Engineers were able to commence work on their second position. (They were assigned sections 107 to 111 inclusive.) Their camp was 4 kilometers south of Mamey in a camp located in the Bois de Puvenelle. Due to topography, going back and forth to the camp took four hours of the day, leaving only four and a half hours to work. Company F of the 51st Pioneers carried stakes and supported the erection of entanglements.

November Report from Regiment Headquarters: 51st PIR H.Q. changed from Menil-le-Tour to Aspelt

Prior to 10 Nov 1918. The 1st and 2nd Battalions of the 51st Pioneers worked on roads and assisted wiring parties of the regiment.

10 Nov 1918. The Battalions of the 51st Pioneers moved up with their corresponding Battalions of the 301st ready to work.

10 Nov 1918. At 0200, there was a field order to the 1st Battalion 301st Engineers and the 1st Battalion 51st Pioneer Infantry. The Fourth Corps was to advance on the front this date at 7 hours. The companies would move at the earliest possible moment, equipment and gas-masks and steel helmets. All transportation in the hands of your companies were to be moved to this point, carrying tools for road repair and bridge construction. Guards would be left with equipment at their current place. Motor transportation with extra tools and rations would be sent to the rendezvous point. Company C of the 51st Pioneer Infantry (with Company A of the 301st Engineers) will move to Woël. Company B of the 51st Pioneer Infantry (with Company B of the 301st Engineers) will move to Joinville. Company D of the 51st Pioneer Infantry will move to Xonville. The main circulation route on which work would commence immediately and en route to the above-named command posts is as follows: From south-to-north, Thiacourt-Xammes-Charey-Saint-Julien-Chambley-Puxiex-Tronville-Vionville-Mars-la-Tour. From north to south, Suzemont-Latourp-Joinville-Woël-Hattonville-via Bois-des Hundronville-Vigneulles. As soon as the companies have moved, an officer with a motorcycle would make reconnaissances of the roads included in the main circulation route, reporting as soon as possible to the regimental command post at the chateau in Saint-Benoit.

10 Nov 1918. Co A 51st PIR held at Post Command at Vigneulles for necessary contingent work. Co B 51st PIR move to command post at Joinville. Co C 51st PIR move to command post at Woel. Co D 51st PIR move to command post at Xonville.

11 Nov 1918. Upon the Armistice, the 1st and 2nd Battalions of the 51st Pioneers returned to the control of their regimental headquarters.

17 Nov 1918. The 51st Pioneer Infantry Regiment proceeded on the march of occupation.

17 Nov 1918. A field order from the 1st Battalion 301st Engineers at 1900 hours ordered the command to enter upon its forward march on 18 Nov 1918. It would proceed by road to Hannonville, Saulx, Riaville, Paroid, Saint-Jean, Mouaville to Fléville where it will billet for the night. The column will consist of the 1st Battalion, 301st Engineers and the 1st Battalion, 51st Pioneer Infantry. The order of march will be Company C 301st Engineers, Company A (which will join the column at Paroid), and Company B. The 1st Battalion, 51st Pioneer Infantry will follow. The 3rd Battalion, 51st Pioneer Infantry will follow from Hannonville. Company C will move out at 4 A.M. and would furnish the advance guard, the other units will proceed immediately afterward. The formation would in columns of squads, until otherwise ordered. The proper distance between platoons would be maintained, as also in the case of the vehicles. The rules of march discipline as set down in F.S.R. will be followed.

18 Nov 1918. The Regimental Headquarters and the 2nd Battalion of the 51st Pioneer Infantry Regiment reached Mouaville at dark. The road to La Marjolaine Farm was impassable, so they had to detour through Gondrecourt and to Fléville. The Companies arrived at 5:30 P.M. but some of the wagons did not arrive until 9:00 P.M.

18 Nov 1918. Companies I and K, 51st Pioneer Infantry to report to the Fourth Corps, for duty at refilling points (by verbal order of the Corps Commander).

20 Nov 1918. The 51st PIR was directed to detail 2 squads from the regiment to work for the Town Major (Capt. Harrington) at 4th Army Corps Headquarters. These men will be used for policing towns and building new Latrines as the Headquarters move from town to town. A truck would be sent to their Headquarters this afternoon to get this detail.

29 Nov 1918. The IV Corps Commander directed that the 1st Battalion, 51st Pioneer Infantry now at FILSDORF be sent on 30 Nov. 1918 to GOSTINGEN, via BOUS - LENNINGEN. Five (5) days rations will be taken. Upon arrival at destination, it will be reported for attachment to the 1st Division for the purpose of guarding structures and buildings along the railways of our line of communication.

The 51st PIR went through northern France via the Duchy of Luxembourg. They entered Germany by following the banks of the Moselle River. (First traveled the Rhine.) They passed through Lorraine, and northern France. They saw the destroyed cities and villages; the Germans shelled, the French shelled German-occupied places. There was no destruction in Luxembourg and Germany. The German people were welcoming.

December Report from Regiment Headquarters: 51st PIR H.Q. changed from Aspelt Luxembourg to Cochem Germany. Companies doing railway guard duty as prescribed by Commanding General 3rd Army.

Before Kochen. Col Deming was relieved, Lt. Col Saulspaugh took charge.

3 Dec 1918. The 51st Pioneer Infantry Regiment crossed the Moselle River into Germany. They followed the stream, and camped Wittlich Alf, Bollens, Caidens. The Medical Detachment crossed bridge into Germany at Gravenmacher, 11:05 AM

3 Dec 1918. The Headquarters Fourth Army Corps requested that Company "I", 51st Pioneer Infantry move from Berncastel to Kobern by rail.

3 Dec 1918. The Headquarters IV Corps directed that the portion of the regiment now under the 51st PIR control march to the town of RIEVENICH, on 4 December, 1918.

3 Dec 1918. The Headquarters 1st Battalion in Longuich, Germany reported that details from that Battalion were on duty at bridges, railroad stations and railroad bridges.

Bridges: over Saar at CONZ 1 N.C.O., 6 men from Company B; over Saar at WILTINGEN 1 N.C.O., 6 men from Company B; Over Moselle at GEVENMACHER 1 N.C.O., 6 men from Company B; over Moselle at WORMELDINGEN 1 N.C.O., 6 men from Company B; over Sauer at WASSERBILLIG 1 N.C.O., 6 men from Company C; over Moselle at SCHWEICH 1 N.C.O., 8 men from Company D;

Railroad Stations on the East Bank of Moselle: CONZ 1 N.C.O., 8 men from Company A; MERZLICH 1 N.C.O., 8 men from Company A; ST MATTHAIS 1 N.C.O., 8 men from Company A; Opposite to WORMWLDINGEN 1 N.C.O., 8 men from Company B; NITTEL 1 N.C.O., 8 men from Company B; WELLEN 1 N.C.O., 8 men from

Company B; TEMMELS 1 N.C.O., 8 men from Company B; OBERBILLI 1 N.C.O., 8 men from Company C; WASSERLIESCH 1 N.C.O., 8 men from Company C

Railroad Stations on the West Bank of Moselle: IGEL 1 N.C.O., 8 men from Company C, ZEWEN 1 N.C.O., 8 men from Company C; EUREN 1 N.C.O., 8 men from Company D; PALLIEN 1 N.C.O., 8 men from Company D; BIEWER 1 N.C.O., 8 men from Company D

In addition to the details mentioned above, the Commanding Officer of Co. "B" was ordered, without delay, to furnish details from the Company to Guard the Railroad Bridge: at PFALZEL 1 N.C.O., 8 men; at the Highway Bridge at MEHRING 1 N.C.O., 8 men; at the Bridge over Moselle at LONGUICH 1 N.C.O., 8 men; at the tunnels at QUINT 1 N.C.O., 8 men. Hdqrs Co. B. was located at No. 32 Matthias St, St Matthias.

The Commanding Officer of Co. "B" was also ordered to furnish details to Railroad Stations: EHRANG & RR Yds 1 N.C.O. & 18 men; QUINT 1 N.C.O. & 6 men; SCHVEICH 1 N.C.O. & 6 men; HETZERATH 1 N.C.O. & 6 men; SALMROHER 1 N.C.O. & 6 men; WITTLICH 1 N.C.O. & 6 men; WENGROHER & RR Yds 1 N.C.O. & 24 men.

The Commanding Officer of Company A was ordered to furnish without delay the following detail for guarding Railroad Stations: PLATTEN 1 N.C.O. & 6 men. (This detail reported to Company B, on the morning of December 4th, not later than 6 a.m., and was thereafter under the direction of the Commanding Officer, Company B.); LIESER 1 N.C.O. & 6 men; BERNCASTEL 1 N.C.O. & 12 men. (The last two named details remained under the jurisdiction of the Commanding Officer of Company A, for supplies, instructions and discipline).

The 51st PIR was ordered to proceed to the town of TRIER and establish Headquarters for the maintenance and administration of the details.

The Command Officers of Companies A, C, and D were each to furnish two Sergeants to the Commanding Officer of Co. "B" to report before 6 a.m., tomorrow, fully quipped and rationed for two days.

4 Dec 1918. The 51st PIR reported to the IV Army Corps that the 51st Pioneer Infantry Hdqrs., and Hdqrs. Co., Supply Co., 2nd Battalion and 3rd Battalion Hdqrs., are located tonight at FOHREN instead of RIEVENICH. This because the 1st Division Billeting Officer informed them that there was no room in RIEVENICH.

The following organizations located tonight at points indicated:

301st Engineers and Train at OLEWIG; 51st Pioneer Infantry, 1st Bn, less Co."B" at BEKOND; 51st Pioneer Infantry, Company "B" at ST. MATHIAS; and 51st Pioneer Infantry, Company "M" at QUINT.

4 Dec 1918.

From: Office of the Chief Engineer, Headquarters Fourth Army Corps

Permanent Railway Guards should be posted at Bridges and tunnels and at culverts of 10 foot or greater span. At long bridges, as in case of those over Moselle River, guards should be established at each end. Guards should similarly be placed at each end of tunnels, and arrangements should be made so that the entire section of the line assigned to each company is patrolled at least once during the day and once during the night.

The following tentative assignment of sections is given, subject to such readjustment as is found to be necessary.

SECTION 1 - Treves (exclusive) to Station N.W. of Schweich (inclusive). One company ½ at Biewer and 1/2 at Quint.

SECTION 2 - Station N.W. of Schweich (exclusive) to black road crossing north of Hetzerath. One company at Föhren.

SECTION 3 - Black road crossing north of Hetzerath to Neuenhof (inclusive). One company at Salinrohr

SECTION 4 – Neuenhof (exclusive) to Station S.W. of Kinderbeuren (inclusive). Line from Wittlich to Berncastel. One company at Wengerchl with detachment at Cues.

SECTION 5 – Station S.W. of Kinderbeuren (exclusive) to R.R. Junction north of Reil (inclusive) also line from R.R. junction to Traben. One company at Bengel with detachment at Traben.

SECTION 6 – R.R. Junction north of Reil (exclusive) to include south end of tunnel north of Eller. One company ½ at Alf or Bullay, ½ at Eller.

SECTION 7 – South end of tunnel north of Eller (exclusive) to Moselle (inclusive). One company at Cochern.

SECTION 8 – Moselle (exclusive) to Moselkern (inclusive). One company at Carden.

SECTION 9 – Moselkern (exclusive) to Lehmen (inclusive). One company at Hatzenoit.

SECTION 10 – Lehmen (exclusive) to Point opposite Lay. One company at Kobern.

SECTION 11 – Point opposite Lay to Coblenz. One company at Guls.

2. Details from Companies of your 1st Battalion placed on guard at R.R. stations and other structure should be relieved and directed to rejoin their companies when the new guards above outlined are established.

3. Companies selected for the several sections should be pushed ahead as rapidly as possible and take over the sections assigned as early as practicable after advance element of the first Division passes.

Relief of Details of 51st Pioneer Infantry Guarding Railroad Stations.

St. Matthias Detail relieved on December 4, 1918, by detail from 6th Infantry – Information furnished by Capt. Thomas, Co. B, 51st Pioneers.

Merzlich Corporal Hull and 8 men – no sick – Notified at 11:45 A.M. 12/5/18. Told Corp. Bull to go by train, if possible.

Conz Corporal Crannell and 8 men – no sick – 2 men with sore feet. Notified at 12:05 P.M. 12/5/18. Told Corp. Crannell to go by train if possible.

Wasserleisch Sgt. Grace and 8 men. One man slightly sick with dysentery. Notified at 1:30 P.M. Told Sgt. Grace to go by train if possible.

Oberbillig Corp. Burley and 8 men. This detail was sent for by Sergeant Grace. No sick. They will accompany Sgt. Grace's detail.

Temmels Corporal Stone and 8 men. No sick. Notified at 2:00 P.M. 12/5/18. Told Corporal Stone to go by train if possible.

Weller Corporal Applegate and 8 men. No sick. Notified at 2:20 P.M. 12/5/18. Told Corporal Applegate to go by train if possible.

Nittel Corporal Mullaney and 8 men. No sick. Notified at 2:50 P.M., 12/5/18. Told the Corporal to return by train if possible.

Wincheringen Corporal Buckley and 8 men. No sick. Notified at 3:20 P.M., 12/5/18. Told the Corporal to return by train, if possible.

Igel Corporal Whelan and 8 men. Corporal Whelan absent drawing rations so told Private Coakley. No sick. Notified at 5:15 P.M., 12/5/18. Told them to return either by train or marching.

Zewen Corporal Aldrich and 8 men. They have 4 days supply of rations on hand, and cannot march and carry the lot. Told him to send runner to Capt. Thomas and endeavor to borrow transportation to carry excess with Co. "B" when they move. No sick. Notified at 5:35 P.M. 12/5/18. Told them to return by rail preferably.

Euren Corporal Battesly and 8 men. No sick. Notified at 5:55 P.M. 12/5/18. Told them to go to Co. B, 51st Pioneer Inf., and mark with that organization.

Pallien Corporal Fischpeck and 8 men. None sick. Notified at 6:25 P.M., 12/5/18. Told them to march.

Biever Corporal McEvany and 8 men. None sick. Notified at 6:50 P.M., 12/5/18. Told them to march.

5 Dec 1918. In a Memorandum to Colonel Robert R. Ralston: This regiment will move to-morrow morning (December 6th, 1918) at 8:30 to, WITTLICH, less Company "F" which goes to WENGEROHR.

8 Dec 1918. 51st Pioneer Infantry Regiment was ordered to move their command out of Wittlich tomorrow, 9 December. Under the circumstances, request that they move that portion of their command now at Wittlich to Alf, or vicinity.

9 Dec 1918. In a Memorandum from Captain Eugene E. Preston, Adjutant, to the Chief Engineer, 4th Army. The location of the elements of the command were reported.

Headquarters	Bullay
Headquarters Company	Bullay
Supply Company	Bullay
Company "A"	Bullay
Company "B"	Bullay
Company "C"	Cochem
Company "D"	Enroute to Carden
Company "E"	Bengel
Company "F"	Wengerohl
Company "G"	Salinrohr
Company "H"	Fohren
Company "I"	Berncastel
Company "K"	Cues
Company "L"	Enroute to rejoin regiment
Company "M"	Biewer and Quint

11 Dec 1918. The 51st Pioneer Infantry was directed to move with their Headquarters, Hdqr. Co., and Band to Cochem on 12 December. Colonel Armitage, Corps Billeting Officer has arranged for billets in Cochem, which they could secure through him. Arrangements to move the Supply Company forward would be made as soon as possible.

16 Dec 1918. Headquarters IV Army Corps, Corps Commander directed that all orders pertaining to units of the 51st Pioneer Infantry, involving construction work, change of station, assignment to duties, etc., shall be published only upon approval of the IV Corps Engineer.

16 Dec 1918. A Telephone message was received by COL Smith from MAJ Foster at 10-00 P.M. 16 Dec. 1918. The III Corps has one Company of Pioneer Infantry in MASBURG and another in the northern outskirts of POLCH. These organizations are to be relieved by troops of the IV Corps. Upon relief they will be sent to rejoin the III Corps at EHRENBREITSTEIN. BASSENHIEM may be used as a staging area if necessary. Relief to be expedited.

17 Dec 1918. The Asst. Chief of Staff, G-3, has approved the following movements of companies:

Company E – Treis to Masburg

Company M – Kobern to Polch

Upon arrival at their destination, they were to relieve troops of the 3rd Corps guarding railroad from Daum to Coblenz.

22 Dec 1918. In a Memorandum from the Headquarters 51st Pioneer Infantry, with mailing address: American Exp. Forces APO 775, the following training schedule was issued:

1. In compliance with Training Memorandum No.12, Hq. IV Army Corps, 17 December 1918, there will be conducted in this regiment a four weeks period of instruction from 23 December 1918 to 18 January 1919. Company Commanders will submit to Battalion Commanders schedule for revision and approval who will in turn, submit schedules to Regimental Headquarters for approval.

2. These approved schedules will be available for Staff Office and Corps Headquarters at all times to ascertain progress made.

3. Each week 25 hrs. Training, exclusive of inspections.

(a) 5 hrs ….. School of soldier & squad & Manual of arms.
(b) 5 hrs ….. School of company & platoon movements.
(c) 5 hrs ….. Instruction in firing & aiming, S.A.F.M. & Target practice. [Small Arms Firing Manual, 1913]
(d) 2 ½ hrs ….. Physical Training. (English system)
(e) 2 ½ hrs ….. Instruction in Bayonet Combat. (English system)
(f) 5 hrs ….. Military Courtesy, pack making, manual of tent pitching and guard duty.
(g) 5 hrs ….. Practicing formation offensive combat of Small Units.
4. In the 2nd two weeks training, sub.par "g" will be substituted for sub.par "f".
5. One hours' school for Officers and non-commissioned officers will be help each evening from 7 to 8 P.M., comprising combat principles I.D.R. Offensive combat for Small Units (Pamphlet, A.E.F. #160) (to be delivered). Critique of days work.
6. Saturday morning will be given to a rigorous inspection of units by company commanders and all officers of the organization.
7. Every effort will be made to attain perfection during this training.
8. No drills or schools Saturday afternoon and Sunday.
By order of Lt. Col. Saulpaugh

25 Dec 1919. "The Stars and Stripes" of 3 Jan 1919 reported Christmas along the Rhine: In a report about Christmas along the Rhine, "Down along the river at Cochem, where men of the 51st Pioneers are installed, a huge cross was erected on the turret of an ancient ruined castle, where it shone forth like a beacon light up and down the valley."

2 Jan 1919. In Kochen near Coblenz the Regimental Command was established. The Companies were billeted in small towns around Coblenz.

3 Jan 1919, 2-15 P.M. The IV Corps Commander directed that Company "I", 51st Pioneer Infantry, from BERNCASTEL to KOBERN, by rail this date.

17 Jan 1919. In a Memorandum from the Headquarters 51st Pioneer Infantry, with mailing address: American Exp. Forces APO 775, the following training schedule was issued:

1. The following is submitted for your information for Training Period from January 20th, 1919 to January 27th, 1919.
(a) 5 Hrs. Close order; platoon and company, Battalion, if ground is available.
(b) 10 Hrs. Instruction Aiming and Firing, Target practice.
(c) 2 ½ Hrs. Physical Training. (English)
(d) 2 ½ Hrs. Bayonet, combat. (English)
(e) 5 Hrs. Ceremonies and guard duty.
2. Schools one (1) hour each evening, critiques of days work. Ceremonies, combat formation, Manual of Courts Martial.
3. Exactness will be insisted upon in all close order formations and Manual of Arms.
4. Saturday Morning will be given to a rigorous inspection of units by company commanders and all officers of the organizations.

18 Jan 1919. In a Memorandum from the Headquarters 51st Pioneer Infantry, the following training schedule was issued:

Training Memorandum: Four (4) Weeks beginning January 27th, 1919.
Training schedule to be followed unless orders are received to contrary.

<u>1st Week</u>
5 Hrs. Close order, squads and platoons.
5 Hrs. Aiming and firing instructions, S.A.F.M.

15 Hrs. Offensive Combat – Attack of platoons on machine gun nests.

2nd Week
5 Hrs. Close order, squads and platoons.
5 Hrs. Offensive Combat – Company in attack on machine gun nests and strong points.
15 Hrs. Practical field exercises, prepared and conducted by Battalion Commanders.

3rd Week
5 Hrs. Close order, squads and platoons.
5 Hrs. Offensive Combat. Same as 2nd Week.
10 Hrs. Field Exercises – Offensive – prepared and conducted by Battalion Commanders.
5 Hrs. Field exercises – Offensive – prepared and conducted by Regimental Command.

4th Week
Same as 3rd Week.

Special instruction to scouts, always working in pairs, and squads for the necessity of covering with fire, the advance of the other.
Importance of reconnaissance and rapid selection and occupation of positions to be instilled into the men.
Use of cover and distribution in depth will receive special attention.
Daily target practice – not over 12 men per target.
Fifteen (15) minutes gas drill weekly, with inspection of masks Saturday morning by Gas Officer.
Schools for Officers and non commissioned officers, of one hour duration, each evening; Reconnaissance, F.S.R. [Field Service Regulations] – Offensive Combat, I.D.R. [Infantry Drill Regulations], Manual of Courts Martial.
One (1) company daily alternating from the 1st and 3rd Battalions, will improve the road from Moselkern to Lehman.
Battalion Commanders will submit outline of field exercises, to this office for approval, not later than Friday, January 27th, 1919.
By order of Lt. Col. Saulpaugh

19 Jan 1919. Col J. L. Gilbreth assumed command.

27 Jan 1919. In a Memorandum from the Headquarters 51st Pioneer Infantry, the following training schedule was issued:

Training Memorandum: Four (4) Weeks beginning January 27th, 1919.
Training schedule to be followed unless orders are received to contrary.
1st Week
5 Hrs. Close order, squads and platoons.
5 Hrs. Aiming and firing instructions, S.A.F.M.
15 Hrs. Offensive Combat – Attack of platoons on machine gun nests.
2nd Week
5 Hrs. Close order, squads and platoons.
5 Hrs. Offensive Combat – Company in attack on machine gun nests and strong points.
15 Hrs. Practical field exercises, prepared and conducted by Battalion Commanders.
3rd Week
5 Hrs. Close order, squads and platoons.
5 Hrs. Offensive Combat. Same as 2nd Week.
10 Hrs. Field Exercises – Offensive – prepared and conducted by Battalion Commanders.
5 Hrs. Field exercises – Offensive – prepared and conducted by Regimental Command.
4th Week
Same as 3rd Week.

Special instruction to scouts, always working in pairs, and squads for the necessity of covering with fire, the advance of the other.

Importance of reconnaissance and rapid selection and occupation of positions to be instilled into the men.

Use of cover and distribution in depth will receive special attention.

Daily target practice – not over 12 men per target.

Fifteen (15) minutes gas drill weekly, with inspection of masks Saturday morning by Gas Officer.

Schools for Officers and non commissioned officers, of one hour duration, each evening; Reconnaissance, F.S.R. [Field Service Regulations] – Offensive Combat, I.D.R. [Infantry Drill Regulations], Manual of Courts Martial.

One (1) company daily alternating from the 1st and 3rd Battalions, will improve the road from Moselkern to Lehman.

Battalion Commanders will submit outline of field exercises, to this office for approval, not later than Friday, January 31st, 1919.

By order of Colonel GILBRETH

11 Feb 1919. From the Commanding Officer, Coblenz Central Post School: The 51st Pioneer Infantry has been moved from Ehrenbreistein to Cochem. Transfer cards for students of the Post School should be made accordingly.

25 Feb 1919. The Third Army, Chief of Staff ordered a detail of (1) Company of Pioneer Infantry from the 51st Pioneer Infantry, now stationed at GULS, to report daily to Lieutenant Cherry at Evacuation Hospital No. 9, for duty in connection with road construction near that Hospital. The work will require the services of one company for about four days. The Third Army would furnish truck transportation daily at GULS at 7:30 A.M. to transport this company to its work and will return company to GULS each evening. This detail will commence on February 26, 1919, on which date trucks will report at 7:30 A.M. The noon meal should be carried daily by the company.

25 Feb 1919. Telephone message received from Capt. Clark, G-3, Third Army, 25 Feb. 19, at 12-00M. by A.P.C. Hoffman, G-3, IV A.C.

From: Chief of Staff, Third Army
To: Commanding General, IV Army Corps
Subject: Detail of Pioneer Infantry
1. The Commanding General directs that you detail one (1) Company of Pioneer Infantry from the 51st Pioneer Infantry, now stationed at GULS, to report daily to Lieutenant Cherry at Evacuation Hospital No. 9, for duty in connection with road construction near that Hospital. The work will require the service of one company for about four days.
2. G-4, Third Army, will furnish truck transportation daily at GULS at 7:30 A.M. to transport this company to its work and will return company to GULS each evening.

This detail will commence on February 26th, 1919, on which date trucks will report at 7:50 A.M. The noon mean should be carried daily by the company.

28 Feb 1919. Capt. Edgar C. Niles, Co. D, 51st Pioneer Infantry, American E.F. sent the Commanding Officer of the 51st Pioneer Infantry a report on road work 1st and 3rd Battalion, from 16th -28th February. He noted that trucks withdrawn, not successful.
(a) River road between Lehmen and Cattenas
(b) Number of kilometers on which work was done   3
(c) Resurfacing, refilling holes, improving drainage
(d) Amount of stone used   Gondorf Quarry, Cubic meters   180
     Cattenas Quarry " "   225
     Total   405
(e) Total number men days work   4003
(f) Total   "   Truck days   13
(g) Total   "   Wagon days   106

1 Mar 1919. In a Memorandum from the Headquarters 51st Pioneer Infantry, American Exp. Forces, the following training schedule was issued:

Week beginning March 1st to March 10th.
4 Hours, I.D.R. (Provisional) by platoon.
4 Hours, S.A.F.M.
4 Hours, Engineers Field Manual. Knots, Lashings, Miniature bridges, etc.
4 Hours, Manual Interior Guard Duty.
4 Hours, Physical Training (English) Bayonet exercises.

Week of March 10th to 17th, 1919.
8 Hours, I.D.R. (Provisional) by Section, Platoon and Companies.
4 Hours, S.A.F.M.
4 Hours, Physical Training and Bayonet exercises.
4 Hours, Engineers Field Manual.

Week of March 17th to March 24th, 1919.
10 Hours, Musketry, G.O. 27, GHQ, C.S.
4 Hours, I.D.R. (Provisional)
4 Hours, Engineers Field Manual.
2 Hours, Instructions, Saluting and Courtesies.

Week of March 24th to March 31st, 1919.
10 Hours, Musketry, G.O. 27, GHQ, C.S.
10 Hours, Offensive Combat, up to and including battalions. (Provisional I.D.R.)

All drills to be held in forenoons.
Afternoons to be chiefly given over to athletics and educational activities.
Saturday morning, rigid inspection by Company Commanders under supervision of Battalion Commanders.
Battalion Commanders will submit schedules of training to conform to above. Copies of same will be held at hand for use of inspectors at all times.
Schools of one hour each day in I.D.R. (Provisional) will be held for all officers and non commissioned officers at such time that it will not interfere with engineering work of training schedule until all can be awarded certificated of proficiency.
By order of Colonel GILBRETH

3 Mar 1919. Capt. Daniel J. Cassidy, the Commanding Officer of Co. E. 51st Pioneer Infantry, sent a memo to the C.O. of the 51st Pioneer Infantry a report of work on roads for month of February:
In compliance with Memo Chief Engineer, IV Army Corps, dated 20 Feb. 1919, the following is a report of the work done on roads by this organization from Feb. 15, 1919 to Feb.28, 1919 incl.
    (a) Section of road between Evacuation Hospital #9 and American Cemetery, Coblenz, Germany.
    (b) Work done on one kilometer.
    (c) Refilling holes and improving drainage.
    (d) Six cubic meters of stone were used which was taken from hills.
    (e) 210 man days work, 70 men per day for three days.
    (f) No trucks were employed.
    (g) No wagons were employed.

14 Mar 1919. Capt. E. C. Niles, the Commanding Officer of Company D, stationed at Lehmen, Germany, sent the Adjutant, 51st Pioneer Infantry, a report on road work for the 1st and 3rd Battalions, 51st Pioneer Infantry, March 1st to 15th, inclusive:
    (a) River road between Lehmen and Cattenas
    (b) Work done of three kilometers
    (c) Resurfacing
    (d) Stone used   Gondorf Quarry 215

| Cubic meters | Cattenas Quarry | 87 |
| | | 302 |

(e) Man days work	1058
(f) Truck days	None
(g) Wagon days	72

18 Mar 1919. Gen Pershing reviewed the Regiment.

31 Mar 1919. Capt. E. C. Niles, the Commanding Officer of Company D, stationed at Lehmen, Germany, sent the Commanding Officer, 51st Pioneer Infantry, a report on road work for the period of March 16th to 31st:

  (a) River road between Lehmen and Hatzenport
  (b) Work done on six kilometers
  (c) Drainage and resurfacing
  (d) Stone used cubic meter, Cattenas quarry 100
  (e) Man days work----- 344 ½
  (f) Truck days ----------none
  (g) Wagon days---------- 2 ½

18 April 1919. Headquarters 51st Pioneer Infantry Office of Athletic Officer, Cobern, Germany. The following is a list of names from the 51st Pioneer Infantry who desire to enter the 4th Corps Tennis Tournament. Gardiner, Ray C. – Co. K – Corporal, Honsberger, Clare A. – Co. B – Private, Dietzer, M. L. – Co. I – 1st Lt

May 1919. The Headquarters of the Third U.S. Army Telephone Directory for the Army of Occupation in Coblenz, Germany of May 1919 lists the phone number "127" for the 2nd Battalion of the 51st Pioneer Infantry in Guls.

2 May 1919. "The Stars and Stripes" of this date reported that the Third Army put on a four day horse and motor American Mardi Gras carnival show, featuring from slow mules to fast planes.

10 May 1919. The 51st Pioneer Infantry left the 4th Corps to be assigned as Third Army troops.

11 May 1919. The 51st Pioneer Infantry Newspaper reported that the following companies will move to Wengerohr. Germany, to build Remount Station the first part of the week: Second Battalion – Co's. E, F, G and H; First Battalion – Co's. A and C. A company has been located at Loef on the Moselle for some months past, while C company has held firmly to Cond on Moselle. The balance of those companies E. F, G and H. have been at Guls, just across the Moselle from Coblenz.

12 May 1919. The Third Army, Army of Occupation, requested the following troop movements. Headquarters 51st Pioneer Infantry will move from its present station to Wittlich, Germany. The remaining companies of this regiment, except those stations at Wengerohr, Germany, will be disposed of as follows: 1 company Mayen, Germany; 1 company to Hollschlog [Hallschlag?], Germany; 1 company to Ettlebruck, Luxembourg; 2 companies to Esch [Esch-sur-Alzette], Luxembourg; 1 company to Bitburg, Germany.

12 May 1919. There was a request made to the Headquarters 51st Pioneer Infantry to move from its present station to Wittlich, Germany. The remaining companies of this regiment, except those stations at Wengerohr, Germany, were to be disposed of as follows:

  1 company Mayen, Germany,
  1 company to Hollschlog, Germany.
  1company to Ettlebruck, Luxembourg
  2 companies to Esch, Luxembourg
  1 company to Bitburg, Germany

G-4 will furnish the necessary transportation for this movement and will notify the Commanding Officer of the 51st Pioneer Infantry as to the hours of departure of trains. Instructions governing the duties to be performed by these organizations upon their arrival at the stations mentioned above will be issued by G-4, 3rd Army direct to the Commanding Officer, 51st Pioneer Infantry."

12 May 1919. Even though the 51st Pioneer Infantry would no longer be attached to the Third Army, the Commanding General, IV Corps, sent a memo to the Commanding General, Third Army, to request that some of the men from the 51st Pioneer Infantry be retained with the IV Corps for Athletic Purposes. It was requested that the following named men from the 51st Pioneer Infantry be placed on special duty with this Corps, for the purpose of engaging in athletics. These men are at the present time representing the Corps in the various athletic activities. Their relief would seriously impair the chances of the IV Corps in the Baseball League, and the A.E.F. Track and Field Meet. Those on the Track Team qualified for entry in the A.E.F. Track and Field Meet to be held at PARIS, and they have been in training for some time for this meet.

TRACK AND FIELD TEAM: Lt. K. Grace, Co. G; 2nd Lt. B.S. Hensley, Co. I; 2nd Lt. E.F. Field, Co. F; Private J. McGee, Co. E; Pvt. W. Hutchinson, Co. E; Cpl. J. Wheeler, Co. F; Sgt. L.P. Shea, Co. G; Pvt. H.M. Morse, Co. G; Pvt. I. Salzberg, Co. G; Pvt. F. Gross, Co. H; Cpl., S.F. Field, Co. I; Pvt. Harry E. Purcell, Co. I; Pvt. Carmelo Crucitti, Co. I; Pvt. Charles F. Hobbs, Co. I; Pvt. Phil K. Lombardi, Co. K; Cpl. E.S. Weinsheimer, Co. K; Pvt. L. Carulo, Co. K; Cook C.J. Perry, Co. K.

MEN ON THE TUG O' WAR TEAM: (Capt.) Sgt. Oliver Crooks; Pvt. Clarence Barlow; Sgt. Lionel S. Higgins; Pvt. Chester Czarniki; Horseshoer Wm. R. Vaughan; Pvt. Loren C. Bond; Pvt. Thomas P. Maroney; Pvt. Henry C. Tack; Pvt. Dewey J. Carpenter; Pvt. George Dahlberg; Pvt. Joe L. Anding; Pvt. 1 cl Abraham Barron.

BASEBALL TEAM: 1st Lt William J. Starr, Co. D; Lt. McLeod, Pvt. Edw. Lewis, Co. I; Pvt. 1 cl. Chas. A. Wagner, Co. E; Pvt. 1 cl. Frank Fountain, Co. I; Cpl. John H. Simmons, Co. I; Cpl. Valentine Melvin, Co. C; Mech. Edward Martin, Co. C; Sgt. Wm. E. Parks, Co. L; and Cpl. Jas. De Motta, Co. I. (These men are on the baseball team, which, without them, would be disbanded.)

13 May 1919. All members of 51st Pioneer Infantry that were on special duty with organizations of IV Army Corps are returned to their organizations. All members of 51st Pioneer Infantry that were on special duties with their organization were directed to immediately return to 51st Pioneer Infantry.

14 May 1919. The Advanced Embarkation Section, SOS, sent a message to update the entraining schedule for fifty-first pioneer infantry has been changed to read as follows: first train departs Trier 00:17 May 26. Second train departs Trier 07:47. May 26. Third train departs 09:02 May 27.

15 May 1919. The Headquarters Third Army requested that Company I, 51st Pioneer Infantry, proceed from Mayen, Germany, to Kripp, Germany, for station, reporting upon arrival to the Commanding Officer, Army Remount Depot., for duty. G-4, 3rd Army, will furnish truck transportation for this movement.

18 May 1919. The 51st Pioneer Infantry Newspaper reported that: immediately after the severance of all connection with the Fourth Army Corps during the latter part of last week commenced movement of troops in the 51st Pioneer Infantry into the lower Rhein Province and parts of Luxemburg. The movement of companies A and B on Sunday, May 11 led the Exodus of the whole 51st Pioneer Infantry Regiment and during the ensuing week a succession of order set in motion the remaining Companies, until none but Headquarters and Supply remain in the old quarters.

Company A moved Sunday, May, 11th at 1:25 in the afternoon. It hiked from Loef on Moselle, where it had been quartered for almost six months past, to Cattenes where it entrained for Wengerohr. It is billeted at Altrich about 6 kilos southwest of Wengerohr and has been detailed to remount construction in that vicinity.

Company B moved Sunday, May, 11th at 1:45 in the afternoon from Hatzenport, for Wengerohr. This company had likewise been situated on the banks of the Moselle for the past six months. It is billeted at Buescheid just north of Co. A and detailed to remount construction.

Company C which had been firmly established at Cond on Moselle for some time past, doing railhead duty in Cochen, just opposite Cond, moved out Wednesday May 14th for Bitburg. There are now working on the 7th Corps Ammunition Dump at that place.

Company D, which had been located at Lehmen on Moselle, immediately placed guard details in Loef and Hatzenport when Companies A and B moved out of those towns Sunday. These details were picked Wednesday by Co D when relieved by other units. Company D then moved to Hallschlag where its duties will consist of guarding an ammunition plant.

Companies E and F of the 2nd Battalion previously located at Guls are now occupying the Barracks at the Wengerohr railroad station and are detailed to remount construction duty.

Company G of the 2nd Battalion formerly located at Guls is now at Dorf and detailed to remount construction duty.

Company H of the 2nd Battalion formerly located at Guls is now at Bombogen about four miles north of Wengerohr and detailed to remount construction duty.

Company I moved Friday A.M. for Lippk am Rhein near Remagen.

Company J of the 3rd Battalion formerly located at Cobern left Wednesday about 12:30 in the afternoon for Eitelbruck, Luxembourg.

Companies L and M of the 3rd Battalion, formerly located at Cobern left at 12:30 Wednesday for Esch, Luxembourg, situated southwest of the City of Luxembourg.

18 May 1919. From the Advance Embarkation Section: The 51st Pioneer Infantry and Laundry Unit No. 325 were to remain on duty with Third Army Troops per authority of G.H.Q. [General HQ]

18 May 1919. The 51st Pioneer Infantry Newspaper reported that men at schools were recalled. All men at the Academic, Mechanic and Trade schools have been called back to their companies. A stream of men immediately began pouring into Cochem Friday in seek of their organizations. These men came from Neuenahr, Brohl and Mayen. The history of the 301st Engineers told that when the Fourth Corps was about to be disbanded, the 51st Pioneers were the first students to be returned from their school.

21 May 1919. The Pioneer Infantry Regiment was ordered to assemble for Station at TRIER, upon being relieved by organizations of the 4th Division. The organizations of this regiment were to proceed on D day and h hour from their present stations, with the movement to be completed before 18:00 hours on 25 May 1919, as follows:

The Regiment (less 1st, 2nd, and 3rd Battalions, Supply Co., and Med. Detachments) from COCHEM.
1st Battalion (less A, B, and D) and Med. Detch., from BITBURG.
2nd Battalion, A and B Cos, and Med. Detch., from WENGEROHR.
3rd Battalion (less I & K Co.s) and Med. Detch., from ESCH, LUXEMBERG.
Co. I, and Med. Detch., from KRIPPS
Co. K, and Med. Detch., from ETTELBRUCK, LUXWMBERG.
Supply Co., from GULS.
Co. D, and Med. Detch., from HALLSCHLOG.

The Third Army was to furnish such rail and truck transportation as may be necessary for these moves and will be notified by these Headquarters of date and hour of departure of organizations.

23 May 1919. Company K was ordered to assemble at TRIER, GERMANY, upon being relieved by organizations of the 4th. Division. This company was to proceed on D day and H hour from its present situations as follows:
Company Post Command & detch & Med Detch from ETTELBRUCK.
Detch. From DOMMELDINGEN.
This Post Command will close upon departure of troops and move to TRIER with them.

23 May 1919. The Advanced Embarkation Section, SOS, sent a message that the 51st Pioneer Infantry would entrain May 25 and 27 for Le Mans. Entraining Point Trier, destination Noyen Le Mans area. First Train departs Trier 00:17 Second Train departs 07:47 Third train departs Trier May 27 09:02. Each train will consist of one American box car for kitchen one for rations, two for baggage, twenty four for Enlisted men, one for officers and one first class coach for officers.

25 May 1919. The 51st Pioneer Infantry Newspaper reported about: Le Mans to Port of Embarkation Then Home. We are informed by courier today that regiment has rolled packs and pulled sales for Trier. The regiment is billeted in that city for two nights, and will entrain for Le Mans from Trier. The 1st Battalion, Co's A, B, C and D and 100 men from Headquarters Company are due to be on the train ready to pull away for Le Mans at midnight Sunday. Second Battalion with the balance of Headquarters Company is scheduled to be aboard troop train at 7:00 Monday morning en route for Le Mans. Of the Third Battalion we have received no word as yet, the presumption being that they will naturally follow closely upon the heels of the Second Battalion. At Le Mans the usual cleaning process will be observed, then rapid movement to the port of embarkation, the gang plank, all hands aboard ship, the Statue of Liberty, a port of debarkation, and Home!

The 51st Pioneer Infantry traveled from Coblenz to LeMans, France by "side car" Pullmans which were quicker than the trains they took going. LeMans had narrow crooked streets and no indoor plumbing. People had to bathe at the bath houses. At LeMans the 51st Pioneers were deloused, and given new uniforms and underwear.

23 June 1919. Part of the Fifty-First sailed from St. Nazaire on the "Wilhemina" to Hoboken, NJ. [Regimental Headquarters, Headquarters Company, Supply Company, Ordnance and Medical Detachments, and Companies A, B, C, D, E, and F.]

19 July 1919. Strength at 89 Officers and 3082 Enlisted Men.

25 June 1919. Companies G, H, I, K, L, M and the Medical Detachment of the 51st Pioneer Infantry sailed from Brest, France, on the U.S.S. Mongolia.

After the war, the companies of 51st Pioneer Infantry were consolidated with the New York Guard 10th Infantry Regiment. In 1921, several companies from this Regiment were redesignated as the 132nd Ammunition Train.

Sources

Lerwil, Leonard L. "The Personnel Replacement in the United States Army", CMH_Pub_104-9, August 1954.

Department of the Army Lineage and Honors Headquarter and Headquarters Detachment, 104th Military Police Battalion (Poughkeepsie Invincibles), https://history.army.mil/html/forcestruc/lineages/branches/mp/0104mpbn.htm, accessed 11 Dec 2017.

Department of the Army Lineage and Honors, 442D Military Police Company, https://history.army.mil/html/forcestruc/lineages/branches/mp/0442mpco.htm, accessed 11 Dec 2017.

Department of the Army Lineage and Honors, 28th Infantry Division Band, https://history.army.mil/html/forcestruc/lineages/branches/bands/band-028id.htm

1st DIVISION COMPOSITION. https://history.army.mil/books/wwi/ob/1-comp-OB.htm, accessed 11 Dec 2017.

"51st Pioneers Got New Designation After World War I." Kingston Daily Freeman September 11, 1947, Kingston, NY.

Martin, Clarence S. "Three Quarters of a Century with the Tenth Infantry New York National Guard 1860-1935" (1936) by. Chapter XI covers the Tenth Infantry

OFFICIAL HISTORY and STATION LISTS

The history in this chapter was found in the pages of "The 51st Pioneers", Germany's Greatest Newspaper, Cochem Germany, and in the National Archives and Record Administration (NARA) Record Group 165 (RG 165). The version of the regimental history, the History of Company K, and the station lists that appear in RG165 have their Classification Cancelled by authority of the Adjutant General, John J. Mick Capt Cav, 18 APR 1947, AGPA-G 334 (27 June 46), 8 July 48. While serving in the Army of Occupation, the 51st Pioneer Infantry published "Germany's Greatest Newspaper". It contained news about the Companies of the Regiment, and articles of interest to all the soldiers.

The 51st Pioneers Newspaper.

The station list for each company has been inserted after the history of each company (when one exists) to show the movements. Highlights from the Morning Reports from Company B have also been combined with the history. Station lists end during the Army of Occupation. Some gaps do appear in the chronology; keep in mind that the troops traveled by train, and also moved at overnight to be at a location at a certain time, or to conceal their movements by cover of the night. Highlights of the Morning Reports for Company B are also included.

The element that appears here were transcribed by the author. Slight typographical errors have been corrected for readability.

HISTORY OF THE 51ST PIONEER INFANTRY.
The Old Tenth.

The entry by the United States into the great war on April 6, 1917, found the 10th New York National Guard scattered throughout the State, each separate Company engaged in performing guard duty at arsenals, bridges and over other National and State property. Following the declaration of war came a discussion of ways and means to make our declaration more than an idle threat. Not by declarations alone nor by prolonged exchange of notes could the war be settled, that had clearly been learned. Obviously, the first thing to do in order to wage a war on land was to create an army. To do this meant starting practically at the bottom. We had the men, some ten million or more between the ages of 21 and 30, but the country had long labored under the delusion that in a democracy where all men are at least theoretically equal, the pacifist and those too proud to fight can not only pursue their way unmolested but can even strike with freedom at the common weal. But we had the experience of our Allies to guide us and we were awake to the fact that not only for the winning of the war but in order to prevent a German victory, time was very much of the essence. Hence draft and elective service early became familiar terms, at first spoken casually, and, as the patriotic pulse increased its beat, talked of widely as the one way of meeting the situation. At about that time Marshal Joffre came to America and beneath all the ceremony and state functions that crowned his visit lay a serious mission. He came to plead for men, for an army and not in a year but at once. At last our War Dept. and our legislators were aroused to the necessity of acting and the first draft bill was passed. By its terms the new National Army was to be created, the small Regular Army and the National Guard to act as both an example and preceptor. The National Guard at this time was in each State a local military body, organized within the State and subject to Federal control only in remote instances. These limitations had to be removed and the National Guard was drafted into the armed forces of the United States on August 5th, 1917.

It was in the later part of October 1917 that the 10th New York National Guard under the command of Colonel John F. Kline was Finally assembled at Camp Wadsworth, S. C., on the site which had been designated for the camp. A forest of pine trees covered the ground, only the kitchens and mess halls having been previously erected. Then followed days of great activity, cutting the trees, clearing the ground and putting up tents. This and much other work accomplished attention was turned to drill. Not unobserved were these Companies of the old 10th, employed in putting into practice their accurate knowledge of the Infantry Drill Regulations Major General John F. O'Ryan was at just this time on the alert for men for the 17th Division, also at Camp Wadsworth. What he saw of the 10th New York evidently pleased him, with the result that orders came for the transfer of Officers and men, orders which came so often that before they had finished three fourths of the Regt. had been transferred. Only a small handful of Officers and non-coms were left to form the nucleus of a new organization.

Period of Preparation.

Around the first of the Year, 1918, the Provisional Depot for Corps and Army Troops was created at Camp Wadsworth, with Brig. Gen. Guy V. Carleton, since promoted to Major Gen., as Commanding Officer. In G. O. 1 emanating from its Headquarters Jan. 4th, 1918, and treating of certain transfers not of interest in this history, paragraph 2 contains the following statement:

"2. When these transfers have been effected, the infantry, regiments will be organized and trained as Pioneer Inf. The 1st N. Y. Inf. Will hereafter be designated as the 1st Pioneer Inf., the 14th N. Y. Inf. as the 2nd Pioneer Inf., the 10th N. Y. as the 51st Pioneer Inf.

(c) The 51st and 52nd Pioneer Infantry with the 3rd Anti-

Aircraft Machine Gun Battalion attached will constitute a command designated as the 1st Provisional Brigade, Army Troops."

This was therefore the inception of the 51st Pioneer Infantry and its history dates from the publishing of that G. O.

However, the giving or changing of a designation lacks much of creating a Regiment. The Officers and men remained the same, the same routine of guard and K. P. duty was the lot of the men and for a time everything but the name remained the same as before. About the middle of January, 1918, other changes began to be noted. Colonel Kline, who had built the old 10th up to that state of military efficiency which made its members so desirable in the eyes of Maj. Gen. O'Ryan, had received his honorable discharge Dec. 29th, 1917, under the provisions of Sec. 9 of the Act of Congress approved May 18th, 1917. On January 14th, 1918, by the provisions of S. O. 10, Hdqtrs. P. D. C. & A. T. Col. J. Guy Deming, N. G. was assigned to the 51st Pioneer Inf. Regt. for duty, and with him came Captain and Adjutant Eugene E. Preston, N. G. On the following day Major Willis Bacon, N. G. arrived and on succeeding days Officers began to pour in. By the end of the month the full complement of Officers was reached.

And now began the period of preparation, the getting ready for the men whenever they might arrive. By orders of the Commanding General schools were organized in all the regiments and all Officers not on other military duty required to attend. The first school, for the study of Field Engineering and Infantry Drill Regulations, was scheduled to commence Feb. 1st and end Feb. 15th. Lieut. Col. William E. Downs, 52nd Pioneer Inf., was designated as the director and the first instructors selected from the 51st were Major Willis Bacon and Major Gilbert V. Schenck. Knot tying became a popular indoor sport and rare engineering feats were accomplished from a few light sticks supplemented by a ball of twine. Other schools followed that the military education and the theoretical knowledge of the Officers might grow and prosper. During the course, for it continued uninterrupted until the arrival of the drafts, the subjects of Field Service Regulations, Musketry, Guard Duty, Sanitation and Hygiene, Court Martial, Physical Training, Field Engineering, Sketching, and Practical Military Engineering were covered and it may be mastered by some. Even in so brief a history of regimental achievement as this record must needs be, some slight mention in passing should be made of the construction of a mammoth bridge, a monument to its designer, over the trickling waters of Spartansburg Creek. In the course of this work, the Officers of this regiment and of other Pioneer Regiments, who were also allowed to share in this honor, learned much that served them in good stead in the trying days that were to come. Still another feature of the instruction for Officers were the lectures and conferences conducted by the various Brigade Commanders, on Saturday mornings under orders of Major Gen. Carleton. At these lectures the new methods of trench warfare and the varied development of military science were brought off with the assistance of pamphlets issued by the War Dept.

During this period of instruction for the Officers, the few remaining non-commissioned officers and fewer privates in the various companies of the regiment were busy at guard duty. The ranks were so depleted that the Sergeant of the guard for one tour of duty would in a day or so go on as Corporal in charge of a relief or it might be serve as a Private, even in the rear rank. There was not much variety to the continuous guard duty, save an occasional turn at K. P. or some other working detail, but the men stuck to their duties and accredited themselves well no matter how humble the task. Before the arrival of the drafted men work had to be done in leveling the ground and erecting floors and tents on the slope toward the bath houses and latrines. To this work also, the men, nearly all of them Sergeants and Corporals, applied themselves with a will, preparing the way and making it easier for the drafted men once they should arrive. To anyone familiar with the sharp lines of demarcation drawn in the Army and the respect which is demanded of the subordinate for the superior, this points the quality of the old men in the organization and represents a fine spirit of patriotism.

Sanitation and hygiene have long since become by-words in American Army annals. There was a time when they were not so well known, in the days when we suffered more by a hundred times from pestilence and disease than from the enemy's fire. But that was before Surgeon General Gorgas had caught the ear of those responsible for our military affairs. Surgeon Gen. Gorgas could have had no more rigid disciple than was Major Gen. Carleton at Camp Wadsworth. And the mere belief of General Carleton in anything having to do with the conduct, maintenance etc., of troops under his control was a sufficient guarantee that those Officers commanding under him saw to it that his belief was practiced by the men of their command. There were numerous orders during the spring of 1918 having to do with sanitation and hygiene in their application to the troops, their quarters, the mess halls etc., and there were even more frequent inspections to see that these orders were enforced. That they were followed, to the credit of the regiment as well as to the personal well being and satisfaction of all concerned, was made evident by the very complimentary words of Major Gen. Carleton himself, on the eve of the regiment's departure from Camp Wadsworth.

Reflecting no discredit upon the sporting records of the regiment was the clean cut baseball championship of Camp Wadsworth, won during the months of May and June by the regiment's nine, composed almost entirely of men Co. I.

Making the Regiment.

Finally, after many false reports, many rumors having no foundation, the first increment of the draft, made up entirely of New York State men, was assigned to the regiment on May 27th, 1918. All night long the long line of trucks could be heard bringing the men of the draft from the railroad yards up to the headquarters of the Depot for Corps and Army Troops, and all night long the lights burned in the kitchens along the regimental street, the cooks ready to serve a hot meal to the new men. Finally as day was beginning to break, small groups, having resemblance to anything but a military unit, each under the guidance of an officer or non-com, wended their way to one or another of the company streets. And on the following night more men arrived and the same procedure was followed. On his arrival each man was sent down to the new bath house for a hot shower and on his return breakfast was waiting for him. A contrast inevitably suggests itself between the forest which greeted the 10th N. Y. on its arrival the previous fall and this open handed, absolutely looked after reception, extended the new men.

No sooner had the men arrived and the various examinations before personnel boards, physical and psychological examination boards etc., been gone through than the training of the recruit began in earnest. The following list of service calls governed during the training period. The need for trained soldiers was urgent, and four hours in the forenoon and four hours in the afternoon the new men were instructed in the life of a soldier.

In due quality to the quality of their instruction and to their own intelligence it may be said that they learned very quickly, becoming good soldiers almost over night. They had not learned the entire game but they were catching on and working hard in a spirit that was admirable. As an indication of the progress made it need only be said that the companies were executing battalion drill in the third week after the arrival of the new men. Along every line such progress was made that within seven weeks after the first assignment the 51st Pioneer Infantry successfully stood the field examination, made by Major General Carleton and staff, and was ready for foreign service.

On July 17th, the regiment entrained for the port of embarkation and two days later reached Camp Merritt, N. J. Here the finishing touches, the final preparations for departure had to be made. Service records must be checked and rechecked, passenger lists prepared, complete issue of clothing and equipment made to all men, and every- thing completed for departure at a moment's notice. It was done, a remarkable achievement when one considers that New York was almost within stones throw, and none of the Officers and men knew whether they should return to enjoy it again.

Friday morning July 26th, at 3:30 A.M. the regiment moved out from the camp and followed the road down to Alpine Landing. At this point ferry boats were waiting and soon transported the troops to the docks at Hoboken. No time was lost in loading the organization on board the Kroonland, lying in dock. Ladies of the Red Cross took advantage of the temporary delay and refreshes the Officers and men with hot coffee and buns. At 4 P.M. on Friday July 26th, the Kroonland steamed out of New York Harbor and the voyage was begun.

HEADQUARTERS

PROVISIONAL DEPOT FOR CORPS AND ARMY TROOPS
CAMP WADSWORTH, S.C.

GENERAL ORDERS)   June 3, 1918.
)
  No. 35   )
            1. The following service times for the troops of this command will be
      observed commencing June 3, 1918.

MONDAYS,TUESDAYS,THURSDAYS AND FRIDAYS.

Reveille
    First Call --------------------------------------5.30 A.M.
    March --5.40 A.M.
    Reveille and Assembly ----------------------5.45 A.M.
Mess Call --6.15 A.M.
Fatigue Call ---6.45 A.M.
Stable Call --6.45 A.M.
Sick Call --7.00 A.M.
Morning Instruction Period
    First Call --------------------------------------7.25 A.M.
    Assembly ---------------------------------------7.30 A.M.
    Recall ---11.00 A.M.
First Sergeants Call ----------------------------------11.35 A.M.
Mess Call -- 12.00 M.
Afternoon Instruction Period
    First Call --------------------------------------12.55 P.M.
    Assembly ---------------------------------------1.00 P.M.
    Recall ---5.00 P.M.
Guard Mounting
    First Call --------------------------------------5.10 P.M.
    Assembly ---------------------------------------5.15 P.M.
Retreat
    First Call --------------------------------------5.40 P.M.
    Assembly ---------------------------------------5.45 P.M.
    Retreat --5.50 P.M.
Mess Call --6.00 P.M.
Tattoo ---9.30 P.M.
Call to Quarters ---------------------------------------9.45 P.M.
Taps --10.00 P.M.

WEDNESDAYS AND SATURDAYS.
Same as above omitting afternoon drill calls.

SUNDAYS.
Same as above omitting drill calls.
Church call at hour to be designated by regimental and
    Independent unit commanders.

              By Command of Brigadier Gen. Carleton
                        J.F.COHN
                    Colonel, National Army
                      Chief of Staff

OFFICIAL:
  A.E.Tuck

The Voyage.

Slowly the great ship lined with men of the regiment made her way through the harbor and out to join the other ships in the convoy. She was well guarded by many small vessels of the mosquito fleet and by a sea plane, which circled above until the sky line of New York had faded away into the distance. Aboard the Kroonland in addition to the 51st Pioneer Infantry was the Advance Section of the 7th Division. No sooner had the tallest of New Yorks skyscrapers melted away in the haze than organization for the voyage was begun. The submarine was the dread enemy; how to combat or guard against the menace was the problem. A roster of Officers with assignment to the numerous lookout posts about the ship was immediately prepared. To make doubly sure a detail of men was selected to watch from the bridge. At all hours of the day and night the lookout posts were occupied and eyes were strained for the first gleam of a periscope or the ripple of foam where it cuts the water.

Below deck the men were tumbled into compartments having the bunks arranged in triple tiers. It was sometimes hot and always stuffy but the discomfort was not so serious as to affect one's health or even one's disposition. And furthermore, this was duty with the A.E.F., dating with the departure from New York, an honor compensating for all the suffering undergone. In the early morning hours bell calls rang throughout the ship summoning the men to "stand to". Then for an hour or more, until the dawn of day had lighted up the waters of the surrounding sea, the Officers and men, all of those on board, stood with life preservers close beside the raft to which they had been assigned.

The Kroonland followed a southerly course, until, some distance off the Norfolk Capes other transports were met and the course changed to an easterly direction. The convoy at this time consisted of five transports, a cruiser and two destroyers.

It may have been thought by those unversed in matters naval that a voyage, even in war times, would be a complete rest for those wearing the Army uniform. Such theories if held, were violently up- rooted and soon went by the board. Details were asked for continually, and in many cases for work requiring special and highly trained ability. Painting, plumbing, welding, carpentry, decorating, waiting, printing and engraving were among the vocations whose rep-representatives were granted the opportunity of practicing their trade and thus avoid getting rusty while on ship board. At one time as many as 2200 men from the regiment were on detail, and it was rumored that so many men could be doing nothing less that rebuilding the ship. Beside the work there was no lack of entertainment, concerts by the band, vaudeville performances by well known artists, and several well-matched bouts. In addition, the shower baths furnished no little entertainment as well as cleanliness and comfort. A sailor with a nozzle in his hand playing a stream of cold water upon a group of squirming men of every description, all clad in only their first issue garments, remains as one of the lasting memories of the voyage.

The voyage, lasting eleven days, dragged out wearily but uneventfully. At one time the Finland, sister ship to the Kroonland, developed engine trouble and lagged behind but later rejoined the convoy. There were the customary rumors of a man overboard, a sailor said to have slipped from his hammock on the hurricane deck, but this was not confirmed.

On August 4th, eight destroyers hove in sight and took over the convoy from the cruiser Huntington and the two destroyers who had performed their duty well. Then through the dangerous submarine infested waters of the Bay of Biscay and at 1 P.M. Aug. 6th, land was sighted. In single file the long line of transports followed the narrow winding channel, lined with mines for the over venturesome U-boat, safely into the magnificent harbor of Brest.

The Landing and the Rest Camp.

All through the night of the 6th of Aug. details worked at un- loading barracks bags, overseas boxes, Officers bedding rolls and all the travelling paraphernalia of a regiment. On the morning of the 7th the troops were landed and immediately formed for the hike to the rest camp. The people of Brittany, wearied as they were after four long years of war and having at times almost despaired of victory, rejoiced at the sight of American soldiers in their streets. Children ran along the column, reaching out to touch the hands of those who were passing and all the while asking for cigarettes and souvenirs. Many interesting groups were passed on the short hike but one which lingered in many minds was of three or four little tots, the eldest not over five, singing away lustily "Hail hail the gangs all here. What the hell do we care now." Pontanezen Barracks were reached but the was no room within and the regiment passed on to the open field assigned it. Shelter tents were pitched and a camp established under anything but favorable conditions. The Pontanezen Barracks, buildings of stone long since erected, had been used by the great Napoleon to shelter his troops following a campaign. Hence the term rest camp had originated and survived. Only the name survived, however, as no sooner were the 51st Pioneers encamped on the site allotted to it, then orders for working details began to pour in. These details would report at the docks in Brest early in the morning storing and assorting material, or whatever work was required of them. This continued until Aug. 14th when the following order was received from Headquarters IV Army Corps.

"1. Pursuant to instructions from American General Headquarters the 51st Pioneer Infantry Regiment is under orders to move by rail."

The time of departure off the battalions which were to travel separately was also stated in the order. According to schedule the troops were entrained at Kermor Station, Brest, and the journey across France commenced.

A queer collection of cars went to make up these trains. There were a few cars bearing the dignified 1 Cl. on their sides but dis- closing in their interior little to justify the claim, there were many 11 Cl. and 111 Cl. cars and a few cars marked with the well known "Cheaveux 8 Hommes 40" were thrown in for good measure. Through St. Brieuc, Rennes, Laval, Tours, Bourges, Nevers, Lecreusot, Dijohn and many smaller towns the journey ran until Is-sur-Tille was reached on August 16th. The great distributing agencies of the Quartermaster and Ordance Corps were here, mammoth warehouses stretching far on every side, and each battalion halted a few hours while gas masks and helmets were issued. On the following day, Saturday the 17th of Aug., the regiment detrained at Maron on the Moselle, having passed through Andilly, Nefchateau and Toul. Now for the first time the term billeting, of which many had but slight know- ledge of the meaning, took on new and real significance. Its flexibility, one of many characteristics, permitted the calling of a house, a barn, any four walls with or without a roof above, a billet for the shelter of men. The adaptability of the Americans was once more displayed and the men were quickly provided for. Headquarters, the 1st and 3rd battalions remained in Maron while the 2nd battalion under Major Dooley marched to the adjoining town of Sexey-aux-Forges and billeted there.

<u>War Work.</u>

During all this time of preparation for service the regiment had remained intact, but now that the time had come for it to play its part with the forces in the field, it was divided into many units of varying sizes and scattered throughout the zone of the advance. This separation of the companies meant the absence of possible achievement by the regiment acting as a whole, but as the whole is equivalent to the sum of all its parts, so must the regiment stand upon the records of its companies.

On the 19th of August the following secret order from Headquarters First Army AEF was received by Col. Deming, "1. Under authority from GHQ [General Headquarters] the following assignment has this day been made

Unit	51st Inf. Pioneers
Assignment	4th Corps
Remarks	Under tactical control 32nd French Corps

(sgd) R. McCreave
Col. General Staff
G-3

From the receipt of this communication the 51st Pioneer Inf. became a part of the IV Corps and remains so at the present time. Its history is inseparably bound up with the achievements, the successes or the reverses, if any, of that military unit. If the IV Corps has played its part, if it has stood the test and merited the confidence of its leaders and the Commander in Chief, then the Officers and men of the 51st Pioneer Infantry, who have never faltered when the Corps Commander or his chosen representatives have directed, may well have a justifiable and well-grounded pride in their regiment. From this assignment to the IV Corps we shall follow the activities of the regiment through the work of the battalions and more often separate companies, which for a great part of the remaining days of the war acted as independent organizations. The towns of Maron, Sexey-aux-Forges and Chaligny were all within a short distance of Nancy and Pont St. Vincent and within two weeks after their landing the Officers and men knew the peculiar motor whir of the Boche avions. With "le clair de lune" reflected in the winding Moselle enemy aviators made frequent bombing expeditions over Nancy and the nearby villages. It was during one of these nocturnal raids that one man of M Co. was killed and several men injured from the explosion of a bomb.

On August 20th, the following order marked "Secret, Urgent" was received by Colonel Deming from Col. Pare commanding the Engineers of the 32d French Army Corps.

"The Colonel commanding the 51st Regiment U. S. Infantry Pioneers) will go to Pagny-sur-Meuse on the 21st inst., to replace and relieve the Colonel commanding the 63rd Regiment Territorial Infantry (French) in the command of the position of barrage in the sector of Lucey. We will receive all information needed by him for the execution of his work from the Officer whom he relieves.

2. One battalion will go to Toul and remain there on the 21st, on the 22nd it will go to Pagny, there to relieve the battalion of the 63rd Regiment Territorial Infantry having in charge the barrage work in the zone of Lucy".

In compliance with this order the 1st Battalion, minus A Co., which had been left at Camp Merritt and assigned to special duty there, left Maron on August 21st, marching at night, as was always the case in the advance zone, and reached Pagny-sur-Meuse the 22nd. Co. A rejoined the battalion here on the 29th, and the entire force engaged in erecting barbed wire entanglements and digging trenches for the third line of defence. On Aug. 24th, Companies E and F of the 2nd battalion left Sexey-aux-Forges in order to take over from the French certain forts guarding the city of Toul. Battalion head- quarters and companies G and H remained at Sexey until the night of Aug. 29th, when under orders received that day the hike to Troussey was commenced. This town was not reached until 2 A.M. August 31st, at which hour the natives were roused from their slumber and the men billeted. During this period the 3rd battalion had been scattered even more than either the 1st or 2nd. Co. I had on the 22nd reached the village of Lay St. Remy and begun the erection of barbed wire entanglements at strategical points outside of the village. Co. K leaving Maron with the battalion on the 21st had continued to Rogeville, four miles from the front. Here the company, working by platoons, was engaged in the clearing of the right of way for a projected railway line. Co. L had on the 22nd been ordered to Minorville and there undertook its first Pioneer work, building pill boxes and digging trenches and dugouts. On the 26th the company began work on the construction of a military railway on which the large naval guns for the bombardment of Metz were to be carried forward. The work was under German balloon observation, and the men were frequently subjected to shell fire while at work. Co. M had moved off on August 22nd, from Chaligny across the river to Pont St. Vincent, and up until Sept. 6th, was busy at the large steel plant located in that city, loading cars with material for shipment to the front.

During the night of Sept. 2-3, Headquarters Co., Supply Co. and Cos. A, C, G, H and I marched to Toul and were billeted in the Bautzen barracks just beyond the city. Within the next few days Cos. B, K, L and M were recalled and joined the regiment at Toul. This was the last time during the war that so large a proportion of the regiment was assembled. All the companies, with the exception of D at Domjermain, and E and F occupying the French forts guarding Toul were now grouped in Bautzen Barracks.

The ever-increasing preparations for a drive, which were being made, during the early days of Sept. were now rapidly nearing a head, and on Sept. 10th, orders reached the Commanding Officer 51st Pioneer Infantry which called for certain Companies to move out toward the St. Mihiel front. Two companies, B and D, were attached to the 1st Division and ordered to move the night of Sept. 10-11th, from their station to bivouac in the woods in the vicinity of Leonval Dump. Pursuant to the same order Companies G and K were attached to the 42nd Division and Companies H and L to the 89th Division. On the morning of Sept. 12th, 1918, the first concerted offensive operation of the American Expeditionary Forces, the operation to reduce the St. Mihiel salient, was delivered. The complete success of the movement marks it as one of the remarkable achievements of the entire war. The three Divisions referred to were all actively engaged and the Companies of the 51st, attached to the Engineers for duty, followed closely behind the advance and participated both in the attack and in the subsequent organization of the position. On Sept. 17th, the following General Order was published from Headquarters IV Army Corps:

"The Corps Commander takes great pride in repeating the Following telegram received by him from the Commander in Chief of the American Expeditionary Forces. 'Please accept my sincere congratulations on the successful and important part taken by the Officers and men of the IV Corps in the first offensive of the First American Army on Sept. 12 and 13. The courageous dash and vigor of our troops has thrilled our countrymen and evoked the enthusiasm of our Allies. Please convey to your command my heartfelt appreciation of their splendid work. I am proud of you all. Pershing'.

By Command of

Major Gen. Dickman.

Stuart Heintzelman

Chief of Staff."

In order to follow more closely the participation by Officers and men of the 51st in this great offensive, short accounts written by Officers whose companies bore a part are included herein.

[Separate histories for several of the companies were not included. Station lists have been inserted into this section of the available histories. Highlights from the Morning Reports of Company B are also included.]

HEADQUARTERS COMPANY STATION LIST

STATION LIST OF UNIT SINCE ARRIVAL IN THE AMERICAN E.F.   Arrived: France Aug. 6, 1918.

Unit: 51st   Pioneer
Infantry   Company: Headquarters Co.

On Transport Kroonland   At: Brest

STATION	ARRIVED	LEFT	AUTHORITY	ATTACHED OR ASSIGNED TO	DETACHMENTS STATIONED AT
Brest, France	August 7, 1918	Aug.14/18	Reg. S.O.		None
Maron, France	Aug.17/18	Sept.7/18	Reg. S.O.		Pagny Sur-Meuse
Toul, France	Sept.7/18	Oct.22/18	Reg. S.O.	4th Army Corps	None.
Menil-la-Tour	Oct.23/18	Nov.16/18	Reg. S.O.	" "	None.
Buxiers, France	Nov.16/18	Nov.17/18	" "	" "	None.
Hannonville, France	Nov.17/18	Nov.18/18	" "	" "	None.
Mouaville, France	Nov.18/18	Nov.21/18	" "	" "	None.
Trieux, France	Nov.21/18	Nov.22/18	" "	" "	None.
Wollmeringen, France	Nov.22/18	Nov.23/18	" "	" "	None.
Aspelt, Luxemburg	Nov.23/18	Dec. 2/18	" "	" "	None.
Wormeldingen, Luxemburg	Dec. 2/18	Dec. 3/18	" "	" "	None.
Cons, Germany	Dec. 3/18	Dec. 4/18	" "	" "	None.
Fohren, Germany	Dec. 4/18	Dec. 6/18	" "	" "	None.
Wittlich, Germany	Dec. 6/18	Dec.9/18	Reg. S.O.	4th Army Corps	None.
Bullay, "	Dec.9/18	Dec. 11/18	" "	" "	"
Cochem, "	Dec. 11/18				

SUPPLY COMPANY

STATION LIST OF UNIT SINCE ARRIVAL IN THE AMERICAN E.F.   Arrived: France August 6, 1918.

Unit: 51st Pioneer Infantry   Company: Supply Company

On Transport Kroonland   At: Brest

STATION	ARRIVED	LEFT
Brest, France	Aug.7, 1918	Aug.13/18
Maron, France	Aug.17/18	8/22/18
Toul, France	8/22/18	8/23/18
Pagny SurMeuse, Fr	8/23/18	9/2/18
Toul, France	9/3/18	10/23/18
Menil la Tour, France	10/23/18	11/16/18
Buxerulles, France	11/16/18	11/17/18
Hannonville, Fr.	11/17/18	11/18/18
Mouaville, France	11/18/18	11/21/18
Trieux, France	11/21/18	11/22/18
Wollmeringen, Fr.	11/22/18	11/23/18
Aspelt, Luxemburg	11/23/18	12/2/18
Wormeldange, Lux.	12/2/18	12/3/18
Konz, Germany	12/3/18	12/4/18
Fohren, Germany	12/4/18	12/6/18
Wittlich, Germany	12/6/18	12/9/18
Bullay, Germany	12/9/18	12/16/18
Poltersol, Germany	12/16/18	12/17/18
Carden, Germany	12/17/18	12/19/18
Treis, Germany	12/19/18	1/10/18
Guls, Germany	1/10/18	

M. M. McMahon, Ph.D.

MEDICAL DETACHMENT

STATION LIST OF UNIT SINCE ARRIVAL IN THE AMERICAN EXP.FORCES.

Unit: 51st Pioneer Inf.   Detachment: Med. Dept.   Arrived: France
Aug. 6, 1918.

On Transport No. 74   At: Brest, France

[STATION]	ARRIVED	LEFT	AUTHORITY
Pontanezen Bks.	Aug.7/18	Aug.14.18	per VO.CO.51st.Pioneer.In.

Left Brest Station on train 5AM. Aug.15/18

[STATION]	ARRIVED	LEFT	AUTHORITY
Maron	Aug.17/18		per VO.CO.51st.Pioneer.Inf.
Toul Bks.			
Pagny / Meuse			
Toul	Sept.2/18	Oct.24/18	per VO.CO.51st.Pioneer.Inf.
Menil-la-Tour	Oct.24/18	Nov.16/18	per VO.CO.51st.Pioneer.Inf.
Bruxieres	Nov.16/18	Nov.17/18	per VO.CO.51st.Pioneer.Inf.
Hannonville	Nov.17/18	Nov.18/18	per VO.CO.51st.Pioneer.Inf.
Mouaville	Nov.18/18	Nov.21/18	per VO.CO.51st.Pioneer.Inf.
Trieux, France	Nov.21/18	Nov.22/18	per VO.CO.51st.Pioneer.Inf.
Wollmeringen, France	Nov.23/18	Nov.24/18	per VO.CO.51st.Pioneer.Inf.
Aspelt (Luxemburg)	Nov.24/18	Dec.2/18	per VO.CO.51st.Pioneer.Inf.
Wormeldingen	Dec.2/18	Dec.3/18	per VO.CO.51st.Pioneer.Inf.

Crossed bridge into Germany at Gravenmacher, 11:05 AM Dec.3/18

[STATION]	ARRIVED	LEFT	AUTHORITY
Conz	Dec.4/18	Dec.5/18	per VO.CO.51st.Pioneer.Inf.
Fohren	Dec.5/18	Dec.6/18	per VO.CO.51st.Pioneer.Inf.
Wittlich	Dec.6/18	Dec.9/18	per VO.CO.51st.Pioneer.Inf.
Bullay	Dec.9/18	Dec.11/18	per VO.CO.51st.Pioneer.Inf.
Cochem	Dec.12/18		

Men and Officers from this Detachment have been on Detached Service
wherever Companies and working parties of this regiment have been
since their arrival in France.

COMPANY A STATION LIST

STATION LIST OF UNIT SINCE ARRIVAL IN THE
AMERICAN E.F.

Unit 51st Pioneer Inf. Company, A

On transport Rochambeau	At Bordeaux	Arrived France Aug 20/18			
STATION	ARRIVED	LEFT	AUTHORITY	ATTACHED OR ASSIGNED TO	DETACHMENTS STATIONED AT
Camp Genicart, Bordeaux, Gironde	Aug 20/18	Aug 23/18	Hq. Base 2 SOS	Separate	
Pagny-sur-Muses Dept of Meuse	Aug 29/18	Sept 2/18	Hq 51 P.I.		
Toul, Muerthe et Moselle	Sept 2/18	Oct 23/18	Hq 51 P.I.		Goodneiu, A.D. Royameizx, A.D. Toul, M.P. Trodes A.D. Troussey Bdge Montaville (construction)
Xivray, Meuse	Oct 23/18	Nov 10/18	4th AC Eng	4th ACEng	Toul, railhead Montaville Troussey Bdge
Vignulles, Dept Muese.	Nov 13/18	Nov 16/18	(unreadable) 1 Bn Hq 51PI	4th ACEng	
Thillot, Dept Muese.	Nov 17/18	Nov 18/18	1 Bn Hq 51PI	4th ACEng	
Fleville, Muerthe et Moselle	Nov 18/18	Nov 21/18	1 Bn Hq 51PI	4th ACEng	
Lomeringen, Lorraine	Nov 21/18	Nov 22/18	Hq 51PI	51 Pinf	
Kanfen, Lorraine	Nov 22/18	Nov 23/18	Hq 51PI		
Filsdorf, Luxembourg	Nov 23/18	Nov 30/18	Hq 51PI	1st Div	
Gostingen, Luxembourg	Nov 30/18	Dec 1/18	1 BnHq 51PI		
Wasserliesch	Dec 1/18	Dec 3/18	1 Bn. Hq 51PI		

Longuich	Dec 3/18	Dec 4/18	1 Bn. Hq 51PI	4th A.C.
Becund	Dec 4/18	Dec 6/18	1 BnHq 51PI	
Wittlich	Dec 6/18	Dec 8/18	Hq 51PI	51 PI
Bullay	Dec 8/18	Dec 17/18	Hq 51PI	
Neef	Dec 17/18	Dec 26/18	Hq 51PI	
Kond	Dec 26/18	Dec 27/18	Hq 51PI	
Loef	Dec 27/18	to date	Hq 51PI	

COMPANY 'B'

"In compliance with the foregoing order, (Field Order No. 12 Hq. IV Army Corps Sept. 8, 1918 and Field Order No. 36 Hq. 1st Div. AEF Sept. 9, 1918) Company B was formed in Buxierauois Woods at 1:30 A.M., during a drizzling rain and inky darkness, except from the flashes of the artillery, which had begun a violent bombardment at 1 A.M. The company marched from this station, with gas masks at the "alert" and ready for any emergency, to their position north of Beaumont in the rear of the front infantry line trenches, arriving at the designated point at 4:45 A.M. It was during this advance that the Co. came into the shell fire zone for the first time. The hour for the Infantry advance was set for 5 o'clock, and Co. B moved forward in rear of the infantry lines. At the outskirts of the village of Seichprey, the company was divided into working parties, filling the shell holes in the road to make the passage of ammunition carts, engineering material, rations and other supplies possible. Two or three small bridges were built north of Seichprey. At a point about midway between Seichprey and St. Baussant, where the main German trench ran at right angles across the road, and had been filled with new earth earlier in the morning by the Engineers, and word sent to the rear that the road was passable, the company met its hardest problems in road construction. Vehicles of all character had been coming up the roadway, and the second large truck that attempted the passage at this point mired to the axle in the loose earth, blocking up the road for hundreds of yards. B Co. was assigned the job of rebuilding the road while the German shells, in great numbers, fell in the immediate vicinity. After several hours of very hard work, and by the taking of timbers from the nearby dugouts and laying them on the road, in courduroy fashion for a distance of more than 150 feet, the roadway was made passable, and vehicles of all descriptions followed the advancing infantry lines once more. It was now past noon day, and the German shell fire had been silenced. The men of the company had performed their several tasks, including the liberation of six pieces of field artillery, which had mired in the mud in a nearby field, with spirit and energy although they had not eaten food since the night before. Several more bridges were constructed and many shell holes between this point and St. Baussant were filled up. The company arrived at St. Baussant at 5:30 P.M., and after a cold meal, snatched from their packs, billeted themselves on the stony ruins of the destroyed village, to snatch what sleep and rest they could. The following two days, the command was engaged in repairing roads in the village of St. Baussant. The company marched from St. Baussant at 5 P.M. Sept. 14th, and arrived in the LeFaux Bois Nauguisard, near Monsard, where they billeted at 2 A.M. The German had extensive camps and gardens in this area, even the woods still held many wandering Germans who were only too anxious to surrender. The second night a German bombing plane flew very low over the woods, where the company was encamped. The following night the woods were bombed, but the company had moved out. On September 15th, the company left Le Faux by auto trucks at 2 P.M. arriving at Royaumeix at 5 P.M. the same date. During the three days following, the company was employed in work on ammunition dumps at Royaumeix and Lafauene".

COMPANY B STATION LIST

HEADQUARTERS, COMPANY B, 51st PIONEER INFANTRY   Hatsenport, Germany

STATION LIST OF UNIT SINCE ARRIVAL IN THE AMERICAN E.F.

Unit: Co. B, 51st Pioneer Inf.   Arrived: France August 6, 1918.

On Transport "Kroonland"   At: Brest

STATION	ARRIVED	LEFT	AUTHORITY	ATTACHED OR ASSIGNED TO	DETACHMENTS STATIONED AT
Brest	Aug. 6	Aug. 14	Hqts. 51 Pion. Inf.	Fourth Corps	
Maron	Aug. 17	Aug. 21	"		
Pagney-Sur-Mouse	Aug. 23	Sept. 7	"		(Trondes
Toul	Sep. 8	" 10	Hqts.4th -- Corps	-1st -Div. ---	- (Gounod
					(Pagnay
Vusieranice Woods	Sep. 11	Sept. 12	1st Div.		(Washington Aux
St. Baussant	Sep. 12	Sept. 14	"		((Dump
LeFaux Bois Nauguisard	Sep. 15	Sept. 16	"		(McCormack "
Royaumeix	Sep. 16	Sept. 19	4th Corps	4th Corps	
Toul	Sep. 19	Oct. 21	Hqts. 51 Pion. Inf.	301 Eng,	
St. Baussant	Oct. 21	Nov. 10	301 Eng.		
Vigneulles	Nov. 10	Nov. 16	"		
Voel	Nov. 16	Nov. 17	Hqts. 51 Pion. Inf.	4th Corps	
Thillot	Nov. 17	Nov. 18	"		
Fleville	Nov. 18	Nov. 21	"		
Lomeringen	Nov. 21	Nov. 22	"		
Kanfan	Nov. 22	Nov. 23	"		
Pilsdorf	Nov. 23	Nov. 30	"		
Costigen	Nov. 30	Dec. 1	"		
Wasseliesch	Dec. 1	Dec. 3	"		
Longuich	Dec. 3	Dec. 4	"		
St. Matthias	Dec. 4	Dec. 6	"		
Fahren	Dec. 6	Dec. 7	"		
Wittlich	Dec. 7	Dec. 9	"		
Bullay	Dec. 9	Dec. 10	"		
Clotten	Dec. 10	Dec. 11	"		
Hatsenport	Dec. 11	===========			

HIGHLIGHTS of the Morning Reports Company B
From July 1918 – June 1919

17 July 1918. Entrained at Fair Forest, SC 11:00 AM

18 July 1918. Enroute

19 July 1918. Arrived at Camp Merritt 10:15 AM

25 July 1918. Lost by transfer – Max Baum by request of Sec of State

1 – 7 Aug 1918. On board.

6 Aug 1918. Arrived France 3:35PM

14 Aug 1918. Entrained 5:00AM

15 – 16 Aug 1918. Enroute

17 Aug 1918. Arrived

4 Sep 1918. Several soldiers to special duty carpenter's detail

12 – 16 Sep 1918. No remarks. [St. Mihiel Offensive]

17-19 Sep 1918. some soldiers from duty to sick in Evacuation Hospital No.12

10-20 Oct 1918. Multiple soldiers sick in quarters.

21 Oct 1918. Left Toul 11:55 A.M. Arrived St. Baussant 3:15 P.M. by motor truck.

1-10 Nov 1918. St Baussant: Co repaired roads around St Baussant.

2 Nov 1918. Detail of Company ordered to second line position at 9:30. Occupied this position at 10:00 A.M.

15 Nov 1918. Left St. Baussant 6:30 A.M. Marched to Vigneulles arrived 11:30 A.M.

16 Nov 1918. Left Vigneulles 8 P.M. marched to Woël Arrived 11:30 P.M. Distance marched 12 K's

17 Nov 1918. Left Woël 6 A.M. marched to Thillot. Arrived 8:45 A.M. Distance marched 4 K's. 9 horses attached.

18 Nov 1918. Left Thillot 4:30 A.M. marched to Fleville [Fléville-Lixières]. Arrived 4:15 A.M. Distance marched 35 K's. 2 horses attached.

19-20 Nov 1918. Fleville [Fléville-Lixières], France: Usual Camp Duties

20 Nov 1918. 4 horses and a wagoner from the Supply Company were attached.

21 Nov 1918. Fleville, France[Fléville-Lixières]: Left Fleville 8:45 A.M. Arrived 4:00 P.M. Distance marched

22 Nov 1918. Lommeringen [Lommerange]: Left Lommeringen 8:30 A.M. Arrived 4:00 P.M. Distance marched

21 Nov 1918. Kanfen: Left Kanfen 8:30 A.M. Arrived Filsdorf, Luxembourg 1:45 P.M. Distance marched

24 – 29. Nov 1918. Filsdorf, Luxembourg: Usual camp duties.

30 Nov 1918. Filsdorf: Left Filsdorf 8:00 A.M. Arrived Gostingen, Luxembourg 3:00 P.M. Distance marched 18 km

1 Dec 1918. Gostingen, Luxembourg: Left Gostingen 7:20 A.M. Arrived Wasseleisch, Germany 4:00 P.M. 23 Km. Several soldiers assigned to guarding bridges (Moselle + Sarr).

2 Dec 1918. Wasseleisch: Usual camp duties. Several soldiers sent to special duty at Temmels, Germany; Wellen, Germany; Wormoldingen [Wormeldange], Luxembourg; 3 medical men attached.

3 Dec 1918. Wasseleisch: Left Wasseleisch: 8:00 A.M. Arrived Longuich, Germany 3:30 P.M. Distance marched 24 Km. Several men attached to special duty on Wagon Train.

4 Dec 1918. Longuich, Germany: Left Longuich 7:20 A.M. Arrived St. Matthias 2:00 P.M. Distance marched 15 Km, Details sent out at various points en route to guard bridges and railroad stations along Moselle River

5 Dec 1918. St. Matthias: Usual camp duties

6 Dec 1918. St. Matthias: Left St. Matthias 1:00 P.M. Arrived Föhren 6: 20 P.M.

7 Dec 1918. Föhren, Germany: Left Föhren 8:00 A.M. Arrived Wittlich 2:30 P.M.

9 Dec 1918. Wittlich, Germany: Left Wittlich 8:00 A.M. Arrived Bullay 4:30 P.M. Distance marched 24 Km

10 Dec 1918. Bullay, Germany Left Bullay 8:00 A.M. Arrived Klotten 6:30 P.M. Distance marched 33 Km.

11 Dec 1918. Klotten, Germany: Left Klotten 8:30 A.M. Arrived Hatzenport 1:00 P.M. Distance marched 16 Km.

12-20 Dec 1918. Hatzenport, Germany: Company patrolled railroad from Moselkern, Germany to Lehmen, Germany.

19 Dec 1918. A Wagoner from the Supply Company and 4 horses attached.

21-31 Dec 1918. Hatzenport, Germany: Company relieved of railroad guard Dec 23 3:00 P.M. Taking up usual camp duties.

1-10 Jan 1919. Hatzenport, Germany: Usual camp duties.

11-20 Jan 1919. Hatzenport, Germany: Usual camp duties.

21-31 Jan 1919. Hatzenport, Germany.

Feb 1919. Throughout the month changes in soldiers' status were recorded.

1 Mar 1919. Hatzenport, Germany.

11-20 Mar 1919. Hatzenport, Germany.

18 March 1919. Entrained at Hatzenport 6:45 A.M. Arrived Cochem, Germany 8:00 A.M. via motor trucks to Kaisereisch [Kaisersesch?]. Reviewed by General John G. Pershing10:30 A.M. Left Kaisereisch 12:00 M. via Motor Trucks to Cochem by Rail to Hatzenport arriving back at Station 4:30 P.M. Distance traveled by rail 44 Km by Truck 33 Km.

9 April 1919. The Company commenced target practice.

20 Apr 1919. The Company held target practice.

30 Apr 1919. The Company held target practice.

10 May 1919. The Company held target practice.

11 May 1919 Hatzenport, Germany. Left Hatzenport 12 M. Marched to Railroad Station at Hatzenport distance 1 Kilometre. Entrained and left Hatzenport at 2:00 P.M. Arrived at Wengerohr, Germany 4:30 P.M. distance by rail 50 Kilometres. Marched from Wengerohr to Büscheid distance marched 3 Kilometres.

12 May 1919. Büscheid, Germany.

24 May 1919. Left Büscheid marched to Wengerohr 3 kilos. Left Wengerohr 2 P.M. arrived W. Trier 4 P.M. marched to Trier 4 Kilos.

25 May 1919. Left Trier, Germany. Marched to W. Trier 4 Kilos Left Trier by train.

28 May 1919. Arrived Noyen [Noyen-sur-Sarthe], France. Marched to Malicorne [Malicorne-sur-Sarthe]. Distance marched 6 Kilos.

31 May 1919. Malicorne [Malicorne-sur-Sarthe], France.

10 June 1919. Malicorne [Malicorne-sur-Sarthe].

11 June 1919. Left Malicorne [Malicorne-sur-Sarthe], France, at 2:30 P.M. and marched to Noyen [Noyen-sur-Sarthe]. Distance 7 Kilometres. Entrained and left Noyen at 6:25 P.M.

12 June 1919. Arrived at Clisson 7:00 A.M. Distance by Rail 100 Kilos. Marched to Gorges [?]. 3 Kilos.

18 June 1919. Marched to Clisson 3 Kilos. Entrained at 9:30 A.M. for St. Nazaire. Arrived St. Nazaire 3 P.M. Marched to Camp No. 2. Distance 3 ½ Kilos.

19 June 1919. Left Camp No. 2 St. Nazaire, France, and marched to Camp No. 1. St. Nazaire. Distance 1 Kilo.

20 June 1919. Camp No. 1. St. Nazaire.

23 June 1919. Left Camp No. 1. St. Nazaire. 2:30 P.M. Marched to Dock #3. 2 Kilos. Embarked on U.S.S. Wilhelmina at 4:00 P.M.

24 June 1919. Sailed from St. Nazaire.

30 June 1919. U.S.S. Wilhelmina at sea.

COMPANY C STATION LIST

STATION LIST OF UNIT SINCE ARRIVAL IN THE
AMERICAN E.F.

Unit: 51st Pioneer Infantry   Company "C"   Arrived: France August 6/18

On Transport "Kroonland"   At: Brest, France

STATION	ARRIVED	LEFT	AUTHORITY	ATTACHED OR ASSIGNED TO	DETACHMENTS STATIONED AT
Brest,	Aug. 6th.	Aug, 13th	Hq. 51st P.I.		
Marrone,	Aug. 17th	Aug 21st	"		
Toul.	Aug. 21st	Aug. 22nd	"		
Trondes	Aug. 22nd	Sept. 2nd	"		
Toul	Sept. 2nd	Oct. 22nd	Hq 4th Corp	4th Corps	Menil-a-tour
					Pagny
					Pont-a-Maison
					Brossy
					Woinville
Mont Sec	Oct. 22nd	Nov. 10th	" " "		
Viguelles	Nov. 10th	Nov. 11th	" 2 "		
Hattonville	Nov. 11th	Nov. 16th			
Woel	Nov. 16th	Nov. 17th			
Thillot	Nov. 17th	Nov 18th			
Flaville	Nov. 18th	Nov 21st			4th Corp Hq.
Lommeringer	Nov. 21st	Nov. 22nd			
Kanfen	Nov. 22nd	Nov. 23nd			
Filsdorf					
Luxembourg	Nov. 23nd	Nov. 30th			
Costigan	Nov. 30th	Dec. 1st			Wasserbillig
Wasserlisch					
Germany	Dec. 1st	Dec. 3rd			Oberbillig
Longuich "	Dec. 3rd	Dec. 4th			
Becond "	Dec. 4th	Dec. 6th			
Wittlich "	Dec. 6th	Dec. 8th			
Bullay "	Dec. 8th	Dec. 9th			
Cochem "	Dec. 9th	Dec. 23rd			
Cond "	Dec. 23rd				

COMPANY 'D'.

"Company D, 51st Pioneer Infantry was stationed at Domgermain, France, doing Pioneer work in the Engineer dump on Saturday Sept. 10th, 1918, when the order came to move into the advance area north of Toul, in the vicinity of Hamonville. The men were under shelter tents, and it had been steadily raining for three days. The order called for the start to be made at 2 P.M. The rain did not abate, and it was necessary for the men to roll their packs in a downpour, all of their belongings being soaking wet, and their packs almost doubly heavy. The route of march was from Domgermain through Choloy, Menillot, Foug, and Lay St. Remy to Trondes. At Trondes one hour halt was made to eat supper and to rest. At 7 P.M. the march was resumed. The route was northward from Trondes to a point between Boucq and Sanzcy where it had been first ordered that a halt would be taken for the night. But upon arrival at this place, it was found that orders had been changed, and that the march would be continued to final destination in the Foret de Reine. Therefore, after a halt of less than an hour in the rain and mud the march was resumed at 10 P.M. The roads were jammed with traffic and the slow progress was particularly trying to the heavily laden men.

The company was attached to the first battalion of the 1st Engineers and the Engineer's camp was reached about 4 A.M. of Sept. 11th, and the men bivouaced in the woods. That day the company rested in the woods.

At 3 A.M. Sept. 12th, the company left the camp in Foret de Reine and marched on Beaumont, through Mandres-aux-Tours. Beaumont was reached a few minutes before 5 A.M., the time specified. There the company was divided to take care of the several roads running forward in the sector of the 1st Division for the advance of the artillery. Captain Niles with Lieuts. Potter and Stauffer had one half of the Co. on the road from Seichprey to Richecourt. This half company encountered heavy shell fire, and suffered casualties, Corporal Slattery (3344424) Robert A. (killed), Mech. Schaumann (1228223) Carl, (slightly wounded), Privates Balletta (3190128) Donato (slightly wounded) and Soin (3184296) Max (slightly wounded). Lieut. Cooper had one platoon on the road from Beaumont to the main road, Bouconville-St. Baussont. Lieutenants Noell and Starr with one platoon were on the road, Rombucourt-Xivray and later on road, Xivray- Richecourt. About noon this detachment joined Capt. Niles at Richecourt and the two detachments worked energetically to open the road to Le Hayville and St. Baussont, and the road through the village of Richecourt, and before six o'clock the immense amount of traffic of all descriptions, artillery, machine guns, supply wagons and ambulances, which was blocked in the rear was able to move forward again. The men bivouaced that night in the ruined village of Richecourt, being joined by Lieut. Cooper's detachment which during the day had worked to St. Baussont, the original assembly place, but learning that the remainder of the company was in Richecourt returned there during the night. This change was made necessary because the road was damaged more greatly than had been anticipated.

Early the next morning, the company moved forward to St. Baussont and Sept. 13-14th, were spent in repairing the Kivray-St. Baussont and the Seicheprey roads. For two days the men were without rations, except the one day emergency rations which they carried, but in spite of hunger, they worked faithfully at their job.

On the 14th, the order came to move forward. The company started at 5 P.M. the line of march being through Essey, Pannes, Nonsard to the woods near Heudicourt, reaching the destination about 11 P.M. and going into bivouac for the night.

On the 16th, the order came to be relieved, the company being transported to Royaumeix in auto trucks".

COMPANY D STATION LIST

STATION LIST OF UNIT SINCE ARRIVAL IN THE AMERICAN E.F.

Unit: 51st Pioneer Infantry   Company "D"   Port of Debarkation: Hoboken, N.J.

On Transport U.S.S.Kroonland   At: Brest, France

STATION	ARRIVED	LEFT	AUTHORITY	ATTACHED OR ASSIGNED TO	DETACHMENTS STATIONED AT
Brest, France	Aug.6/18	Aug.14/18	Hq. 51 P.I.		
Maron, France	Aug.17/18	Aug.21/18	Hq. 51 P.I.		
Bagny-sur-Meuse, France	Aug.22/18	Sept.3/18	Hq. 51 P.I.	4th Corps	
Domjermain	Sept.3/18	Sept.10/18	Hq. 51 P.I.	4th Corps	
Reine Woods	Sept.10/18	Sept.12/18	Hq. 1st Div	1st Div	
St. Baussont,	Sept.13/18	9/14/18	Hq. 1st Div	1st Div	
Royaumeix	Sept.16/18	9/19/18	Hq. 51 P.I.	4th Corps	
Toul	Sept.19/18	Oct.21/18	Hq. 51 P.I.	4th Corps	
Mont Sec	Oct.21/18	Nov.9/18	Hq. 51 P.I.	4th Corps	
Vigneulles	Nov.9/18	Nov.17/18	Hq. 51 P.I.	4th Corps	
Wohl,	Nov.17/18	Nov.18/18	Hq. 51 P.I.	4th Corps	
Thillot	Nov.18/18	Nov.19/18	Hq. 51 P.I.	4th Corps	
Fleville	Nov.19/18	Nov.22/18	Hq. 51 P.I.	4th Corps	
Lommeringen	Nov.22/18	Nov.23/18	Hq. 51 P.I.	4th Corps	
Filsdorf Luxembourg	Nov.23/18	Nov.30/18	Hq. 51 P.I.	4th Corps	
Gostigen, Luxembourg	Nov.30/18	Dec.1/18	Hq. 51 P.I.	4th Corps	
Wasserlick, Gy.	Dec.1/18	Dec.3/18	Hq. 51 P.I.	4th Corps	
Longuich, Gy.	Dec.3/18	Dec.4/18	Hq. 51 P.I.	4th Corps	
Becond, Germany	Dec.4/18	Dec.6/18	Hq. 51 P.I.	4th Corps	
Witlich, Germany	Dec.6/18	Dec.8/18	Hq. 51 P.I.	4th Corps	
Bullay	Dec.8/18	Dec.9/18	Hq. 51 P.I.	4th Corps	
Sehl	Dec.9/18	Dec.10/18	Hq. 51 P.I.	4th Corps	
Carden, Germany	Dec.10/18	Dec.28/18	Hq. 51 P.I.	4th Corps	Clotten, Galgenberg, Pommern, Muden, Moselkern
Lehmen, Germany	Dec.28/18		Hq. 51 P.I.	4th Corps	

<u>COMPANY E STATION LIST</u>

STATION LIST OF UNIT SINCE ARRIVAL IN THE AMERICAN E.F.

Unit: 51st Pioneer Infantry   Company "E"   Arrived, France Aug. 6, 1918

On Transport #74 (S.S.Kroonland)   At: Brest, France

STATION	ARRIVED	LEFT	AUTHORITY	ATTACHED OR ASSIGNED TO	DETACHMENTS STATIONED AT
Brest	Aug,6/18	Aug.13/18	S.O.219 Base Sec. 5 Oper. O.2		none
Sexey-aux-Forges	Aug.17/18	Aug.24/18	IV Corps	IV Corps	none
Laneuville	Aug.24/18	Sept.18/18	O, 51st Pio. Infty	"	Ouvrage de la Cloche Ouvrage de Bouvron Fort de Trondes
Toul	Sept.18/18	Sept.20/18	"	"	
Sezieuria	Sept. 21/18	Sept. 21/18	"	"	none
Puvenelle Wds	Sept. 22/18	Sept. 23/18	"	"	none
Fey-en-Heye	Sept. 23/18	Oct. 5/18	"	"	none
Limey	Oct. 5/18	Nov. 16/18	"	"	Puvenelle Wds
Zammes	Nov. 16/18	Nov. 17/18	"	"	Puvenelle Wds
Hannonville	Nov. 17/18	Nov. 18/18	"	"	none
Thermoville	Nov. 18/18	Nov. 21/18	"	"	none
Trieux	Nov. 21/18	Nov. 22/18	"	"	none
Wollerinden	Nov. 22/18	Nov. 23/18	"	"	none
Aspelt	Nov. 23/18	Dec. 2/18	"	"	none
Wollmerdingen	Dec. 2/18	Dec. 3/18	"	"	none
Conz	Dec. 3/18	Dec. 4/18	"	"	none
Fohren	Dec. 4/18	Dec. 6/18	"	"	none
Wittlich	Dec. 6/18	Dec. 7/18	"	"	none
Bengel	Dec. 7/18	Dec. 15/18	"	"	Traben-Trabach
Ettiger	Dec. 15/18	Dec. 16/18	"	"	none
Treis	Dec. 16/18	Dec. 18/18	"	"	none
Masburg	Dec. 18/18	Dec. 30/18	"	"	none
Kerben	Dec. 30/18	Jan. 1/19	"	"	none
Guls	Jan. 1/19				

COMPANY F STATION LIST

51st. Pioneer Inf.   "F"

#74 (Kroonland)   Brest, France   Aug.6, 1918

		1918			
Brest	Aug.6,1918	Aug.13,	V.O. CO.51 P.I.		
Sexey-aux-Forges	Aug,18	Aug 23,			
St. Etienne	Aug.24	Sept.18	Orders 6659, 3rd.sec 8th.Army (French)		Francheville Ropage Vieux Carton Mordant
Toul	Sept. 18	Sept. 20	VOCO.51 P.I.		
Fey-en-Haye	Sept. 22	Oct. 7	VOCO.2nd.Bn.51 P.I.		
Remenauville	Oct. 7	Oct. 13		4th.Corps	
Xivray	Oct. 13	Oct. 23	Memo.O.Ch.Eng 4th.Corps	4th.Corps	
Mamey	Oct. 23	Nov.10	Memo.O.Ch.Eng 4th.Corps	4th.Corps	
Thiacourt	Nov.10	Nov.16	Memo.O.Ch.Eng 4th.Corps	4th.Corps	
Xammes	Nov.16	Nov.17	VOCO.2nd.Bn. 51 P.I.	4th.Corps	
Suzemont	Nov.17	Nov.18	VOCO.2nd.Bn. 51 P.I.	4th.Corps	
Thurerville	Nov.18	Nov.20	VOCO.2nd.Bn. 51 P.I.	4th.Corps	
Trieux	Nov.20	Nov.21	VOCO.2nd.Bn. 51 P.I.	4th.Corps	
Wohlmeringer	Nov.21	Nov.22	VOCO.51st P.I.	4th.Corps	
Aspelt, Luxenbourg Wilmerdinden,	Nov.22	Dec.2	VOCO.51st P.I.	4th.Corps	
Luxembourg	Dec.2	Dec.3	VOCO.51st P.I.	4th.Corps	
Konz. Germany	Dec.3	Dec.4	VOCO.51st P.I.	4th.Corps	

COMPANY 'G'.

"Left Bautzen Barracks, Toul Sept. 11th, hiked to Bernecourt and attached to Co. F, 117th Engineers, 42nd Division. Company messed in an old barn, then marched to open field outside the village where they dug in, in a pouring rainstorm. This was done in anticipation of enemy shell fire. At 1 A.M. Sept 12th, a barrage commenced with all calibres of guns and continued till about daylight. There was no enemy fire in our sector, consequently no casualties. Left Bernecourt in detachments: 1st Det. left 6 A.M.; 2nd Det. 9 A.M. and 3rd Det. 11 A.M. Our gun fire then was very slight. Detachments marched to Flirey about 5 kilometers, passing many prisoners on the way halted for mess and continued the march to a point in the woods, between Flirey and Essey and occupied the dugouts just vacated by the enemy, where we camped till the 14th., engaged in repairing roads for line of communication. The system of trenches and dugouts was very complete and substantial and had been occupied by the Germans for four years. One of our men found a young German hid away in a deep dugout who yelled "Kamerad" when discovered and was brought to the open stricken with terror. He was turned over to the M. P.'s in charge of the almost continuous line of prisoners who were passing along the Bernecourt and Metz road while we camped there. Left on the morning of Sept. 14th and proceeded to woods 2 kilometers south of St. Benoit, where Co. and the Engineers made camp and pitched pup tents in the woods digging shrapnel proof holes alongside. Gas guard was posted every night. Frequent enemy planes came over for observation and everybody ducked out of sight. Heavy shell fire went over our heads every night, the objective being four heavy field batteries in the woods in our rear. Co. was engaged in cutting and pointing stakes for wire entanglements. A commodious balloon shed furnished ample room for kitchens, Officers mess, office and store room. Pursuant to Memo No. 15 S-3 Hq. 42nd, Div. we were returned to Toul Barracks by truck on the morning of Sept. 18, proud to have had a part, however small in the famous offensive that brought great credit to our Army".

M. M. McMahon, Ph.D.

COMPANY G STATION LIST

STATION LIST COMPANY "G", 51st PIONEER INFANTRY, SINCE ARRIVAL IN THE A.E.F.

ARRIVED FRANCE AUGUST 7, 1918 -- TRANSPORT "KROONLAND" AT BREST.

STATION	ARRIVED	LEFT	AUTHORITY	ATTACHED OR ASSIGNED TO	DETACHMENTS STATIONED AT
Brest	Aug 7/18	Aug 14/18	R.O.	----	------
Sexay-au-forges	Aug 17/18	Aug 28/18	R.O.	----	------
Troussey	Aug 30/18	Sep 2/18	R.O.	----	------
Toul	Sep 3/18	Sep 11/18	R.O.	----	Trondes-Commercey Dougermain-Gudenear.
Bernecourt	Sep 11/18	Sep 12/18	R.O.	117th Engrs Co. "F"	------
	Sept 12/18	Sep 14/18	----	" "	------
Ft. Benoit	Sep 14/18	Sep 18/18	----	" "	------
Toul	Sep 18/18	Sep 21/18	----	----	------
Saizerais	Sep 22/18	Sep 22/18	R.O.	----	------
Griscourt (Puvenelle Woods)	Sep 23/18	Sep 24/18	R.O.	----	------
Thiacourt & Mrtz Rds	Sep 24/18	Oct 3/18	R.O.	6th Army Corps	------
Euvezin Woods near Remmenauville	Oct 3/18	Nov 16/18	R.O.	----	------
Xammes	Nov 16/18	Nov 17/18	R.O.	----	------
Hannonville	Nov 17/18	Nov 18/18	R.O.	----	------
Thurmeville	Nov 18/18	Nov 21/18	R.O.	----	------
Trieux	Nov 21/18	Nov 22/18	R.O.	----	------
Wooleringen	Nov 22/18	Nov 23/18	R.O.	----	------
Aspelt (Luxemburg)	Nov 23/18	Dec 2/18	R.O.	----	------
Wormeldang	Dec 2/18	Dec 3/18	R.O.	----	------
Conz	Dec 3/18	Dec 4/18	R.O.	----	------
Fohren	Dec 4/18	Dec 5/18	R.O.	----	------
Salmrohr	Dec 5/18	Dec 13/18	R.O.	----	------
Cochen	Dec 13/18	Dec 14/18	R.O.	----	------
Guls	Dec 14/18				

COMPANY 'H'.

By order of the Commanding General IV Army Corps, dated Sept. 10th, 1918, Co. H, now attached to the 89th Division left Toul and proceeded to Lagny there being directed to continue to Grosrouves and join the 314th Engineers. The latter part of the march was made during a heavy rainstorm and the men miserable and weary from the long hike tumbled into the abandoned and war-scarred houses and barns of Grosrouves sometime after midnight.

About 3 P.M. the following day orders were received from the acting Commander of the 1st Battalion of the 314th Engineers to send the Co. divided into two platoons, to Bernecourt immediately, to help in the construction of Bangalore Torpedoes. A drive was scheduled for the following morning with the object of straightening out the famous four-year-old St. Mihiel salient and the combined forces of the Engineers and Pioneers were to use these torpedoes to blow up the wire entanglements in No Mans Land just before the zero hour o'clock - and clear the path for the doughboy.

The two platoons reached Bernecourt and remained there until about 8:30 P.M. Then they moved forward separately, along the traffic-choked road, and entered the trenches in the vicinity of Flirey a few hours later. At 1 o'clock began the terrific four hour barrage. This was the first time the company had experienced the nerve shattering fire of artillery but every man stood the test well. When zero hour came the first wave of the attacking American Infantry went over the top in the face of bursts of machine gun fire and rather spasmodic Germany artillery action. One platoon of Co. H attached to the 356th Inf. followed close behind. Before the German trenches were reached Sergt. William E. Harris made the supreme sacrifice, being killed instantly. A moment later Private Alfred J. Young feel badly wounded. The other men never faltered behaving like seasoned veterans.

The other platoon with the 314th Engineers moved in the wake of the ever-advancing doughboys and cleared and constructed roads for the forward movement of artillery and supplies. The work was done under incessant Boche shell fire but the men toiled hour after hour with a steadiness of old campaigners. For a week this platoon labored, feverishly working along the roads in the vicinity of Essey, Pannes, Euvizen and Thiacourt. Eating and sleeping were out of the question for the first few days and the men, when finally relieved, were thoroughly tired out. The platoon with the 356th Infantry remained with them for five days occupying the front line in the woods north of Beney. Here they helped dig hasty entrenchments and organized the ground, in addition to supplying patrols to reconnoiter in No Mans Land. After being relieved the platoon left the infantry and joined the Engineers at Beney. Two days later the whole Co. assembled at Toul".

COMPANY H STATION LIST

STATION LIST OF UNIT SINCE ARRIVAL IN THE AMERICAN E.F.

Unit: 51st Pioneer Infantry   Company H   Arrived: France Aug. 6/18

On Transport U.S.S.Kroonland   At: Brest, France

STATION	ARRIVED	LEFT	AUTHORITY	ATTACHED OR ASSIGNED TO
Brest, France	Aug. 6/18	Aug. 14//18	Hdqrts.	
Sexey-aux-forges	" 17/18	" 29/18	Hdqrts.	
Chaloy, France	" 30/18	" 30/18	Hdqrts.	
Troussey, "	" 31/18	Sept. 2/18	Hdqrts.	
Toul, "	Sept. 2/18	" 10/18	Hdqrts.	
Grosrouves, "	" 10/18	" 11/18	Hdqrts.	89th Div
Flirey, "	" 12/18	" 17/18	Hdqrts.	" "
Essey, "	" 17/18	" 18/18	Hdqrts.	" "
Toul, "	" 19/18	" 20/18	Hdqrts.	
Saizerais, "	" 21/18	" 22/18	Hdqrts.	
Fay-en-Hays, "	" 22/18	Oct. 8/18	Hdqrts.	
Euvazin Woods, "	Oct. 8/18	Nov. 16/18	Hdqrts.	
Xammes, Franche	Nov. 17/18	" 17/18	Hdqrts.	
Hannonville, "	" 17/18	" 18/18	Hdqrts.	
Thumerville, "	" 18/18	" 21/18	Hdqrts.	
Trieux, France	Nov. 21/18	Nov. 22/18	Hdqrts.	
Wolleringen, Luxemburg	Nov. 22/18	Nov. 23/18	"	
Aspelt, "	Nov. 23/18	Dec. 2/18	"	
Wormeldanger, Luxemburg	Dec. 2/18	Dec. 3/18	"	
Conz, Germany	" 3/18	" 4/18	"	
Fohren, "	" 4/18	" 14/18	"	
Wittlich, "	" 14/18	" 15/18	"	
Alf, "	" 15/18	" 17/18	"	
Sehl, "	" 17/18	" 18/18	"	
Treis, "	" 18/18	" 27/18	"	
Lehmen, "	" 27/18	" 28/18	"	
Gulz, "	" 28/18			

COMPANY I STATION LIST

STATION LIST OF UNIT SINCE ARRIVAL IN THE AMERICAN E.F.

Unit: 51st Pioneer Infantry   Company I   Arrived: France
Aug. 6/18
On Transport U.S.S. Kroonland   At: Brest, France

STATION	ARRIVED	LEFT	AUTHORITY
Brest, France	Aug.6th/18	Aug.14/18	R.S.O.
Maron, France	Aug.18/18	Aug.21/18	R.S.O.
Toul, France	Aug.22/18	Aug.22/18	R.S.O.
Lay St. Remy, France	Aug.22/18	Sep.2/18	R.S.O.
Toul, France	Sep.3/18	Oct.22/18	R.S.O.
Menil-la-Tour, France	Oct.22/18	Nov.16/18	R.S.O.
Vegneulle, France	Nov.16/18	Nov.17/18	R.S.O.
Mars-la-Tour, France	Nov.17/18	Nov.18/18	R.S.O.
Buzzy, France	Nov.19/18	Nov.19/18	R.S.O.
Conflans, Alsace	Nov.19/18	Nov.25/18	R.S.O.
Ardun, Alsace	Nov.25/18	Nov.26/18	R.S.O.
Bettemburg, Luxm.	Nov.26/18	Dec.4/18	R.S.O.
Berncastle-Cues, Germany	Dec.5/18	Jan.4/19	R.S.O.
Coburn, Germany	Jan.4/19		

COMPANY 'K'.

"One Sept. 11th, the company hiked to Mandres, behind the front lines, where it took part in the opening of the St. Mihiel offensive, on the morning of Sept. 12th.

The work of the company during the first individual offensive of the American Army, deserves special mention. From the beginning of the attack until the establishment of a new line had been effected, the Officers and men of the command worked indefatigably at the tasks assigned to them, often times under hazardous conditions penetrating far into the zone of enemy fire and, in small numbers, even reaching during this period of their baptismal fire was sustained on a high plane at all times. No casualties were suffered during the seven days in which the Co. advanced behind the combat forces as far as St. Benoit and the Bois de Thiacourt, among the points of farthest advance in the offensive.

In the course of this action the four platoons of the command were assigned to duty respectively with the 165th, 166th, 167th and 168th Regiments of the 42nd Division. On Sept. 16th, the Company was re-assembled and returned to Toul".

History of Company K, 51st Pioneer Infantry.

The history of the company, under its present designation, dates from January 6th, 1917, when, at Camp Wadsworth, Spartanburg, S.C., it was formed from the existent nucleus of Company K, 10th New York Infantry. Previous transferal of officers and men for service with the 27th. Division, U.S.A., had reduced its personnel to 43 men. The company was brought up to full strength by the assignment of men of the selective service and casuals during May and June.

The officers --- Frank X. Kearns, Captain; Arthur W. McFarland, 1st. Lieut.; Dwight J. Harris, 1st. Lieut.; Allison Armour, 1st. Lieut.; Reginald Havill, 2nd. Lieut.; and Victor A. Means, 2nd. Lieut., had been assigned to the company about the first of February, 1918.

Following a period of seven weeks' intensive training at Camp Wadsworth, the company left with the regiment on July 17th. for Camp Merritt, Tenafly, New Jersey, and sailed from Hoboken on the 26th. for France, on the U.S.S. Kroonland.

Brest was reached on August 5th., the company remaining with the regiment in rest camp near that port for nine days, departing on August 14th. under battalion command for Maren, on the Moselle River, between Toul and Nancy, where it was billeted from the 18th. to the 21st. On the railroad journey the company had been equipped with helmets and gas masks at Is-sur-Tille and had gone through the gas chamber there, on August 16th.

On the 21st. of the same month, the company left Maron with the battalion for Toul, was quartered there overnight, and left the following morning, alone and on foot, for Regeville, four miles from the front. At this place the company, working in platoons, was engaged in the cleaning of a right of way for a projected railroad line. This work was completed by September 6th., when the command returned to Toul for five days.

On September 11th. the company hiked to Mandres, behind the front lines, where it took part in the opening of the St. Mihiel Offensive, on the morning of September 12th.

The work of the company during the first individual offensive of the American Army, deserves special mention. From the beginning of the attack until the establishment of the new lines had been effected, the officers and men of the command worked indefatigably at the tasks assigned to them, often times under hazardous conditions, penetrating far into the zone of enemy fire and, in small numbers, even reaching out beyond the foremost lines. The morale and discipline if the men during this period of their baptismal fire was sustained on a high plane at all times. No casualties were suffered during the seven days in which the company advanced behind the combat forces as far as St. Benoit and Bois de Thiacourt, among the points of farthest advance in the offensive.

In the course of this action, the four platoons of the command were assigned for duty respectively with the 165th, 166th, 167th, and 168th. Regiments of the 42nd Division.

On September 18th. the company was reassembled and returned to Toul. From that date until October 21st. it was occupied with S.O.S. [Services Of Supply] detail work at the Toul rail-head. On October 21st. it removed to Sanzey, where barracks were constructed. Details sent out for Pioneer work at Essey and Evacuation Hospital returned to the command at this time.

On November 14th. The company received orders to join the newly established Third Army for the occupation of German soil, being attached to the Fourth Army Corps and assigned to rail-head duty. Moving northward, by truck, rail and foot, the company made stops at from one to eight days at Verdun, Baroncourt and Audun-le-Reman, in France; at Aumetz, in Lorraine; at Bettemburg, in Luxemburg; and at Trier, Castellaun, Carden and Mayen. in Germany, for assigned work.

Mayen was left on December 23rd. and the company was billeted the same night in Coborn, its present headquarters.

On October 15th. The company sent two sergeants, J.K. Mannain and T.C. Stuart, to Officers' Training Camp.

On November 1st. three Lieutenants - Arrmour, Means and Havill and one sergeant- W.M. LeRoy- left the company for Infantry Weapon School at Chatillen-sur-Seine, rejoining it December 23rd. On November 8th. fifteen men, under charge of the 1st. Sergeant, were sent to Aix-le-Bains for a week's furlough.

The present strength of the company is six officers and two hundred and fifteen men.

M. M. McMahon, Ph.D.

COMPANY K STATION LIST

Station List of Unit since arrival in the American E.F.

Unit- 51st Pioneer Infantry, Co. K,   Arrived in France August 7, 1918

On Transport Kroonland   At Brest, France

Stations	Arrived.	Left.	Authority	Attached or Assigned to	Detachments stations at
Pantanezzen Barracks	Aug 7/18	Aug. 14/18	R.V.O.		
Maren	Aug. 18/18	Aug. 21/18	R.V.O.		
Toul	Aug. 21/18	Aug.22/18	R.V.O.		
Regeville	Aug.22/18	Sept.6/18	R.V.O.		
Toul	Sept.6/18	Sept.11/18	R.V.O.		
Mandres	Sept.11/18	Sept.13/18	4th Corps. V.O.	117th.Eng.	
Essey	Sept.13/18	Sept.18/18	42nd Div. V.O.	42nd Div.	
Toul	Sept.18/18	Oct.21/18	42nd Div.		Royamieux
Sanzey	Oct.21/18	Nov.14/18	R.V.O.		Essey
Menil-la-Tour	Nov.14/18	Nov.16/18	R.V.O.		
Wienville	Nov.16/18	Nov.17/18	R.V.O.		
Nammenville	Nov.17/18	Nov.18/18	R.V.O.		
Buzy	Nov.18/18	Nov.19/18	-A.C., V.O.	4th, A.G. Hq.	
Etain	Nov.19/18	Nov.20/18	"	"	
Baroncourt	Nov.20/18	Nov.21/18	"	"	
Aumetz	Nov.21/18	Nov23/18	"	"	
Audun-le-Roman	Nov23/18	Nov25/18	"	"	
Bettemburg, Luxemburg	Nov25/18	Dec. 1/18	"	"	
Trier, Germany	Dec. 1/18	Dec.8/18	"	"	
Castellaun	Dec.9/18	Dec. 13/18	"	"	
Carden	Dec. 13/18	Dec.16/18	"	"	
Mayen	Dec.16/18	Dec.23/18	"	"	
Cobern, Germany	Dec.23/18		R.V.O.		

90

<u>COMPANY 'L'.</u>

"On Sept. 6th the Co. was ordered back to Toul, but returned to Noviant four days later to take part in the St. Mihiel offensive. In this offensive L Co. was attached to Co. E 314th, Engineers to do engineer and pioneer work. It reached the trenches shortly after the first line crossed the top, and began to cut wire and bridge the trenches so that the artillery and lines of communication could go forward. Much of the work of the day was under shell fire, but there were no casualties. Euvizen was reached in the first days advance, and in the afternoon the Co. was formed for attack and held in reserve for a German counter attack but none came. The work was continued on the second day and Bullionville was reached. The Co. was now ordered back to Flirey to work with the Grave Registration Service. This work continued four days. The battle ground surrounding Flirey and Essey was reached and the dead registered and buried. A small ammunition dump was located at Essey, and no night passed without German shell fire reaching us. The Grave Registration Service having been completed the Co. was ordered to Menil-la-Tour (Sept. 18th) attached to IV Corps Hq., and took charge of the German prison stockade".

COMPANY L STATION LIST

STATION LIST OF UNIT SINCE ARRIVAL IN THE AMERICAN E.F.

Unit: 51st Pioneer Infantry   Company L

Arrived: France Aug. 6, 1918

On Transport Kroonland   At: Brest, France

STATION	ARRIVED	LEFT	AUTHORITY	ATTACHED OR ASSIGNED TO	DETACHMENTS STATIONED AT
Brest - Finistere	Aug. 6, 18	Aug. 14, 18	-	-	-
Chaligny - Meurthe	Aug, 18. 18	Aug.21, 18	-	-	-
Toul -- "	Aug.21, 18	Aug.22, 18	-	-	-
Minorville "	Aug. 23, 18	Sept.2, 18	G.O.143, 32 Army Corps French	Attached	-
Ansauville "	Sept.2, 18	Sept.6, 18	V.O.C.O. 89th Div.	"	-
Toul "	Sept.6, 18	Sept.10, 18	V.O.C.O. 51st Pio.INF	-	-
Noviant "	Sept.11, 18	Sept.13, 18	Field order #12, Hq. 4th Army Corp	Attached	-
Flirey "	Sept.13, 18	Sept.15, 18	Hq.89th Div No.126	"	-
Essey - Meurthe	Sept.15, 18	Sept.18, 18	V.O.C.O. Co. L	Attached	-
Menil-la-Tour "	Sept.18, 18	Nov.16,18	-	"	Lagney, Lucey, Bruley, Pagney, Ecrouves, Aulnois, Lay St Remy Troussey, Laneuve-ville, Trondes Boucq.
Buxerelles - Meuse	Nov.16,18	Nov.17,18		-	-
Hannonville "	Nov.17,18	Nov.18,18		-	-
Mouaville "	Nov.18,18	Nov.20,18		-	-
Bouligny - Meurthe	Nov.20,18	Dec.4,18	Hq.4th Corps G-3 Memo #675	-	Audun, Baroncourt, Landres, Mercy la Haut

COMPANY M STATION LIST

STATION LIST OF UNIT SINCE ARRIVAL IN THE AMERICAN E.F.

Unit: 51st Pioneer Inf. Company "M"   Arrived: France Aug. 6, 1918

On Transport U.S.S. Kroonland At: Brest, France

STATION	ARRIVED	LEFT	AUTHORITY	DETACHMENTS STATIONED AT
Brest	Aug.7/18	Aug 14/18		
Chaligny	Aug 18/18	Aug 22/18	V.O. Hq 51st P.I.	
Pont St. Vincent	Aug 22/18	Sept 6/18	V.O. Hq 51st P.I.	
Toul	Sept 7/18	Oct 26/18	V.O. Hq 51st P.I.	Menil le Tour
				Mennecourt
				Woinville
Menil-le Tour	Oct 26/18	Nov 16/18	V.O. Hq 51st P.I.	Bernecourt
Bruxerelles	Nov 16/18	Nov 17/18	V.O. Hq 51st P.I.	
Hannonville	Nov 17/18	Nov 18/18	" "	
Mouaville	Nov 18/18	Nov 21/18	" "	
Trieux	Nov 21/18	Nov 22/18	" "	
Wollmeringen	Nov 22/18	Nov 23/18	" "	
Aspelt	Nov 23/18	Dec 1/18	" "	
Wermwldingen	Dec 1/18	Dec 2/18	VO Hq 51st P.I.	
Conz	Dec 2/18	Dec 3/18	" "	
Biewer	Dec 3/18	Dec 12/18	" "	
Wittlich	Dec 12/18	Dec 13/18	" "	
Kaaiseresche	Dec 13/18	Dec 14/18	" "	
Kehrig	Dec 14/18	Dec 15/18	" "	
Cobern	Dec 15/18	Dec 18/18	" "	
Kerben	Dec 18/18	Dec 26/18	" "	Bassenheim
Dieblich	Dec 26/18	Dec 29/18	" "	Bassenheim
Cobern	Dec 29/18	To date	" "	Metternich
				Bassenheim

These accounts told by those who were not only eye witnesses but actors in the living drama, are representative of the work done and the part played by those Officers and men of the 51st Pioneer Infantry who were in the St. Mihiel drive.

Not so spectacular but not less important was the work being done by the remainder of the regiment, operating from Toul as a base. Not all the fighting is done at the front, and there was work of tremendous import going on continuously in the advance zone well within range of the enemy artillery, work that called for steady nerves and unremitting labor. Illimitable were the orders which rained upon headquarters for details and varied was the work which they were called upon to perform. An idea of the number and variety of these details may best be had by taking a few examples from the report on the Strength and Disposition of the Regiment as of September 14th. Some of the details and the number of men from the regiment employed thereon were as follows:

Military Police	170
Red Cross Hut	7
Troussey	41
Menil-la-Tour	112
Ammunition Dumps	403
Camp Guard	46
Carpenters	20
Salvage	22
Clerks, Town Major	4
Railhead	100
Gasolene Detail	21
42nd Division	352
89th Division	335
1st Division	322
French forts guarding Toul	438

Similar quotations might be taken from other reports on the Strength and Disposition of the Regiment at different times, but this one will suffice to show how busily the companies were engaged in furthering, in a great variety of ways, the winning of the war.

On Sept. 20th, S.O. No. 90 was received by the Commanding Officer from Hq. IV Army Corps stating,

"Pursuant to authority contained in Par. 1 S.O. 252
Hq. 1st Army dated Sept 19, 1918, one battalion
51st Pioneer Infantry will proceed without delay by
marching to Saizerais, reporting upon arrival to
Commanding General 6th Army Corps, at that place,
for duty.
By command of Maj. Gen. Dickman
Stuart Heintzelman
Chief of Staff".

In compliance with that order the second battalion under Major Dooley moved out from the Bautzen Barracks Toul on Sept. 20th, and Hiked to Saizerais. From there the hike was continued to Fay-en-Haye, a stop over night being made in the Puvenelle Woods. At Fay-en-Haye the troops were quartered in dugouts where available, those men not being so accommodated, pitching shelter tents in the woods. Co-operating with the 2nd Battalion 301st Engineers, the task assigned was that of repairing and reconstructing altogether in many places the Fay-en-Haye----Vilcey road. This road, lying between the artillery positions and the front line, and being one of the main arteries for the transport of supplies was subject at all times to shell fire. Running for the most part through open country, across the trench system and what was No Mans Land before the Franco-American advance, it lay well within the observation of enemy balloons. Hardly a day passed that the Officers and men, busy on the road or in the ruined village, were not many times within an ace of losing their lives. And during the nights the danger continued for the woods and the old trench system were subjected to frequent shelling. Despite the hardships suffered and the risks involved the work continued until its completion on Oct. 6th. Following the completion of this task, the 2nd Battalion with Hq. at Limey engaged in the repair of the Remnauville-Euvizen road, a task with which it was still occupied when the armistice was signed.

Headquarters remained at Toul during the month of Sept. and until later in October and during this time working details from the Companies there assemble were continually required. There were details   for ammunition dumps scattered throughout the forward area, for railheads, for salvage work, for gasoline stations, for carpentry work   and always the omni-present guard details. The band was kept busy playing frequently at Army hospitals in the Toul area and in so doing helped by lightening the other fellows load. The Supply Co., always busy, were during these trying days busier than ever, if such were possible. The magnitude of their task and the merit of its successful accomplishment stand revealed in the following statement:

"From Toul, we were not permitted to ration the various detachments by day, and night was the only time to perform this very necessary work. No lights were allowed to be used and this made traveling no easy task. To reach some of the place where detachments were located, moving troops to the front during the hottest days of battle, through rain and mud, getting tangled up with French truck trains, proved easily that a real war was on. Aeroplanes followed our movements, the bombing of the road, looked to us at times that to get to our Cos., would be impossible but with the "Never give up" motto always before us, we traveled on and always made our destination. Many a time we were held up for hours as the shell fire was so steady, and to proceed would have been suicide. While the fighting was at its height, the following are some of the places the Supply Company Officers and men were sent- McCormack Ammunition Dump, Fort de Trondes, Trondes, Launeville, Xivray, Ville St. Etienne, Fay-en-Haye, Saizerais, Griscourt, Rogeville, Minorville, Mont Sec, Richecourt, Thiacourt, Villers-en-Haye, Francheville, and many other places which were under fire from the enemys guns. Not only did the task of supplying necessities to the men fall upon this Company, but transporting troops was another duty assigned to us, which we were called upon to perform on many occasions. By constant travel, Officers and men of the Supply Company knew every town and road in the advance zone".

At the time of the separation of the regiment into its component parts the medical Officers and their assistants, the non-commissioned officers and privates in the Sanitary Detachment had been assigned to the battalions. From this time on therefore first aid treatment or more expert medical aid when needed was always near at hand for all the companies. And due to the presence and the watchfulness of these Officers and men the health of the various companies was maintained and under very trying conditions.

In the latter part of October, a number of Lieutenants from the regiment, each Company being represented, were selected to attend the Infantry School for Officers at Chatillon-sur-Seine. The course of instruction, involving an intensive study and practice with all the offensive and defensive weapons of warfare, as well as the study of combat principles, continued until the end of November. It was some weeks later before the Officers had located their Companies, then well into Germany.

During October a number of enlisted men were selected to attend Army Candidates Schools. Only the signing of the armistice before the completion of the course prevented the granted of commissions, and the certificated of eligibility for commissions awarded may yet be redeemed by the War Dept. that merit of a high order may not go unrewarded.

M. M. McMahon, Ph.D.

On October 7th, the regiment was distributed as per the following memorandum:

HEADQUARTERS, FIFTY-FIRST PIONEER INFANTRY,
American E. F.

October 7th, 1918.

MEMORANDUM FOR MAJOR SCHUYLER.

DETAILS AND WHERE DISTRIBUTED.

	OFF.	MEN
Toul and Vicinity; Guard Detail, Railhead, Road Detail, Salvage Detail, etc.	13	1,103
Menil le Tour, (Company L),	7	233
Detail at Troussey,		24
Salvage Detail,	1	22
Trondes,		75
Evacuation Hospital No. 12,		40
Carpenters with Engineers,		25
Non-Commissioned Officers Staff,		9
Rail Orderlies,		4
1st, Mess, Supply Sergeants; Cooks and Regimental Details,	4	182
Sick,		22
	25	1,739

Total strength of Companies (Hq., Supply, A, B, C, D, I, K, L, and M) from which these details are taken .... 2,115.

Second Battalion, with Sixth Army Corps, ... 907.

EUGENE E. PRESTON,
Captain, 51st Pioneer Infantry,
Adjutant.

On the 23rd of October, Headquarters, Headquarters Co. and Supply Co. were transferred to Menil-la-Tour, a considerable forward move, seeming to presage a participation in the expected offensive. Within a few days Cos. I and M were assembled at the same station. Co. L was already there, in charge of the prison stockade, which duty the Co. was still performing when the signing of the armistice brought hostilities to an end.

The order transferring Regimental Hdqtrs. To Menil-la-Tour, affected the disposition of several of the Companies and is for that reason copied here at length:

HEADQUARTERS IV ARMY CORPS,
AMERICAN EXPEDITIONARY FORCES, FRANCE,
THIRD SECTION, CHIEF OF STAFF
TROOP MOVEMENTS OFFICE

g-3 MEMORANDUM)
:
No. 193   )

19 October, 1918

16 Hours.

To: Commanding Officer,
51st Regiment, Pioneer Infantry.

96

1. Regimental Headquarters, Headquarters Company, Supply Companies "I", "K" and "M" will proceed to MENIL-la-TOUR and ROYARMEIX.

2. Company "F" will proceed to FORET de PUVENELLE (7231) for duty under Corps Engineer.

3. Headquarters 1st Battalion and two companies of 1st Battalion will proceed to MONTSEC for duty under Chief Engineer.

4. One company of 1st Battalion will proceed to XIVRAY for duty under Chief Engineer.

5. One company of 1st Battalion will proceed to ST. BAUSSANT for duty under Chief Engineer.

6. Precautions to prevent hostile aerial observation will be taken.

BW/RLB   By command of MAJOR GENERAL MUIR:

OFFICIAL   BRIANT H. WELLS,

BERKELEY ENOCHS   Chief of Staff.

Col., G.S., G-3

DISTRIBUTION:

Chief of Staff	(1)	Adj. Gen'l	(1)
G-1	(2)	Rep. Off. G-3	(1)
G-2	(1)	TMO G-3	(1)
G-3	(2)	Second Army	(1)
Sig. Off.	(1)	5th Corps	(1)
Chief Air Ser.	(2)	CO 51st Reg.,	
Chief Engineer	(1)	Pioneer Inf	(4)
Surgeon	(1)	1st Anti-aircraft Machine Gun Bn	(1)
Quartermaster	(1)		

Cooperating with the 1st Battalion 301st these companies of the 1st battalion 51st Pioneers entered into road repair and reconstruction work well up toward the front.

Following the wiping out the St. Mihiel Salient with such pronounced success, preparations were made for another push somewhere along the line. Days and weeks passed during which a steady stream of men, munitions, and all the accessories of war were massed in the forward area. It soon became apparent that the advance would be from the vicinity of Thiacourt. Bearing this out was the secret order dated Nov. 6tth, received by the Commanding Officer 51st Pioneer In- fantry. Its subject was that of the plan for defense of the second position, the taking into account by the Commanding General of the possibility of a counter attack and the reception to be made therefor.

This order stated

"In case of a surprise attack by the enemy, the second position will be manned and defended by the Army and Corps Pioneer Infantry, Engineers and Service troops and other units in the Thiacourt zone not assigned to defense of first positions".

All the companies of the 1st and 2nd battalions were assigned positions in the various sub-sectors named in the secret order and each Co. Commander familiarized himself with the sub-sector assigned his Co.., and the possibilities his location therein afforded for defense. The occasion was never presented to defend this line but had it come the Hun would have found in the Companies of the 51st foemen not to be despised.

During these early days in November negotiations were being entered into for a settlement of the Great War. The Germans well tired of it and for many reasons, internal trouble with the socialists, the falling away of their allies and as much as anything else the hammering away by the American Army in the Argonne, a thrust at their main line of communications which was not to be denied, all operating to inculcate in the German mind a fervent desire for peace. Diplomacy was resorted to in a final attempt to wrest from the Allies their well won victory, but to no purpose. The terms dictated by Foch, in supreme command of the Allied Armies, was "Unconditional Surrender". Finally the German Commissioners selected to convey the decision of the German Staff in regard to the ultimatum left German Imperial Headquarters and at a prescribed hour made their way through the trench system of friend and foe until they had come to Marshal Foch's headquarters. This was on Nov. 8th.

With peace hanging in the balance there was a redoubling of activity all along the Allied front, as though to make the Hun pay in these last few hours for all the devastation and death he had wrought. At 3 o'clock on the morning of Nov. 10th, Major Dooley, commanding the 2nd battalion, received Field Order from the Commanding Officer 301st Engineers. In it the following information and orders were contained:

"1. IV Corps will advance on this front this date at seven hours.

1. You will move your companies to a rendezvous at Thiacourt at the earliest possible moment. Equipment, rifles, gas masks and steel helmets -------

2. At H hour following the infantry advance you will move towards the following command posts.

Co. D 301st Eng.)	
Co. G 51st Pio.)	St. Julien
Co. E 301st Eng.)	Dompvitoux
Co. E 51st Pio.)	Donmartin
Co. F 301st Eng.)	
Co. F 51st Pio.)	Chambley
Co. H 301st Eng.)	will be held at your P.C. at Thiacourt for such contingent work as you may deem necessary".

A similar order to this was received by the Commanding Officer 1st battalion 51st Pioneer Infantry, in this case Vigneulles being named as the rendezvous. Pursuant to G-3 Memo No. 233, issuing from Headquarters IV Corps Nov. 10th, 1918, Co. K then at Sanzey was ordered to report without delay to the Commanding General 28th Div. for temporary duty and Co. M was ordered to report to the Commanding General 7th Division for temporary duty. These orders were followed immediately and the troops took the positions designated.

The anticipated advance, however did not materialize, whether because of the very heavy fog on the morning of the 10th or for other reasons is unknown. On the following day the armistice was signed at 5 in the morning and at 11 all hostilities ceased along the entire front.

Four days after the signing of the armistice orders were issued from Hq. IV Army Corps placing the 51st Pioneer Infantry under the direction of Col. Robert R. Ralston, Corps Engineer, and his instructions to move Headquarters and the 3rd battalion to Buxerulles were received at the same time. This was the beginning of the now famous hike to Germany. The other battalions received orders to move forward and on Nov. 16th, all were under way. By a variety of routes which it is not the purpose of this history to record, the Companies of the Regiment made their journey through the fighting zone, with its intricate trench systems through the devastated sections on into Lorraine and Luxembourg and finally into Germany. Great was the joy of the emancipated people of Lorraine, and in many villages arches of victory decked with garlands greeted the Americans, while from every flag staff waved the Tri-color of France. Some of the larger towns along the course of the hike were Fleville, Trieux, Wollmeringen, Aspelt, Konz, Trier, Föhren, Wittlich, Bullay and Cochem.

During this hike particular attention was paid to bringing the organization to a high standard of discipline and general military efficiency, and, whenever rests were made for a period exceeding one day, drill schedules were enforced.

On December 2nd, G-3 Memo 262 issued from Hq., IV Army Corps, then located at Luxembourg, and marked secret, was received. It created new activities for the regiment as follows:

"1. The 51st Pioneer Infantry will protect the vital points on the Trier-(Excl) Wengerohr-Bullay-Pommern-thence along the Moselle to Coblenz railway.

2. A guard will be placed at all bridges, large culverts and tunnels as the leading elements of our troops come abreast of any such points.----------

By command of Maj. Gen. Muir".

This duty was continued until Dec. 19th, when by orders from Chief of Staff IV Corps to Commanding General 3rd Division, 4th Division and 42nd Division, the guard maintained by the 51st Pioneer Infantry was relieved.

In December, Lieut. Col. Willis Bacon, attached, was relieved from duty with the regiment and assigned to the 805th Pioneer Infantry. On December 13th, Col. J. Guy Deming, was relieved from duty. Following his departure Lieut. Col. Albert Saulpaugh was actively in command of the regiment until Jan. 26th, 1919, when Colonel J. L. Gilbreth assumed command pursuant to authority contained in Par. 10 S.O. 25 Hq. IV Army Corps.

Beginning with the first of the year a period of training was entered into by all troops in the Army of Occupation and still continues. In addition to the drills and the study of combat principles, schools have been organized for the better education of the men. These schools, created for the purpose of preparing soldiers for their return to civilian life have met with a ready response on the part of the men. Broadened by their experiences, men who have had but limited, if any opportunities, and who heretofore knew not the incentive to learn, are now crowding to these Post Schools. It is a clear-visioned and far-seeing policy, for upon these men who have made the winning of the great war a possibility realized, the United States rests its hope not only in a World Safe for Democracy, but in a World Democratized.

[signed]
John A. Selby,
1st Lieut. 51st Pioneer Inf.

COMING HOME

On 23 June 1919, part of the 51st Pioneer Infantry sailed from St. Nazaire on the U.S.S. Wilhelmina. The 51st Pioneer Infantry onboard included: Headquarters, Headquarters Company, Supply Company, Ordnance and Medical Detachments, and Companies A, B, C, D, E, and F of the 51st Pioneer Infantry traveled on that ship. There were 4595 people on that trip.

After the Armistice, the U.S.S. Wilhelmina made seven round trips returning the American Expeditionary Force (AEF) troops from France. She was decommissioned on or after 6 Aug 1919 and on 16 Aug 1919 she was returned to the Matson Navigation Company. She was originally bought to carry passengers and cargo between the west coast of the US and Hawaii. She was purchased by a British shipping company and sunk by a U-boat in 1940 while in a convoy between Nova Scotia and Liverpool.

On 3 July 1919, they arrived in Hoboken, N.J. On 4 July they were sent to Camp Mills. On 6 July they left Camp Mills for Camp Upton and were mustered out.

On 25 June 1919, Companies G, H, I, K, L, M and the Medical Detachment of the 51st Pioneer Infantry sailed from Brest, France, on the U.S.S. Mongolia.

On 6 July 1919, they arrived in Boston, MA. They traveled to Camp Devens, MA. These companies of the 51st Pioneer Infantry were deloused and rested for four days. Then, they went to Camp Upton, Yaphank, Long Island. These troops were discharged beginning on 12 July 1919.

Sources

Naval History and Heritage Command Photography Collection, http://www.history.navy.mil/our-collections/photography.html

RG ATS records, NARA, Records of the Office of the Quartermaster General, 1774-1985, Record Group 92.

U.S.S. Wilhelmenia NH 47885, Naval History &
Heritage Command

Troops on Board Ferry Lighter Traffic, 1919, NH 105416,
Naval History and Heritage Command

Camp Mills, Mineola, Long Island, NARA, 165-ww-
528D3

U.S.S. Mongolia, Naval History and Heritage Command
NH 105722

Return of the 51st Pioneer Infantry on the U.S.S. Mongolia. From the Author's Collection.

NOTABLE MEMBERS

Along the journey, I have gathered some photos of and stories about members of the 51st Pioneer Infantry. Among the men were entertainers, future ministers and police officers.

Louis Borach (Lew Brice), CORP, Company A, Company M, Headquarters Company

Louis Borach was born in Newark, NJ, on October 26, 1893.

His stage name was Lew Brice. He was known for a comedian and dancing act in Broadway shows, and for silent movies and musicals. He had a starring role in the silent movie "The Income Tax Collector". He was married to Tillie Zick, Muriel Worth and Mae Clarke. His older sister was Fanny Brice, the subject of the film and play, "Funny Girl".

The "Stars and Stripes", February 28, 1919 column "With the Yanks Along The Rhine" related: "In Trier Thursday evening the 166th and 68th Aero Squadron's fighters and Lou Brice and his O.D. comedians from the 51st Pioneer Infantry furnished one of the most successful entertainments ever pulled off in that area."

Brice entertained men in Company Shows. He began in Company A, then became ill during training at Camp Wadsworth requiring a hospital stay. He joined Company M when he left the hospital. He was with Company M when two men in the company were killed by enemy machine bombs. He was with entertainment committees in Toul, then transferred to the Headquarters Company, where he was promoted to Corporal. According to the 51st Pioneer Infantry newspaper of 19 APR 1919, credited him with exceptionally clever entertainment and he "became one of the most popular entertainers in the army and was known and liked by everyone throughout the entire A. E. F."

CORP Brice received his discharge on 17 Apr 1919, and was mustered out in Liverpool so that he could proceed to London for an English production company.

Lew Brice died of a heart attack on 16 June 1966, in Hollywood, and is buried at the Westwood Memorial Park in Los Angeles, CA.

Kenneth Wilkins Cann, SGT, Company C

In the photo, he is in Freeport, NY, as a Corporal.

Kenneth Cann was born on 1 Feb 1898, in Brooklyn, NY. He was a bookbinder before the war. He served in the Machine Gun Company of the NYNG 10th Infantry, and was on the Mexican border in a wagon train in the 27th Div, NY. During his service, he went from a buck Private, Corporal, Sergeants, Platoon Sergeants, Mess Sergeants, 1st Sergeants. Master Sergeants Engineers in Germany Army of Occupation and on return home, made (temporary) Battalion Sergeant Major.

He recalled singing French songs of the day while marching. His first impressions of service abroad: "I like it. I was taught to take what comes and make the best of it."

During combat, he had very little medical care, and took care of himself for 1 shrapnel and 2 bayonet wounds. One bayonet wound went in his stomach. It was sewed up and he returned to his outfit. Since he was standing, they would not put him in an ambulance.

He said that later, the soldiers had to watch out for trip wires all over the place. He was caught in one and received a wound in his left leg and the back of his neck.

When he retired, he was the foreman of the Print Plant at Ft Belvoir. After his retirement, he was a bookbinder, and the only hand binder in Northern Virginia. He was still working at 84.

Melville Stevens Bulmer, PVT 1CL, Company B

Melville Bulmer was born in Brooklyn, NY, on 22 Jan 1894. He also still lived in Cairo, NY. He was inducted on 27 May 1918, leaving Syracuse University in his Junior year.

During the Army of Occupation, he taught soldiers how to read and write at night. In a letter home, he mentioned his thoughts turning to his home while "in the thick of the fight".

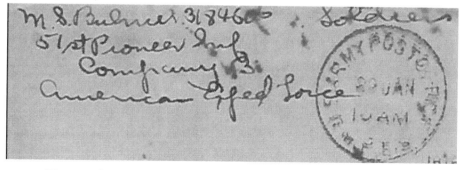

The Reverend Melville Stevens Bulmer would go on to complete his studies and become a pastor. He served pastorates in: Kirkville, NY, Cold Spring Harbor, Westhampton L.I., Ridgefield, CT.

He was honorably discharged on 10 July 1919. In 1920, he was living back to Brooklyn, NY with his parents. He graduated Syracuse University cum laude. After graduation, he worked in the financial department of the American

Trading Company. He received a Master's Degree in Social Psychology from New York University. He was ordained in 1953, after graduating from Drew Theological Seminary. He studied in Grenoble University, France.

On 4 May 1923, he married Bertha Margaret Whiting. He and his wife had one daughter, Mildred. The Reverend Bulmer was the Pastor at Westhampton United Methodist Church in Westhampton, NY, from 1923 to 1927. From 1935 to 1960, the Reverend Bulmer was the Senior Pastor at Stratford United Methodist Church in Stratford, CT.

He counseled WWII soldiers, and was Chairman of the Stratford USO. In his role on the War Council, he placed over 2000 women working in area defense jobs in Stratford homes.

Both he and his wife passed away in 1960. The Stratford United Methodist Church named the Bulmer Memorial Chapel for him.

Jack Carleton (Mathew Carroll), CORP, Company C

Jack Carleton was the stage name for vaudevillian Mathew Carroll. He was born on 12 Nov 1894.

Jack Carleton was in the long running production of "The Honeymoon Express", playing the role of "Constant". The play was described as a mammoth spectacle, involving a car and train onstage. It was the longest-running show to date at the New York Winter Garden, and featured Al Jolson and a huge cast. He was with the "Jazz Nightmare".

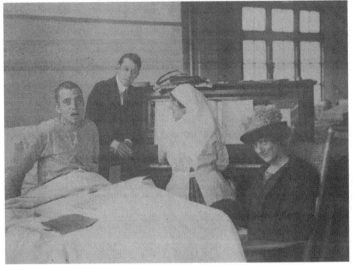

Carleton was a Corporal in Company C of the 51st Pioneer Infantry Regiment. His attendance at Camp Wadsworth was noted in the June 1918 issue of Variety (Vol 51). He was severely wounded in action on 6 Oct 1918. He was determined to be 45% disabled.

He died on 11 Jan 1960, and is buried at the Long Island National Cemetery in Farmingdale, NY.

Jack Carlton, formerly a star with the Honeymoon Express and now of the 51st Pioneer Infantry, is here shown taking his daily vocal exercise, Scenes at Debarkation Hospital No. 5, NARA, 165-ww-251E-011

Olaf Theodore Dahlgren, PVT, Wagoner, Supply Company

Olaf Dahlgren was Born 10 Sept 1894 in Kagerod, Sweden. He lived in Tuxedo Park, NY, and was a gardener before the war. His aunt, Miss Emma Pearsson, also of Tuxedo Park, Orange, NY, was listed as the person to notify in case of emergency. He was promoted to Wagoner 1 March 1919.

The 51st Pioneers newspaper of 18 May 1919 reported that Dahlgren had received another notification of his own death from the U.S. Government. According to the paper, "Last fall he was summoned before his captain and informed that a message had sent from New York asking him to verify that War Department's casual[ty] report. Wagoner Olaf Dahlgren was reported 'killed in action', his supposed death being due to wounds received while on actual duty during the big drive last fall." The story reported that his aunt in New York had been asked if she wanted his remains shipped back to the U.S.

The story continued. On 14 July 1919, he applied for a passport so that he could visit his parents in Sweden to reassure them that the report that he was killed in battle was a mistake.

His death was incorrectly recorded in the books containing the deceased men of the war, "American Soldiers of World War I." (There was an Olaf Dahlgren who was in the U.S. Navy during WWI and died on 10 January 1918.)

Olaf T. Dahlgren, Passport Application.

Floyd Milton Elliott, CAPT, Company M

Floyd Milton Elliot was born in Spring Hills, OH, on 24 March 1891. He lived in Ada, Ohio.

He was in the 2nd Ohio National Guard, and was at Camp Sheridan, AL, before being stationed at Camp Wadsworth. His is the only picture indexed with the 51st Pioneer Infantry at the Photographic Archives at NARA II.

Capt. Elliott was one of the U.S. Army Student Officers assigned to Arts and Science course at the University of Edinburgh. The picture was taken on 29 March 1919. He appears in the front row, the 4th man from left.

Floyd Elliott was discharged on 5 Aug 1917. He died on 9 Nov 1974.

NARA, 111-SC-898 WWI Number 160146.

Fuller, Harold, PVT, CORP, Company G

Harold Fuller was born 2 March 1896 in Middletown, NY. He was inducted at Orange County, NY. He was promoted to Corporal on 7 Sep 1918.

Before the war, he worked as a cook and on a ditching machine for NY Road Department. After the war, he worked in the railroad industry, as a pipe fitter then as a motor mechanic.

Highlights from his war diary are included in this book.

Harold Fuller Honorable Discharge, USAHEC.

Roylance Herbert, PVT, Company D, Headquarters Company

Roylance Herbert was born in New York, NY, on 7 Jul 1896. He was in Company D until 16 July 1918, then in the Headquarters Company until 14 Dec 1918. At that point he was transferred to Headquarters Troops 2nd Army (Hq Tr 2 Army) until his discharge 23 May 1918.

Exterior of Officers Rest Hotel, A.R.C. Left to Right: PVT Herbert Roylance, 51st Pioneers; Miss Ruth Smith, A.R.C.; Miss M.D. Andress, A.R.C.; PVT J. Murphy, 51st Pioneers and Joseph (old faithful) French Man of Affairs. Tour, Meurthe et Moselle, France. (Taken 11 Nov 1918.) 111-SC-33461-ac

Although there were several PVTs with the name J. Murphy in the 51st PIR, this is possibly Murphy, James Arthur, of the Headquarters Company.

William Frederick Lawson, PVT, Company E

William Lawson was born on 14 Oct 1894 in New York, NY. His previous occupation was graphic artist, which he resumed after being discharged.

He recalled being at the firing line at St. Mihiel on Sept 12 when the Hindenberg Line was smashed. He also recalled the long train ride from Brest to the front lines. He was exhausted carrying a full load for the 30 mile a day hikes from Limey, France, to Guls, Germany, during the time between November 1918 and January 1919.

He was stationed at usual guard duty at bridgeheads at Coblenz and Guls, Germany. Army of Occupation, January to May 1919.

During his time in service, he was very concerned about his mother. He was her only child, and her sole supporter. His mother was born in a small German village Neunkircken, near Cuxhaven. In 1906, when he was 11, he and his mother visited his maternal Grandmother in that small village. He stayed for a year, attending school in a one room schoolhouse. His German improved during that time. While there, he met various near relatives. During action he wondered if he had destroyed some cousins or an uncle or two in the German lines. His mother was very fearful of her German origin.

John G. Mansfield, SGT Company B

SGT Mansfield was the 1st SGT of Company B. He was originally in the N.Y.10th National Guard, and was called to active duty when diplomatic relations with Germany were broken, before the beginning on the war. SGT John G Mansfield enlisted in the 10th Inf NY NG on 30 March 1916, and was promoted to SGT 25 July 1917.

SGT John G. Mansfield would return to the U.S. ahead of the rest of the 51st Pioneer Infantry, leaving Brest on 9 Feb 1919, as part of the LeMans Casual Co 1201 (New York) on the U.S.S. Montana. He arrived at Hoboken, NJ, on 23 Feb 1919, and headed to Camp Merritt. Among his fellow passengers were other 1st SGTs from the Pioneer Infantry. He was discharged on 5 March 1919. He kept a journal throughout the war, which is available at the USAHEC. He lived in Albany, NY. His wife, Tess was featured in his journal and had either accompanied him, or met him at various points in his duties and trip to South Carolina.

John Mansfield died on 25 Mar 1959 and is buried at Memory Gardens (also known as Memory's Garden) in Colonie, NY.

John Mansfield Collection, USAHEC

Joseph Francis McMahon, PVT 1CL, Company B

Joseph Francis McMahon was born in Kilrush, County Clare, Ireland, on 29 Aug 1894. In 1907, his Father died. Later than year, at age 11, he departed Ireland with his Mother and younger siblings and sailed to New York City. He became a U.S. citizen. He worked as a telegraph clerk for Western Union in Manhattan. He married fellow clerk, Ella Small on 24 Nov 1917. Upon returning from WWI, he returned to his wife and became a NY Police Officer. They had 2 sons and 1 daughter. He died on 9 Feb 1926, and is buried in Saint John's Cemetery in Queens, NY.

His service inspired the author to research the 51st Pioneer Infantry Regiment across the United States, and write this book and a book about researching WWI ancestors.

Photo from the author's collection.

David Benjamin Pellegrini, PVT, Company F

David Benjamin Pellegrini was born on 28 April 1887 in Longobardi, a village in the southern Italian region of Calabria. Pellegrini came to the US in September 1906; in 1910, when he filed his declaration of intention to become a United States citizen, he was living in New York City. By the time the US entered the war, Pellegrini owned his own grocery store.

Pellegrini was drafted into the Army on 26 May 1918; he was assigned as a private, serial number 3182552, to Company L, 2nd Pioneer Infantry Regiment, at Camp Wadsworth, South Carolina. While there, Pellegrini took advantage of a new law allowing foreign-born military members to become US citizens in an expedited manner; he became a citizen on 8 June, one of thousands of immigrant soldiers to do so during the war.

On 20 June he was transferred to Company F, 51st Pioneer Infantry Regiment, also at Camp Wadsworth. In July, the 51st went to Camp Merritt in preparation for their shipment to France. Pellegrini left the Hoboken Port of Embarkation with his unit, destined for France, on 16 July. The 51st returned to the US on 23 June 1919, and Pellegrini was discharged on 24 July.

This brief story was provided by Peter L. Belmonte. He is the author of the "Calabrian-Americans in the U.S. Military During World War I" series of books, which can be found at Amazon.com.

John Baptist Pizzuto, PVT, PVT 1CL, Headquarters Company

John Baptist Pizzuto was born in Monacilioni, Italy on 26 Apr 1892. He was a naturalized citizen. Before the war he was a clothing designer for Samuel Peck. He worked as a tailor in Paris, France, in 1913. He died 21 Dec 1983 in Laguna Niguel, Orange, CA.

PVT John B. Pizuto, 51st Pioneer Infantry, 26 Years. Home in New York. Born in Italy. Parents and grandparents born in Italy. Cochem, Germany. Taken 17 Jan 1919, NARA, 111-SC-45156-ac

Gordon Van Kleeck, CORP, Company F

Gordon Van Kleeck was born 27 Jan 1894 in Olive Bridge, NY. Gordon enlisted as a Private in 1918 and was in Company F. He was a Corporal when he mustered out on 9 July 1919. He was the historian for his unit and his journal was kept in a small spiral pocket notebook.

The 51st Pioneers newspaper reported that Corp. Van Kleeck slept on an ambulance stretcher every night, which he found necessary to nail to the floor.

He married Genevieve Winne in 1923.

He died on 7 Oct 1977 Kingston, Ulster County, NY, and is buried in the Wiltwyck Cemetery, Kingston, NY.

Photo courtesy of Roxy Triebel.

Wallace Vaughan, PVT 1CL, Company I

Wallace Vaughan was born 30 Dec 1897 in Astoria, NY. He was in Company I of the 10 Inf NYNG, then Company I of the 51st Pioneer Infantry until his discharge on 15 July 1919. He died on 11 May 1953 and is buried in the Long Island National Cemetery. His photo as a boy was donated to the Museum of the City of New York.

Men in Service, Private Wallace Vaughan, Co. I. 51st Pioneer Infantry, now stationed at Battenberg, Germany, X2010_7_1_5455, Museum of the City of New York

Frank Eugene Weeks, SGT, Company H

Frank Weeks was born on 1 Jan 1897 in Pelham, NY. He lived in Mt Vernon, NY. His parents were George H. and Emma Weeks. Before the war, he was in the Motion Picture business. He served in Company H of the 10th NYNG, then Company H of the 51st Pioneer Infantry. He was discharged on 15 July 1919.

He died on 23 Nov 1980 and is buried in the Garden of Resurrection Columbarium, Serenity Gardens Memorial Park, Largo, Pinellas County, Florida.

Photos from the author's collection.

FALLEN

Individual combat units were responsible for burying the deceased soldiers and marking the graves. Then, the Graves Registration Unit (GRU) was responsible for moving the deceased to U.S. cemetery graves. The 51st Pioneer Infantry History tells of GRU work.

Even if the deceased soldier was initially buried overseas, his remains may have been returned to the U.S. in 1920 or 1921. The decision whether to leave a soldier buried in an overseas cemetery or bring his remains home was made by the next-of-kin. In October of 1919, the War Department contacted the next-of-kin of every deceased soldier, and each was given the option to bury the soldier in American military cemeteries in Europe, or have his remains shipped home for burial in a military or private cemetery. 30,000 soldiers' remains were buried in cemeteries in Europe. For the families of these soldiers, the government paid the travel expenses pilgrimages for Gold Star mothers, and widows, to visit these graves. 46,000 soldiers' remains were returned to the United States. It took over $30 million and two years to return the remains of these 46,000 soldiers.

There are similarities between the experiences of Americans and the Australian soldiers, who fought so far from their homeland. However, Australia would not pay for mothers to visit the graves of their sons, as it was a dangerous and expensive proposition.

The American Battle Monument Commission contains a database for the soldiers who fell in Europe, and are still buried in Europe.

The U.S. Army Transport Service records on Ancestry.com can confirm that the soldier's remains were returned to the U.S. These records contain the soldier's serial number and the soldier's military organization.

The author has created a Virtual Cemetery for the graves of members of the 51st Pioneer Infantry Regiment at: https://www.findagrave.com/virtual-cemetery/852267

Soldiers buried in American Cemeteries in Europe

The following is a list of fallen 51st Pioneer Infantry soldiers whose remains were buried in the American Battle Monument Commission's cemeteries in Europe.

Amitrano, George, PVT, Company M, died 8/31/1918 buried in St. Mihiel American Cemetery, died of wounds received in action. (Residence: New York, NY)

Davis, Fay Irving, PVT, Company H, died 10/6/1918 buried in St. Mihiel American Cemetery, killed in action. (Residence: Ft Johnson, NY)

Harris, William Edward, SGT, Company H, History of the 51st Pioneer Infantry killed in action 12 Sept 1918 at St. Mihiel. (Residence: Yonkers, NY)

Higgins, Geradus Backman, PVT, Company F, died 11/25/1918, buried St. Mihiel American Cemetery, died from broncho pneumonia. (Residence: Ellenville, NY)

Hitchcock, Frank, COOK, Company E, died 1/20/1919 buried in St. Mihiel American Cemetery, died from measles and broncho pneumonia. (Residence: Cairo, NY)

Jones, Ben. Jr., PVT, Company F, died 9/16/1918 buried in St. Mihiel American Cemetery, died of disease. (Residence: Kentucky)

Kipling, Alfred Richard, PVT, Company I, died 10/3/1918 buried in St. Mihiel American Cemetery, died from lobar pneumonia. (Residence: Brooklyn, NY)

Messina, Antonio, PVT, Company I, died 10/12/1918 buried in St. Mihiel American Cemetery, died from broncho pneumonia. (Residence: New Rochelle, NY)

Osborne, Albert William, PVT, Headquarters Company, died 2/7/1919 buried in Oise-Aisne American Cemetery, died from broncho pneumonia. (Residence: New York, NY)

Palmer, Frank P., COOK, Company G, died 10/4/1918 buried in St. Mihiel American Cemetery, died from lobar pneumonia, V (Residence: Yonkers, NY)

Sparkman, Acie, PVT, Company L, died 8/24/1918 buried in St. Mihiel American Cemetery, ABMC, Missouri, died of disease. (Residence: Cape Girardeau, MO)

Clinton, Vincent Jerome, PVT, Medical Detachment, MD to death, died 5/29/20 of tuberculosis. (Gardiner, New York)

Fallen Soldiers Returned to the United States for Burial

The following is a list of fallen 51st Pioneer Infantry soldiers whose remains were returned to the United States for burial.

Agrillo, Sam, PVT, Co. F. 51st Pion Inf. Died of lobar pneumonia 13 Feb 1919. Remains returned to U.S. Departed Antwerp, Belgium on 18 Aug 1920 on U.S.S. Princess Matoika. Arrived Hoboken, NJ on 4 Sep 1920. (Residence: New York, NY)

Barry, William E., PVT, Co. G. 51st Pion Inf. Remains returned to U.S. Died broncho pneumonia 13 Feb 1919. Departed Antwerp, Belgium on 18 Aug 1920 on U.S.S. Princess Matoika. Arrived Hoboken, NJ on 4 Sep 1920. (Residence: New York, NY)

Cassidy, Walter C., PVT, Co. D, 51st Pion. Inf. Died of broncho pneumonia on 30 Nov 1918. Remains returned to the U.S. Departed Antwerp, Belgium on 29 Sep 1920 on the U.S.S. Pocahontas. Arrived Hoboken, New Jersey on 18 Oct 1920. (Residence: New York, NY)

Dawe, LeRoy, PVT, Co. F 51st Pion Inf. Died of lobar pneumonia 13 Feb 1919. Remains returned to U.S. Departed Brest, France on 19 Jun 1920 on U.S.S. Princess Matoika. Arrived Hoboken, New Jersey on 21 July 1920. (Residence: Kingston, NY)

Fishman, Isadore, PVT, HQ. Co. 51st Pion. Inf. Died of drowning 20 Aug 1918. Remains returned to U.S. Departed Antwerp, Belgium on 19 Jun 1921 on U.S.A.T. Wheaton. Arrived Hoboken, New Jersey on 2 JUL 1921. (Residence: Bronx, NY)

Fritz, Adolph J., PVT, HQ. Co. 51ST. Pion. Inf. Died of broncho pneumonia on 16 Feb 1919. Remains returned to U.S. Departed Antwerp, Belgium on 18 Aug 1920 on U.S.S. Princess Matoika. Arrived Hoboken, NJ on 4 Sep 1920. (Residence: New York, NY)

Goodman, Samuel, PVT, Co. M. 51st Pion.Inf. Died of broncho pneumonia on 15 Oct 1918. Remains returned to U.S. Departed Antwerp, Belgium on 3 May 1921 on U.S.A.T. Wheaton. Arrived Hoboken, New Jersey on 1921. (Residence: New York, NY)

Garvey, Edward Vincent, CORP, Co. I 51st Pion Inf. Died as result of a railroad accident on 15 Oct 1918. Remains returned to U.S. Departed Antwerp, Belgium on 3 May 1921 on U.S.A.T. Wheaton. Arrived Hoboken, New Jersey on 1921. (Residence: New York, NY)

Hicks, Edward, PVT, Co. D 51st Pion Inf. Died 6 Jan 1919 from wounds received in action. (listed as Co. B on the ATS records). Remains returned to U.S. Departed Brest, France on 19 June 1920 on U.S.S. Princess Matoika. Arrived Hoboken, New Jersey on 21 July 1920. (Residence: Glenmont, NY)

Hornbeck, Percy, PVT, Co. E. 51st Pion Inf. Died from wound caused by sharp object while swimming 1 June 1919. Remains returned to U.S. Departed Antwerp, Belgium on 18 Aug 1920 on U.S.S. Princess Matoika. Arrived Hoboken, NJ on 4 Sep 1920. (Residence: Saugerties, New York)

Isenhart, Jacob W., BUGL, Co. F. 51st Pion Inf. Died of broncho pneumonia on 13 Feb 1919. Departed Antwerp, Belgium on 18 Aug 1920 on U.S.S. Princess Matoika. Arrived Hoboken, NJ on 4 Sep 1920. (Residence: Philmont, Columbia, NY)

McEneany, Edward P., PVT, Co. G 51st Pion. Inf. Died of wounds received in action. 16 Mar 1919. Remains returned to U.S. Departed Brest, France on 19 Jun 1920 on U.S.S. Princess Matoika. Arrived Hoboken, New Jersey on 21 July 1920. (Residence: New York, NY)

McGraw, Willard, SGT, Co. K 51st Pion Inf. Died lobar pneumonia 1 Mar 1919. Remains returned to U.S. Departed Brest, France on 19 June 1920 on U.S.S. Princess Matoika. Arrived Hoboken, New Jersey on 21 Jul 1920. (Residence: Buffalo, NY)

Moore, Robert, PVT, Co. L. 51st Pion Inf. Remains returned to U.S. Departed Antwerp, Belgium on 18 Aug 1920 on U.S.S. Princess Matoika. Arrived Hoboken, NJ on 4 Sep 1920. (Residence: Illinois) 419728

Nemeroff, Harry Lewis, PVT, Co. B. 51st Pion Inf. Died broncho pneumonia 25 Nov 1918. Remains returned to U.S. Departed Antwerp, Belgium on 3 May 1921 on U.S.A.T. Wheaton. Arrived Hoboken, NJ. (Residence: Bronx, NY) He was in the vegetable business.

Poach, Peter P., PVT, 1CL. Co. G 51st Pion, Inf. Died broncho pneumonia 11 Feb 1919. Remains returned to U.S. Departed Brest, France on 19 June 1920 on U.S.S. Princess Matoika. Arrived Hoboken, New Jersey on 21 Jul 1920. (Residence: Sidney, NY)

Quinn, Leonard W., PVT, Co. L 51st Pion Inf. Died of disease. Remains returned to U.S. Departed Brest, France on 19 June 1920 on U.S.S. Princess Matoika. Arrived Hoboken, New Jersey on 21 July 1920. (Residence: Matamoras, Pennsylvania,)

Rhinehart, Walter J., PVT, Co. E, 51st Pion, Inf. Died of pneumonia 19 Feb 1919. Remains returned to U.S. Departed Brest, France on 19 June 1920 on U.S.S. Princess Matoika. Arrived Hoboken, New Jersey on 21 July 1920. (Residence: Highland Falls, NY)

Ribsamen, Charles, PVT, Co. E. 51st Pion. Inf. Died of pneumonia 23 Feb 1919. Remains returned to U.S. Departed Brest, France on 19 June 1920 on U.S.S. Princess Matoika. Arrived Hoboken, New Jersey on 21 July 1920. (Residence: Saugerties, New York)

Robinson, George Keeler, PVT, Co. L. 51st Pion. Inf. Died of pneumonia 6 Feb 1919. Remains returned to U.S. Departed Brest, France on 19 June 1920 on U.S.S. Princess Matoika. Arrived Hoboken, New Jersey on 21 July 1920. (Residence: Mt Vernon, NY)

Slattery, Robert Augustine, Corp, Co. D 51st Pion. Inf. Died of wounds received in action 14 Sep 1918. Remains returned to U.S. Departed Antwerp, Belgium on 23 May 1921 on U.S.A.T. Cambrai. Arrived Hoboken, New Jersey on 6 July 1921. (Residence: New York, NY)

Silverstein, Herman, Second Lieutenant, Band Leader, HQ. Co. 51ST. Pion Inf. Died of lobar pneumonia 17 Feb 1919. Buried at Grave 43 Sec 19 Nenw Mayer Rhineland Germany. Remains returned to U.S. Departed Antwerp, Belgium on 18 Aug 1920 on U.S.S. Princess Matoika. Arrived Hoboken, NJ on 4 Sep 1920. (Residence: Albany, New York)

Sleeper, Clarence, PVT, Co. E 51st Pion Inf. Died broncho pneumonia 14 Feb 1919. Remains returned to U.S. Departed Brest, France on 19 Jun 1920 on U.S.S. Princess Matoika. Arrived Hoboken, New Jersey on 21 July 1920. (Residence: Oswego, NY)

Wheeler, Edward, SGT, Co. F 51st Pion Inf. Died of lobar pneumonia 16 Feb 1919. Remains returned to U.S. Departed Brest, France on 19 Jun 1920 on U.S.S. Princess Matoika. Arrived Hoboken, New Jersey on 21 Jul 1920. (Residence: Seneca Falls, NY)

Young, Wm E, PVT, Co. I 51st Pion Inf. Remains returned to U.S. Departed Brest, France on 19 Jun 1920 on U.S.S. Princess Matoika. Arrived Hoboken, New Jersey on 21 Jul 1920.

Fallen Soldiers Who Died in the United States

The following is a list of fallen 51st Pioneer Infantry soldiers who died in the United States.

Barnhart, John James, PVT, Co. F 51st Pion. Inf. Died of influenza on 13 Nov 1918. (Residence: Kingston, NY)

Clinton, Vincent Jerome, PVT, Medical Detachment, died of tuberculosis on 29 May 1920. (Residence: Gardiner, NY)

Coffey, John Joseph, PVT, Co. I, Co. D 51st Pion. Inf. Died on 2 Jan 1920 of tuberculosis. (Residence: Binghamton, NY)

De Graw, John Henry, PVT, Co. E 51st Pion. Inf. Died of ureamia on 2 Jul 1918. (Residence: Nanuet, NY)

Finnigan, Phillip, PVT, Co. L 51st Pion. Inf. Died of delirium tremens on 27 May 1918. (Residence: Utica, NY)

Hart, William Joseph, PVT, Co. A 51st Pion. Inf. Died on 9 Aug 1918 of falling from 5th floor window to the paved court below. (Residence: Brooklyn, NY)

Kreslein, Adolph Edward, PVT, Co. E 51 Pion. Inf. Died on 23 Jul 1918 of intestinal obstruction. (Residence: New York, NY)

Manniello, James, PVT, Co. M 51st Pion. Inf, 6 Cas Co. Died of lobar pneumonia on 11 Oct 1918. (Residence: New York, NY)

Ranucci, Antonio, Cook, Supply Co. 51st Pion. Inf. Died of tuberculosis, pulmonary on 28 Jan 1920. (Residence: New York, NY)

Fallen New York Soldiers Others from NYNG 10th

The following is a list of fallen soldiers from New York State who were in the NYNG 10th Infantry before it was redesignated, transferred out and died in the World War.

Caridieo, Louis J., PVT, Co. H NYNG 10th to 7 Dec 1917, Co. F 105 Inf. Killed in action 19 Oct 1919. (Residence: Mt. Vernon, NY)

Luny [Lunny], James F., Co F NYNG 10th, Co. L 105th Inf. Killed in action on 31 Aug 1918. (Residence: White Plains, NY)

Mattimore, Edgar J, PVT, CORP, Sn Det 10 Inf NYNG. Died of broncho pneumonia on 11 Dec 1917. (Residence: Albany, NY)

McCaul, James McCaul, PVT, Co. G NYNG 10th to 7 Dec 1917, Co. E 107 Inf Killed in action on 18 Aug 1918. (Residence: Yonkers, NY)

Van Etten, Clarence E., PVT, PVT1CL, Co. I NYNG 10th. Died on 11 Nov 1917 of empyema. (Residence: Jamaica, NY)

Yozzo, Frank, PVT, Co. L NYNG 10th to 7 Dec 1917, Co. E 105th Inf. Killed in action on 19 Oct 1918. Buried in Somme American Cemetery (Residence: Mt Kisco, NY)

Sources

"Lieut. Kerr Killed in Last Big Drive". New York Times (1857-1922); Dec. 16,1918, ProQuest Historical Newspapers: New York Times, pg.10. (Included Harry Lewis Nemeroff)

American Battle Monument Commission, https://www.abmc.gov, accessed 12 December 2017.

Ancestry.com. New York, Abstracts of World War I Military Service, 1917-1919 [database on-line]. Provo, UT, USA: Ancestry.com Operations, Inc., 2013.

Ancestry.com. U.S., Army Transport Service, Passenger Lists, 1910-1939 [database on-line]. Lehi, UT, USA: Ancestry.com Operations, Inc., 2016.

Haulsee, William Mitchell, Frank George Howe, Alfred Cyril Doyle (Residence: compiled). Soldiers of the Great War. Soldiers Records Publishing Association, Washington, DC, 1920

History of the 51st Pioneer Infantry, National Archives and Records Administration II, College Park, RG 165 Box 439.

ROSTER

The National Archives and Records Administration (NARA) National Personnel Records Center (NPRC) holds the rosters for modern military organizations. NARA II in College Park has invaluable sources for obtaining information about the 51st Pioneer Infantry. There have been rosters tucked into company correspondence, names and ranks listed in correspondence and training books, and a trove of information in passenger lists from the U.S. Army Transport Service found in the Quartermasters records (RG 92). The passenger lists themselves are similar to abbreviated censuses; for each service member, they give the name, relationship to the member, and address of the person to contact in case of an emergency. You may find a wife's name, a married sister's last name or a remarried mother's new last name. Additionally, these records provide the service number for each enlisteded soldier on the list (unless it is unavailable).

This book presents an effort to compile rosters from multiple sources. We have manually transcribed the outgoing passenger lists of the ships carrying the 51st Pioneer Infantry to France. When necessary and possible, we have cross referenced other rosters, WWI Draft Registration cards, and the NY State Service Abstract cards.

Information about known deaths during service have been included. The deaths listed in the American Battle Monument Commission (ABMC) have been used. For cause of death, the New York Abstracts of Service have been consulted. Additionally, the History of the 51st Pioneer Infantry was used.

Despite our best efforts, there may be instances of misspelled names. In addition, members who transferred into and out of the 51st Pioneer Infantry between the dates of the available lists may not appear in them. Please feel free to contact us with names and supporting information for those who do not appear, so that they can be added to future publications.

Alien Enemy. This notation appears in the passenger lists, but additional research into the members' service has uncovered that at least one soldier been cleared of all charges and honorably discharged. This designation should indicate that an investigation had been performed; if that paperwork can be located, it might provide more genealogical information about the individual.

Since these rosters were created by hand, some of the abbreviations that are used may be different for each company. A list of the ratings for the soldiers is included below. Below is a table of the abbreviation used in them

Abbreviation	Meaning
1 CL MSN	1st Class Musician
1ST LT	1ST Lieutenant
1st SGT	1st Sergeant
2 CL MSN	1st Class Musician
2 LT	2ND Lieutenant
3 CL MSN	1st Class Musician
ASST BND LDR	Assistant Band Leader
BN SGT MJR	Battalion Sergeant Major
BND CPL	Band Corporal
BND LDR	Band Leader
BND SGT	Band Sergeant
BUG	Bugler
BUGL	Bugler
CAPT	Captain
COL	Colonel
COL SGT	Color Sergeant
EOC	Explosive Ordnance Clearance
INA	Infantry National Army
INF	Infantry
INF N.A.	Infantry National Army
INF NG	INF NG Infantry National Guard
INF RC	Infantry Reserve Corps
ING	Inactive National Guard, part of the Ready Reserve of the U.S. Army
IRC	Infantry Reserve Corps
IRR	individual Readiness Reserve
LT COL	Lieutenant Colonel
LTC	Lieutenant Colonel
MECH	Mechanic
MESS SGT	Mess Sergeant
MS SGT	Mess Sergeant
NG	National Guard
ORD SGT	Ordnance Sergeant
ORDERLY SGT	Orderly Sergeant
RGT SGT MJR	Regimental Sergeant Major
SAD	Saddler
SGT BGL	Sergeant Bugler
STABLE SERG	Stable Sergeant
STBLE SGT	Stable Sergeant
SUP SGT	Supply Sergeant
SUP SGT RGT	Supply Sergeant Regiment
WAG	Wagoner

The following abbreviations used as the author's own, based on the notations observed in the rosters.

ABMC = American Battle Monuments Commission

Alien = transferred to Camp Merritt as Alien Enemy

C = transferred to Casuals in Camp Merritt
Casuals is an indication that the individual had been one of replacements, put in companies were formed at the Embarkation Camp (Merritt) or this may have been shorthand for Overseas Casual Detachment

Disch = discharged

OC = Transferred to Overseas Casual Detachment Camp Merritt, NJ, per G.O. - 26
These soldiers were not assigned to specific units during their transfers overseas. These may have been soldiers who traveling to become replacements for those who died, were injured or became ill.

SOTGW = Information about the soldier appears in "Soldiers of the Great War"

U = Information from the soldier is available at the U.S. Army Heritage & Education Center (USAHEC)

ROSTER

Aceveda, Edelmiro, PVT, Company C, died overseas
Acker, Edward Thomas, SUP SGT, Company C
Ackerman, Stewart Ward, PVT, Medical Detachment
Adams, Ray Harrison, PVT, Company F
Adams, Samuel Ernest, PVT, Company H
Adamski, Louis, PVT, Company C
Adlman, Joseph Martin, PVT, Company L
Adriance, Arthur B., PVT, Company D
Agers, Mathey, PVT, Company C
Agnew, Edward Theodore, PVT, Company G
Agnoli, Mike, PVT, Company K
Agricola, Isidaro, PVT, Company F
Agrillo, Sam, PVT, Company F, died overseas
Ahlborn, Ernest, PVT, Company L
Ahrens, Charles Emil, PVT, Company H
Ahron, Abraham, PVT, Company B
Ainbender, Mayer, PVT, Headquarters Company
Alberighi, Oresta, PVT, Company B
Albers, George, PVT, Company H
Albrecht, Arthur L., PVT, Company D
Albrecht, Charles Philip Joseph, PVT,
  Headquarters Company
Albrecht, Christopher, PVT, Company H
Albright, William Henry, CPL, Company C
Aldrich, William Smith Jr., CPL, Company C
Alexander, Daniel, PVT, Company B
Alexander, Herbert James, PVT, Headquarters
  Company
Allen, Byron, PVT, Company B
Allen, Earl Wright, PVT, Company C
Allen, Frank J., CPL, Headquarters Company
Allen, Harold B., SGT, Headquarters Company
Allen, Harry Wilson, PVT, Company E
Allinger, Robert, CPL, Company H
Alsante, Anthony, PVT, Company M
Altman, Louis, PVT, Headquarters Company
Alvino, Vito, PVT, Company C
Ambrose, Joseph Anthony, PVT, Company I
Amitrano, George, PVT, Company M, died overseas
Amuneson, Oscar E., PVT, Company K
Andersen, Edward W., COOK, Company I
Anderson, Argyle H., PVT, Company G
Anderson, Elmer, PVT, Company M
Anderson, George H., MECH, Company E
Anderson, Harry B., CAPT, ADJ, Regimental
  Headquarters
Anderson, Harry B., CPT, ING, Company C
Anderson, Oscar Arthur, PVT, Company C
Anderson, Sverre, PVT, Company B
Angell, Walter Edward, COOK, Company A
Angenti, Angelo, PVT, Company L
Annarella, Michael Joseph, PVT, Company K
Anopol, Aaron, PVT, Company M
Anselmo, George, PVT, Company F
Anspach, William Sydney, PVT 1CL, Company M
Antezzo, Vincenzo, PVT, Company M
Anthony, Frank Henry, STABLE SERG, Supply
  Company
Antonio, Philip Antonios, PVT, Company G
Anzelmo, Mariomo, PVT, Company K
Apoian, Benjamin, PVT, Company L
Apoyzo, James, PVT, Company M
Appel, Harry, PVT, Company D
Appell, Arthur F., CPL, Company B
Appitito, Tomasso, PVT, Company M
Applegate, William S., PVT, Company B
Areff, Samuel M., PVT, Company B, Alien, Company
  I 51 PI to July 15/18, Company B 51 PI to Hon

Disch Dec 7/18
Arena, Joseph, PVT, Supply Company
Areson, Irving, PVT, Company G
Aristini, John, PVT, Company A
Arlotta, Angelo, PVT, Company B
Arm, Henry Edward, PVT, Company G
Armer, Leon Mathew, PVT, Company M
Armour, Allison A., 1LT, I.R.C., Company K
Armour, John Stewart, CPL, Company C
Armstrong, Guy, PVT, Company L
Armstrong, William Henry, PVT, Company E
Arndt, Gustave Theodore, PVT, Company L
Arnett, Samuel, PVT, Company I
Arnold, Joseph T., PVT, Company M
Aseline, John Lewis, PVT, Company K
Ashe, George L., PVT, Company A
Ashe, John Edward, PVT, Company D
Askey, Arthur Goodenough, PVT, Company A
Athanasopulos, Silas, PVT, Company H
Atherton, Jasper N., PVT, Company K
Augur, Ernest Bradford, CPL, Company C
Aurelio, Thomas Anthony, PVT, Company F
Auris, Herman Max, PVT, Company M
Austin, Furman, SGT, Company G
Austin, Jay Sherwood, PVT, Company A
Avakian, Ashag, PVT, Company L
Avery, Jay, PVT, Company G
Avnet, Henry, CPL, Company M
Axelrod, Benjamin, PVT, Company M
Axelrod, Louis Judah, PVT, Company M
Axthelm, Robert, PVT, PVT1CL, Company I
Ayers, Thomas Lawrence, CORP, Company H
Ayvanizian, Mihran, PVT, Company L
Ayvazian, Lazare Hartioun, PVT, Company F

Babcock, Clarence Adelbert, PVT, Company E
Babcock, Francis Grander, PVT, Company G
Baber, Leonard M., PVT, Company D
Baber, William Alexander, PVT, Company E
Baccaro, Pasquale, PVT, Company A
Bache, William Lowre, SGT, Company L
Bacon, Willis, MAJOR, LTC, ING, 3rd Battalion,
  later 805th Pioneer Infantry
Baedor, William J., PVT, Company B, (Baedar)
Bagnato, Dominick, PVT, Company D
Bahret, Charles Henry Jr., CPL, Company K
Bailey, Irvin D., PVT, Supply Company
Bain, James, PVT, Company L
Baird, Maxwell Aken, PVT, Company D
Baker, George F., PVT, Company D
Baker, Jacob, PVT, Company H
Baker, John Pescud, PVT, Company M
Baker, Tom, PVT, Company I
Baker, William M., SGT, Company B
Baldwin, Dale S., PVT, CORP, Company B
Baldwin, William Lee, CORP, Company L
Balfe, Francis William, PVT, Company E
Ballasty, Henry, PVT, Company C
Ballem, Jake, PVT, Company F
Balletta, Donato, PVT, Company D
Ballmeyer, Ernest Frederick, PVT, PVT1CL,
  Company I
Bamberger, LeRoy A., PVT 1CL, Company I
Bamford, Thomas Harold, CORP, Company H
Banker, Arthur Seward, PVT, Company I
Banker, Philip, PVT, Company D
Banks, Luther Hugh, PVT, Company I

Bannan, Francis Edward, BUG, Company H
Bannister, Harry J, CORP, Company F
Baptiste, Jean Lamont, PVT, PVT1CL, Company E
Barber, Will, PVT, Company I
Bard, Charles Milton, PVT, Company D
Barnard, Frederick R.G., 2LT, INF, Regimental Headquarters
Barnes, Charley Wesley, PVT, Company M
Barnes, James M., PVT, Company K
Barnes, Joseph Daniel, PVT, Company K
Barnett, Harvey, PVT, Company M
Barnett, Max, PVT, Company A
Barnhart, John James, PVT, Company F, died U.S.
Baronas, Myron Stanley, SGT, Company C
Barone, James, PVT, Headquarters Company
Barrett, Myron K., 1LT, IRC, Headquarters Company
Barron, Terence Theodore, PVT, Company L
Barry, James Awolysis, PVT, Company G
Barry, John W. J., CORP, Company I
Barry, William Edwin, PVT, Company G, died overseas
Bartells, John Jr., CPL, Company H
Bartholmae, Herbert Dallis, PVT, Supply Company
Bartlett, Leander Chas., PVT, Supply Company
Bartley, Phillip, PVT, Company G
Baruch, Sidney, PVT, Company G
Basile, James Carlo, PVT, Company G, C
Basinger, Robert V., PVT, Company D
Basso, Angelo, PVT, Company F
Bastian, William Frederick, PVT, Company C
Bates, Carl Forrest, PVT, Company D
Bates, Eugene Edward, PVT, Company D
Bates, Frederick Thomas, PVT, Company G
Bates, Irby Otha, PVT, Supply Company
Bauer, August Michael, PVT, Company E
Bauer, Charles, PVT, Company H
Bauer, Irving, PVT, Company M
Bauer, Theodore Henry, PVT, Company G
Baum, Homer David, PVT, Company A
Baum, Jesse James, PVT, Company A
Baum, Max, PVT, Company B, Discharged, order of Pres. Of U.S., Co E 51 Pion Inf to disch July 25, 1918, Alien
Baumann, Edward W., PVT, Company B
Baus, Charles Adam, PVT, Company G
Baxter, Augustus, PVT, Company G
Bayerle, Charles J., PVT, Company E
Beasley, Lewis Henry, COOK, Headquarters Company
Beatty, Harvey, CORP, PVT, Company E
Becker, Charles J., PVT, Company B
Becker, Joseph Vincent, PVT, Company M
Beckmann, Fred Joseph, PVT, Company I
Bedell, William A., MS SGT, Headquarters Company
Beeber, Herman, SGT, Company H
Beekman, Charles Spurgon, PVT, Company G
Beerle, Charles L., SGT, Company B
Beesmer, Oscar, PVT, Company F
Begge, Ernesto, PVT, Company L
Behan, James, PVT, Company G
Behnken, George Henry, PVT, Headquarters Company
Bell, Frank, PVT, Company H
Bellanca, Luigi, PVT, Company E
Bellew, James Anthony, PVT, Company C
Bellinger, Ralph, SGT, Company H
Bellodi, Sergio, COOK, Company M
Belous, Louis Ted, PVT, Company M
Bench, George T, PVT, Company E
Bender, Frank Joseph, PVT 1CL, Company M
Benjamin, William H., PVT, Company G
BenLahader, Mocktar, PVT, Company B

Bennett, Joseph D., SGT, Company G
Benton, Byron James, PVT, Company H
Berardi, John, PVT, Company F
Berg, David Emanuel, PVT, Company A
Berg, George, PVT, Company M
Berger, August Louis, CPL, Company H
Berger, David, PVT, Company A
Berger, Herbert Julius, BUGL, Company I
Berger, Peter, PVT, Company M
Berinato, Tony, PVT, Company I
Berman, Peter, PVT, Company D
Berney, Benjamin, PVT, Company M
Berrie, Clyde R., PVT, Company B
Bernola, Oscurnza, PVT, Company H
Berrian, Ira Israel, PVT, Company A
Berry, Errol LeRoy, PVT, Company I
Berwick, Andrew Joseph, PVT, Company L
Best, Charles Vincent, PVT, Company D, OC
Betterley, James A., CPL, Company D
Betts, Charles, PVT, Company B
Beyer, Gus, PVT, Company M
Bezaire, Ernest Joseph, PVT, Company K
Biangardo, Andrew, PVT, Supply Company
Bielli, Joseph Dennis, PVT, Company K
Bierds, Frank Preston, PVT, Company E
Bingham, Robert, CPL, Company G
Bishopp, Earl Norris, SGT, Company A
Bissikumer, William Frederick, PVT, Company E
Bisson, Clarence, PVT, Company K
Black, Eber Heston, PVT, Company D
Black, Malcolm F., CORP, Company I
Black, Thomas, PVT, Company E
Blackman, Frederick R., SGT, Medical Detachment
Blackwell, Albert Arthur, PVT, Headquarters Company
Blackwell, Charles Kenneth, PVT, Company E
Bladon, William Joseph, PVT, Company K
Blakeslee, Barnett Jr., PVT, Company F
Blakeslee, Robert Paul, CORP, Company A, Company D 51 Pion Inf to July 25/18; Company A 51 Pion Inf Sept 5/18; Company D 51 Pion Inf to May 11/19
Blanchette, Joseph Anthony, PVT, Company A
Bland, Paul F., PVT, Company D
Blaney, Frank Leo, PVT, Company C
Blank, Abe, PVT, Company M
Blaschke, Herman F., PVT, Company   E
Blauvelt, Floyd, PVT, Company G
Blauvelt, Harold, PVT, Company H
Blauvelt, William Joseph, PVT, Company E
Bleitzhofer, Benjamin Joseph, PVT, Company F
Blonder, Morris, PVT, Company A
Bloomquist, John Walfred, PVT, Company M
Blowers, Arthur Cornelius, PVT, Company A
Bluck, Owen Hugh, PVT, Company G
Blum, Henry, PVT, Company K
Blum, William George, PVT, Medical Detachment
Blumberg, Benjamin, PVT, Company G
Blute, William Francis, PVT, PVT1CL, Company I
Bock, Frederick W., 3 CL MSN, Headquarters Company
Bockis, Martin Francis, PVT, Supply Company
Bockover, Leroy, PVT, Company A
Bodden, Ralph, PVT, Company M
Bodenstein, Charles Henry, MECH, Company K
Bodrewiezz, Stanislaw, PVT, Company E
Bogert, Albert C., CPT, N.G. INF, Company G
Boggio, Remo, PVT, PVT 1CL, Company M, died overseas
Bohman, Nelson Charles, PVT, Company H
Boker, Frank, PVT, PVT1CL, Company I

Bolin, Harry Anthony, PVT, Company H
Bolin, William Roland, PVT, Supply Company
Bolle, Oscar Florian, PVT, Company H
Bolt, Thomas C., 1LT, I.N.A., Company E
Bonamassa, Domenick, PVT, Company L, Supply Company
Bonanza, Rock Joseph, PVT, Company L
Bonavoglia, Giacinto, PVT, Company D
Bond, Theodore, COOK, Headquarters Company
Bonfardeci, John, PVT, Company H
Bongiovi, Charles, PVT, Company F
Boniddio, Antonio, PVT, Company L
Bonk, Anthony (Antonio), PVT, Company K
Bonocorso, Giovanni, PVT, Company K, Co. K to Jul 25/18, served overseas
Boone, Joseph K., PVT, Company B
Borach, Louis, PVT, CORP, Company A, Company M [Lew Brice]
Boren, Joseph, PVT, Company B
Borst, Charles, PVT, Company A
Bossman, Julius Jr., CPL, Headquarters Company
Bottaglia, Salvatore, PVT, Company I
Bottomley, William E., SGT, Company D
Bough, James Anthony, PVT, Headquarters Company
Bourke, Kevin D., PVT, Company B
Bovee, Ward, PVT, Company B [Bovec]
Bowe, William Patrick, SGT, Headquarters Company
Bowen, Edgar T., PVT, Company B
Bowers, Glenn George, PVT, Company H
Bowles, Leonard Charles, PVT, Company H
Bowmaker, Hilton G., CORP, Company A
Bowron, Frank W., PVT, CORP, Company I
Boyce, John Joseph, PVT, Company I
Bracebridge, James Earnest, PVT, Company H
Bradley, George H., PVT, Company B
Brady, Frank John, PVT, Company M
Brady, James Raphael, PVT, PVT1CL, Company I
Brady, Joseph Henry, PVT, Company G
Bragg, Ralph, PVT, Company F
Brall, Ludwig, SUP SGT, Supply Company
Brand, Charles Frederick, PVT, Company H
Brandt, Auguest C., PVT, Company M
Brannely, Hugh, PVT, Company C
Brannock, John J., PVT, SGT, Company B
Brassil, Thomas Joseph, PVT, Company G
Bravo, Stephen Donato, PVT, Company A
Bray, William James, PVT, Company M
Brayton, Horatio Earl, PVT, Company H
Brazie, Matthew, SGT, Company C
Breakstone, Monroe, PVT, Company B
Breckle, Frederick George, PVT, Company I
Breen, Richard John, PVT, Company G
Breese, William Murray, MECH, Company A
Breitenbach, Jerome, PVT, Company M
Bremer, Frank William, PVT, Company H
Bremm, Richard Aloysius, PVT, Company C
Brennan, Thomas Joseph, PVT, Company H, C
Breslin, Gustav George, PVT, Supply Company
Brewer, Delbert, PVT, Company A
Brewton, Daniel G., PVT, Company D
Bricker, Abraham, PVT, Company F
Bridgeman, George Allen, PVT, Company E
Brierley, Samuel Romer, PVT, Company A
Brierly, Mark, PVT, Company H
Briganti, Angelo, PVT, Company E
Briggs, Clarence Truman, CPL, Company H
Briggs, Furman, WAG, Supply Company
Briggs, Sydney H., PVT, Company B
Brinkman, Leon Jacob, PVT, Company A
Britcliffe, Herman, CPL, Company M
Brittain, Earle M., 1 CL PVT, Headquarters Company

Brockway, Roy Frank, PVT, Company H, died overseas
Broderick, Jeremiah J., 1LT, CHAPLAIN, Regimental Headquarters
Brodhead, Alfred Wood, PVT, PVT1CL, Company I
Bronisz, Frank, PVT, Company F
Brooks, Frederick, PVT, Company F
Brooks, Owen Thomas, PVT, Headquarters Compa
Broom, Willie M., PVT, Headquarters Company
Broome, Joseph William, PVT, Company H
Broszio, Marx F., MESS SGT, Company F
Brower, Frank, CPL, Company H
Brower, Homer S., PVT, Company B
Brown, Alvie, PVT, Company D
Brown, Charles Philip, PVT, Company E
Brown, Earle Hudson, PVT, Company C
Brown, Gustav Martin, PVT, Company M
Brown, Harry, PVT, Company F
Brown, Henry Joseph, CPL, Company C
Brown, James Henry, PVT, Company A
Brown, Patrick Joseph, PVT, Company G
Brown, Sanford, PVT, Supply Company
Brown, Thomas Francis, MECH, Company M
Brown, Thomas Gilbert, CPL, Company K
Brown, Vincent, PVT, Company D
Brown, Wesley, PVT, Company D
Bruce, Thomas Moore, PVT, Company L
Brumaghim, Raymond Willard, PVT, Company D
Brune, Herman, PVT, Company B
Bryant, James M., PVT, Company H
Brzostek, Stanislow, PVT, Company C
Buchanan, Robert, CORP, Company F
Buckley, Daniel C., PVT, CORP, Company B
Buckley, John G., 3 CL MSN, Headquarters Company
Buckley, William John, PVT, Company M
Buckley, William Joseph, PVT, Company C
Budd, Thornton, PVT, Company D
Budny, Teofil, PVT, Company D
Bueno, Ferdinand C., PVT, Company B
Bull, Howard V., PVT, Company K
Bull, Howard Wilbur, PVT, Company E
Bull, Raymond Dwitt, CORP, Company A
Bulmer, Melville S., PVT, Company B
Bundy, Virgil Vanwagnen, PVT, Company F
Bunke, Richard Diedrich, CPL, Headquarters Company
Bunn, Earl, PVT, Company C
Buonainto, Michael Vincent, PVT, Company I
Buono, Ferdinand C., PVT, Company B
Burd, Thomas Edwin, PVT, Company L
Burger, Robert Leon, PVT, Company F
Burger, Sidney Joseph, PVT, Company G
Burgess, David Arthur, PVT, PVT1CL, Company I
Burgess, Joseph, PVT, Company I
Burgess, William Thomas, CORP, Company A
Burke, Edward J., SGT, Company L
Burke, George M., PVT, Company G
Burkert, John W., PVT, Headquarters Company
Burley, Raymond Albert, CPL, Company C
Burnett, Charles William, PVT, Company D
Burnett, Raymond Walter, COOK, Company K
Burns, Arthur Patrick, PVT, Company H
Burns, James Joseph, PVT, Company A
Burns, Robert David, HORSESHOER, Supply Company
Burris, Arthur, SGT, Company A
Busch, Johannes William, PVT, Company M
Buschke, Frank Albert, PVT, Company D
Buschman, John F., PVT, Company B
Bush, Oliver Mathren, PVT, Company F
Bush, Otis, PVT, Company C

Busking, Henry, PVT, Company H
Busses, Charles, PVT, Company G
Butkus, Stanley, PVT, Company L
Butler, James Joseph, PVT, Company A
Butters, Harry E., PVT, Company B
Butts, Charles R., PVT, Company G
Byars, Andrew, PVT, Company C
Byrne, James J., PVT, Company B
Byrne, John T., PVT, Company K
Byrne, Joseph Alexander, CPL, Company D
Byrne, Kyran, PVT, Company L
Byrnes, Michael Thomas, PVT, Company F
Bzduch, Francis, PVT, Company K

Caccamaseo, Tony, PVT, Company E
Cacchione, Marziale, PVT, Company B
Cahill, Frank Xavier, PVT, Company F
Cain, James Joseph, PVT, Company E
Caiola, Benny, PVT, Company E
Calamito, Angelo, PVT, Company F
Calandra, John Alfred, PVT, Company D
Calatanatto, Vincenzo, PVT, Company H
Caldiero, Giulo, PVT, Company D, OC
Caldwell, Samuel C., PVT, Company B
Calef, Hyman, PVT, Company C
Callahan, Earl John, SGT, Company D
Callahan, Michael Lawrence, PVT, Company E
Callahan, Timothy Thomas, PVT, Company L
Calloway, George Francis, PVT, Company H
Calzerano, Angelo, PVT, Company E
Calzerano, Charles Angelo, PVT, Company M
Cameron, Duncan, PVT, PVT1CL, Company I
Cammarota, Salvatore, PVT, Company F
Camp, Frank, PVT, Company M
Campanella, Carmelo, PVT, Company H
Campbell, Alexander Henderson, PVT, Company K
Campbell, Daniel J., SGT, Company I
Campbell, Robert Donald, SGT, Headquarters
  Company
Campfield, Charles Moses, PVT, Company A
Campton, Thomas William, PVT, Company M
Candidori, Fioravante, PVT, Company A, PVT 1CL
  Sept 10/18
Canfield, Charles H., CAPT, I.N.G., Company H
Canfield, Julian K., CPL, Company M
Cann, Kenneth Wilkins, MES SGT, Company C, U
Cannon, Louis Wilbert, PVT, Company H
Cappelli, Lorenzo, PVT, Company F
Cappello, Nicolo, PVT, Company C
Cappelly, John, PVT, Supply Company
Caprolichio, Antonio, PVT, Company L
Capuano, Ludovico, CPL, Company G
Caraman, Alexander J., COOK, Company I
Caramenti, Frank, PVT, Company B
Carapelluceio, Emilio, PVT, Company A
Caravetta, John, PVT, Company H
Cardinale, Michael A., MECH, Company E
Caricchia, Emidio, PVT, Headquarters Company
Carle, Harry Arnold, PVT, Company E
Carlson, Fred O., PVT, Company L
Carlson, Fred T, PVT, Company D
Carlson, William Ernest, PVT, Company G
Carman, Charles Andrew, PVT, Company G
Carnright, Joseph Jason, PVT, Company C
Caros, James Genie, PVT 1CL, Company K
Carpender, Clarance Eugene, PVT, Company H
Carpenter, Allan T., CPL, Supply Company
Carpenter, Charles Martin, PVT, Company F
Carpenter, Daniel Latting, PVT, Company L
Carpentieri, Michele, PVT, Company E

Carracceola, Joseph, PVT, Headquarters Company
Carrella, Victor, PVT, Company K
Carretta, Joseph, PVT, Company C
Carroll, Matthew, CPL, Company C
Carroll, Michael Martin, CORP, Company I, OC
Cartaino, Frank Louis, PVT, Company E
Carter, Charles, PVT, Company D
Carter, Irwin Dewitt, PVT, Company A
Carter, John, CORP, Supply Company
Carton, William Henry, PVT, Company C
Caruso, August, PVT, Company E
Carver, Tim, PVT, Company A
Case, Frank L., SGT, Company L
Casey, James William, PVT, Supply Company
Casey, John Francis, MCH, Company C
Casey, Joseph William, PVT, Company E
Casper, Harry Arthur, PVT, Company G
Cassano, Frank J., PVT, Headquarters Company
Casserly, Paul Joseph, PVT, Company D
Cassidy, Daniel J., CAPT, I.N.G., Company E
Cassidy, Walter Clarence, PVT, Company D, died
  overseas
Castelli, Vito, PVT, Company C
Cataldo, Paul, PVT, Company F
Catanzaro, Vito, PVT, Company C
Cater, Barent W., CORP, Company E
Caterini, Pietro, PVT, Supply Company
Cavalieri, Salvatore, PVT, Company F
Cavanagh, James J., PVT, Company B
Cefariello, Amedeo, PVT, Company G, C
Celestino, Peter, PVT, Company F
Celli, John, PVT, Company B
Celmer, Leo Lawrence, PVT, Company C
Censori, Filippo, PVT, Company K
Ceramella, Alosmetro, PVT, Company B
Cermak, Joseph Aloysius, PVT, Company L
Cervone, Matteo, PVT, Company F
Chambers, Martin Joseph, PVT, Company K
Chapman, Landon Lawson, PVT, Company L
Chauvin, Leo, PVT, Company M
Chee, Mahomet, PVT, Company E
Chesbro, Harry, PVT, Company B
Chiacchiri, Luigi, PVT, Headquarters Company
Chianverini, Joseph, PVT, Company L
Chiarello, Guiseppe, PVT, Supply Company
Chickalone, Joseph, PVT, **PVT 1CL**, Company C, died
  overseas
Childs, Edward E., PVT, Company A
Chimenti, Marco, PVT, Company M
Chinnery, Michael A., SGT, Company G
Chirico, Benjamen, PVT, Company M
Chisling, Morris, PVT, Company G
Chittenden, Delbert J, PVT, Company E
Chittenden, Vandervoart Eastman, CORP, Company I,
  [Chettenden]
Christ, William Herman, PVT, Company D
Christensen, Harry, PVT, Company I
Christianna, Daniel Marvin, COOK, Company E
Christiano, Mike, PVT, Company F
Christiansen, Christian, CORP, Company I
Chrysoulakis, George John, PVT, Company D
Cicalo, Giuseppe, PVT, Company D
Cicaloni, Gaetano, PVT, Company H
Ciccotto, Angelo, PVT, Company H
Cicoro, Antonio, PVT, Company B
Cieri, Angelo, PVT, Company E
Cieri, Sylvester, PVT, Company A
Cigliano, Frank Joseph, COOK, Headquarters
  Company
Cilento, Frank, PVT, Company K
Cipiri, Cirillo, PVT, Company G

Cipriano, Joseph, CORP, Company I
Ciskanow, Vincent Edward, PVT, Company H
Civic, Isidor Elliott, PVT, Supply Company
Clancy, Jere James, SGT, Company H
Clark, Andrew Jr, PVT, Company A
Clark, Edward J., CAPT, I.N.A., Company I
Clark, Frank, PVT, Company H
Clark, Hoyt, PVT, Company G
Clark, James Michael, PVT, PVT1CL, Company I
Clark, John H., SGT, Company I
Clark, John William, PVT, Company K
Clark, Loran Simeon, PVT, Company M
Clark, William Wesley, PVT, Company A
Clarke, Edward Joseph, SAD, Supply Company
Clarke, Lafayette Gerbode, PVT, Company K
Clary, William Erwin, SGT, Company K
Clasen, Nicholas, PVT, Company E
Clearwater, John Thomas, PVT, Company F
Clemenza, Luigi, PVT, Company F
Cline, Philip, MECH, Company G
Clinton, Vincent Jerome, PVT, Medical Detachment, died U.S.
Clock, Herbert W., 1LT, IRC, Company C
Clum, Clarence L. Jr., CPL, Headquarters Company
Clute, Nicholas, PVT, Company A
Coakley, Cornelius, PVT, Company C
Cochran, John E., PVT, Company G
Coe, Charles Gabriel, PVT, Company C
Coffey, John Joseph, PVT, Company D, died U.S.
Coffey, Matthew Joseph, COOK, Company K
Coffey, Matthew Joseph, PVT, Company C
Coffey, Robert Eli, PVT 1ST CL, Supply Company
Cohen, Bernard, PVT 1CL, Company M
Cohen, David, PVT, Company A
Cohen, George, PVT, Headquarters Company
Cohen, Joseph, PVT, Company F
Colaiacovo, Vincenzo, PVT, Company L
Colantuono, Antonio, PVT, Supply Company
Coldwell, Kenneth Peirce, CPL, Company C
Cole, Basil Victor, PVT, Company A
Cole, Jacob R. Jr., 2LT, I.N.G., Supply Company
Cole, Jacob, PVT, Supply Company
Cole, Maurice, CPL, Headquarters Company
Cole, Mert, PVT, Headquarters Company
Coleman, David, PVT, Company C
Coleman, Herman, PVT, Company E
Coleman, John, PVT, Company F
Coley, Chester Kenyon, PVT, Company H
Colio, Maritino, PVT, Company H
Colley, Herbert Archer, PVT, Company I
Collins, Albert, PVT, Company A
Collins, Cyril H., CORP, Company I
Collins, Eugene Joseph, PVT, Company D
Collins, Frederick Patrick, CORP, PVT, Company E
Collins, James, CPL, SGT, Company B
Collins, John Joseph, PVT, PVT1CL, Company I
Collins, Patrick Joseph, PVT, Company L
Collins, Timothy Joseph, PVT, Company H
Colucci, Mateo, PVT, Company F
Comber, Martin Matthew, PVT, Company A
Comfort, Dominick, PVT, Company H
Comfort, William W., MECH, Company E
Comins, Albert Harry, PVT, Company I
Compo, Robert, PVT, Company H
Condy, Archibald Little, PVT, Company D
Conforti, Cattelo, PVT, Company C
Conklin, Frank, PVT, Company A
Conklin, James Augustus, PVT, Company G
Conklin, James R., MCH, Company G
Conklin, John Joseph, PVT, Company D
Conklin, William Baker, PVT, Supply Company

Conn, William Joseph, PVT, Company F
Connaughton, Harry Francis, PVT, Company L
Connelly, Francis Edward, PVT, Company C
Conners, Robert George, PVT, Company K
Connolly, Thomas Joseph, PVT, Company G
Connolly, Thomas, PVT, Company H
Connor, George W., PVT, Company D
Conroy, Edward Thomas, PVT, Company A
Conroy, Walter J., PVT, Company H
Considine, Joseph Patrick, PVT, Company F
Consilvie, Amidio, PVT, PVT1CL, Company I
Constable, James H., PVT, Company B
Conte, Robert, PVT, Company B
Conti, Domenico, PVT, Headquarters Company
Coogan, Bernard, PVT, Company B
Cook, Charles F., 2LT, INF, Regimental Headquarters
Cook, Charles Francis, SGT, Company D
Cook, Herbert W., PVT, Company B
Cook, William Guy, CORP, Company K
Cookset, Willard, PVT, Company F
Cooley, Herbert A, PVT, Company I
Cooney, Frank Leo, PVT, Company A
Cooney, William Joseph, PVT, Company A
Cooper, Clarence E., 1st SGT, Headquarters Company
Cooper, George Edward, PVT, Company D
Cooper, Paul H., 1LT, I.N.A., Company D
Cooper, Roy, CORP, Company H
Copp, Otto Erving, PVT, Company C
Coram, Clarence, PVT, Company E
Corbelini, Cesare, PVT, Company D
Corberson, William Joseph, PVT, Company I
Corcoran, Daniel, PVT, Company H
Corey, Frank Simpson, CORP, Company H
Cornwell, Eugene, PVT, Company F
Corrigan, James J., SGT, Headquarters Company
Corrigan, James Thomas Jr., PVT, Company M
Corrigan, John Clement, PVT, Company G
Corrigan, Joseph Vincent, PVT, PVT1CL, Company I
Cosella, John, PVT, Company I
Cosentino, Antonio, PVT, Headquarters Company
Cosgrove, John Joseph, PVT, Company F
Cosgrove, Phillip, PVT, Company G
Coslick, John Percival, PVT, Company A
Cosman, George Hawthorne, PVT, Company G
Costelle, William B. Jr, WAG, Supply Company
Costello, Alphonsus Stephens, PVT, Headquarters Company
Costello, Frederick J., PVT, Company B
Costello, John J., PVT, Company B
Costello, Patrick, PVT, Company B
Costello, William, PVT, Company B
Costigan, Edward J., CPL, Company B
Cottrell, Horace Keeths, PVT, Company A
Cottrell, Howard C., PVT, Medical Detachment
Coughlin, Thomas F., CPL, Company M
Coulson, William James Jr., SGT, Company A
Courto, Anthony, PVT, Company L
Covill, Ralph W., PVT, Company B
Cowan, Byron A, PVT, Company E
Cowen, John Leonard, PVT, Company L
Cown, Robert H., MECH, Company G
Cox, Carlton W., 1LT, INF RC, 1st Battalion (Entertainment Officer)
Cox, Daniel Leo, PVT, Company C
Cox, Fred M., PVT, Medical Detachment
Cox, James S., PVT, Medical Detachment
Cox, Joseph James, PVT, Company G
Cox, Vincent Benedict, PVT, Company A
Coy, John H., PVT, Company K

Craft, Herbert Winfield, CPL, Company K
Craig, Cullen, PVT, COOK, Company H
Craik, Joseph S., SGT, Company I
Cramer, Harry Bud, PVT, Company C
Crandell, Albert Morton, 1LT, I.N.A., Company I
Crannell, Leon Matteson, PVT, Company A
Crawford, George E, COOK, Company F
Crawford, Harrison Morton, PVT, Company G
Crawley, Harry, PVT, PVT1CL, Company I
Credentino, Luigi, PVT, Company D
Crehan, Matthew, PVT, Company A
Creighton, James, PVT, Company G
Creighton, John W., PVT, Company B
Crevling, Raymond Whitfield, PVT, Company C
Crimmins, John B., PVT, Company I
Crippen, Donald Samuel, PVT, Company I
Cristiano, Vito, PVT, Company F
Croce, Pasquale, PVT, Company H
Crofton, Edward, PVT, Company I
Cronin, Edward Francis, PVT, Company E
Cronin, John, PVT, Company G
Cronk, Louis L., PVT, Company D
Croopin, Charles George, CORP, Company A
Cross, Benjamin E., PVT, Medical Detachment
Crow, William Henry, SGT, Headquarters Company
Crowell, Edwin Philip, CPL, Company K
Crowell, Gustav, PVT, Company M
Crowley, John Francis, PVT, Company M
Crowley, Thomas Francis, PVT, Company H
Crowley, William Timothy, PVT, Company G
Crozier, William E., 1LT, IRC, 3rd Battalion
Crucitti, Carmelo, PVT, PVT1CL, Company I
Cuba, Stanley Stephen, PVT, Company F
Cubelli, Vito, PVT, Company C
Cubello, Joseph, PVT, Company C
Cuccia, Peter, PVT, Company F,
Culhane, Richard, PVT, Company M, C
Cullen, Bernard, PVT, Company A
Cullen, Frank Joseph, PVT, Company L
Culnan, Thomas S., PVT, Supply Company
Cummings, Alonzo E., PVT, Company B
Cummings, Joseph Lawrence, CPL, Company C
Cummins, John Francis, PVT, Company G
Curkendall, Howard Jacob, PVT, Company E
Curran, John J., PVT, Company B
Curry, George, PVT, Company H
Curry, Lee D., PVT, Company K
Curtice, Louis, PVT, Company M
Cushing, Rodger R., PVT, Company B
Cushman, Norman Chester, CPL, Company K
Cussins, Daniel Joseph, PVT, Company C
Cuthbertson, John Douglas, PVT 1ST CL, Supply
  Company
Cutlip, Frank T., PVT, Medical Detachment
Cutrona, Salvatore, PVT, Company H
Cymny, Anthony Stanley, PVT, Company F
Czarnicke, Tony F., PVT, Company B
Czuiko, Bolesaw, PVT, Company H

Daddeo, Joseph, PVT, Company F
D'Agati, Frank, PVT, Company B
Dagnall, Wren, PVT, Company D
Dahlgren, Olaf Theodore, PVT, Wagoner, Supply
  Company
Dailey, Francis Aloyius, PVT, Company I
D'Alessandro, Nicholas, PVT, Company B
Daley, James F., CORP, Company L
Dalton, John R., PVT, Company B
Dalton, Leon J., PVT, Company B
Daly, Fielding John, PVT, Company E

D'Amato, James, CORP, Company I
Damels, William, PVT, Company E
Damiano, Giuseppe Antonio, PVT, Company D
D'Amico, Joseph, PVT, Company C
D'Amico, Vincenzo, PVT, Company E
Daml, Elmer Walmer, PVT, Supply Company
Danahy, Dennis Bernard, PVT, Company A
Dandrea, Romualdo, PVT, Company E
Daniels, Amory O., PVT, Company I
Darbee, Frank Lorenzo, PVT, Company G
Daring, Gilbert I., SGT, Medical Detachment
Daronco, Achille, PVT, Headquarters Company
Darrow, Daniel, PVT, Company H
Dauchy, Mallie A., PVT, Company L
Dauchy, Norris Alexander, CPL, Company K
Davelle, Rocco, PVT, Supply Company
Davider, Carl Ernest, PVT, Company H
Davidson, David Reid, PVT, Company C
Davidson, Howard Leslie, CPL, Company C
Davis, Alfred, PVT, Company L
Davis, David Cornelius, PVT, Company G
Davis, Fay Irving, PVT, Company H, died overseas
Davis, Gilbert A., PVT, Medical Detachment
Davis, Harry A., PVT, Company D
Davis, Herbert D., PVT, Company B
Davis, John Mynderse, PVT, Company E
Davis, Lewis A., 1 CL MSN, Headquarters Company
Davis, Richard, CPL, Company H
Davitt, James Edwin, PVT, Company C
Dawe, Leroy, PVT, Company F, died overseas
Dawson, John Wilfred, PVT, Supply Company
Dayton, Raymond, PVT, Company F
Dean, Ira G., PVT, Medical Detachment
Dean, James Henry, PVT, Company C
Dean, John Sutton, PVT, Company C
Deangelis, Celestino, PVT, Company G
Dearborn, Louis G., PVT, Medical Detachment
Decicco, Michael, PVT, Company G
Decker, Ethan S., SGT, Company M
Decker, George H., SGT, Company M
Decker, Nelson White, PVT, Supply Company
Decker, Ralph, CORP, PVT, Company E
Decrino, Gennaro, PVT, Company G
DeDodonato, Dominick, PVT, Supply Company
Dedrick, Charles H., PVT, CPL, Company B, B
Dee, John Bertram, PVT, Company E
Deely, Charles E., PVT, Medical Detachment
Deer, Howard Frederick, PVT, Company H
Deflice, Rocco, PVT, Medical Detachment
Defro, Vincent L., PVT, Company B
Degennaro, Jack, PVT, Company E
DeGraw, John Henry, PVT, Company E, died U.S.
Del Pizzo, Dominick, CPL, Company H
Delamarter, Sylvester, PVT, Company E
Delaney, Francis T., 2 CL MSN, Headquarters
  Company
Delaney, James A, CPL, Company G
Delaney, Robeert Emmett, PVT, Supply Company
Delaney, Thomas Daniel, PVT, Company C
Delappe, John Patrick, CPL, Company H
Dellatto, Michael, PVT, Company C
Dellicarpini, John, PVT, Company H
Delmonte, Ferdinand, PVT, Company E
Delmore, John Joseph, PVT, Company H
DeLong, Darwin C., PVT, Company B
Deluca, Gartano, PVT, Company B
Deluca, Joseph, PVT, Company F
Demacek, Rudolph, PVT, PVT1CL, Company I
DeMaio, Michele, PVT, Company H
DeMara, Rocco, PVT, Company K
Demarest, William A., SUP SGT, Company I

Demeo, Alexander, PVT, Company I
DeMeo, Alexander, PVT, Company L
DeMeo, Fiorie, PVT, Company I
Deming, J. Guy, Colonel, NG, Regimental
   Headquarters
Denner, George Joseph Conrad, PVT, Company K
Denner, Leonard Aloysius, PVT, Company E
Dennis, Enis, PVT, Company M
DeNyse, William John, CPL, Company K
Depaolo, Frank, PVT, Company C
DePaolo, Pasquale, PVT, Company M
DePerna, Camille, CPL, Company B
Deppolito, Amidore, PVT, Company K
Depuy, Lyle MConald, PVT, Company G
Depuzzi, Joseph Fred, CORP, Company L
Derenda, Stanley John, PVT, Headquarters Company
Dermenjian, Arshag Tacvor, PVT, Company M
Dernicola, Guiiseppi Jr., PVT, Company H
DeRosa, Charles, PVT, Company L
Desanti, Pasquale, PVT, Company G
Desantis, Joseph, PVT, Company F
Desimone, Michele, PVT, Supply Company
Desmond, Daniel, PVT, Company B
Dessauer, Jacob Columbus, PVT, Company E
Deutchman, Herman, PVT, Headquarters Company
Devecchis, Joseph, PVT, Company F
DeVincenties, Luigi Pasqual, PVT, Company I
Devitt, Jermiah Thomas, PVT, Company C
Deweese, Wilbur, SGT BGL, Headquarters Company
Dewolf, Samuel Hyman, PVT, Company A
Diagostino, Salvitore, PVT, Company H
Diamond, Soloman Charles, PVT, Company G
Dibble, Frank Leslie, PVT, Company A
DiCaprio, Pancrazio, PVT, Company L
Dickison, John Frederick, SGT, Company F
Dickson, Arthur J., PVT, Headquarters Company
Dickson, Thomas, CORP, Company I
Diehl, Grover Addison, PVT, Company L
Diehl, Philip, COOK, Company K
Dietrich, Daniel, MECH, Headquarters Company
Dietz, Sherman Eugene, PVT, Company M
Dietzer, Mortimer Lyman, 1LT, I.R.C., Company I
DiFazio, Cesare, PVT, Company H
Digiovanni, Amerigo, PVT, Company F
Dillenbeck, Clayton Adelberg, PVT, Company G
Dillon, Thomas Anthony, PVT, Company C
Dilmore, Wilbur Earl, PVT, Company K
Dilorenzo, Joseph, PVT, Company H
Dimartino, Carmelo, PVT, Company F
Dimella, Modesto, PVT, Company C
Dimpfl, George Jr., PVT, Company L
Dinan, David Joseph, PVT, Company G
DiNardor, Pasquale, PVT, Company K
Dingman, Earl Orlis, PVT, Company H
Dingo, John, PVT, Company G
Dinote, Peter, CPL, Company G
Diroma, Frank, PVT, Company E
Dirubba, Gabriel, PVT, Company H
D'Ischia, Tony, PVT, Company F
Disegni, Michael Henry, PVT, Company D
Disisto, Frank, PVT, Company E
DiStefano, Nicolo, PVT, Company E
Dixon, Charles T., 1ST SGT, Company M
Dixson, Frank N. W., PVT, Company G
Doberstein, Andrew, PVT, Company F
Doberstein, Frank, PVT, Company F
Dodd, Bettino, CPL, Company H
Doherty, Richard B., SGT, Company D
Doherty, Robert, PVT, Company B
Dolan, Frank E., PVT, Company B
Dolan, George Anthony, PVT, Company I

Dolan, John, PVT, Company I
Dolan, Thomas J., PVT, Company B
Dolan, Thomas Peter Jr., SUP SGT, Supply Company
Dolato, Frank, PVT, Company K
Doll, Frederick Joseph, PVT, Company L
Dominy, Melville James, CPL, Company D
Donahue, John J., CPL, Company B
Donahue, Terence, Jr, MECH, Headquarters Company
Donahugh, Raymond William, PVT, Company K
Doncourt, Carlton L., SGT, Company I
Donlon, Hugh Patrick, PVT, Company C
Donlyn, Dominick Thomas, PVT, Company K
Donnelly, Frank John, PVT, Company I
Donnelly, Thomas Joseph, SGT, Company D
Donohue, John Joseph, PVT, Company M
Donovan, Edward Francis, PVT, Company E
Donovan, John Joseph, PVT, Company I
Doody, James Michael, CPL, Company C
Doody, Patrick Henry, PVT, COOK, Company E
Dooley, Thomas J., MAJOR, ING, 2nd Battalion
Dooley, William Anthony, PVT, Company F
Dooling, William Patrick, PVT, Company F
Doonan, Thomas Joseph, PVT, Company L
Doran, James L., PVT, Company B
Doran, Thomas Walter, PVT, Company F
Dorbs, Frank B., COL SGT, Headquarters Company
Dorfman, Jacob, PVT, Company M
Dorman, John Joseph, PVT, Company G
Dornbaum, Oscar, COOK, Company B
Dory, Roderick Edward, PVT, Company D
Douch, Anthony, PVT, Company E
Dougherty, Daniel Richard, PVT, Company H, C
Dougherty, Harold Edward, PVT, Company K
Dougherty, William A., PVT, Company G
Douglas, Milton John, SAD, Supply Company
Dowling, John Joseph, PVT, Company K
Downling, John Joseph, PVT, Headquarters Company
Doyle, Frank Peter, CORP, PVT, Company E
Drake, Charles, PVT, Company D
Drake, James Samuel Jr, SGT, 2LT, Company A
Dreher, Norman Joseph, PVT, Company F
Dreier, Charles William, PVT, Company E, [Drier]
Dreier, Frank Homer, PVT, Headquarters Company
Drew, John Vincent, PVT, Supply Company
Drombrowski, Waclaw, PVT, Headquarters Company
Drury, George W. Jr., CORP, Company L
Due, George, CPL, Company D
Duff, Alonzo, PVT, Company K
Duff, William Robert, PVT, Company D
Duffy, Charles Francis, PVT, Company G
Duffy, John Joseph, MECH, Company L
Dugan, Arthur Benedict, PVT, Company H
Dugan, John Joseph, PVT, Company M
Duggan, James Clarence, PVT, Company F
Dunbar, Joseph C., PVT. MECH, Company B
Dunn, Earl Douglas, PVT, Company D
Dunn, Fred Norman, PVT, Company G
Dunn, Joseph Leo, PVT, Company G
Dunsky, Isaac, PVT, Company G
Durkin, James, CPL, Headquarters Company
Durland, Joseph Livermore, PVT, Company G
Duryea, Charles, MECH, Company A
Dwyer, Francis Herbert, PVT, Company D
Dwyer, Gerald John, PVT, Company H
Dwyer, Philip, PVT, Company C
Dwyer, William J., SGT, Company B
Dzierzanoski, Henry, PVT, Company H
Dzyedzul, John, PVT, Company F

Eadon, Edgar James, PVT, Company F, C, Co F Pion

Inf to Aug 1/18; Co L 56 Inf to disch
Eagan, Charles F., PVT, Company B
Eagan, John Michael, PVT, Company A
Eaione Dominick, PVT, Company B
Eben, Chappell Belmont, PVT, Company C
Eck, Eddie, PVT, Company G
Edelson, Morris, PVT, Company M
Eden, Van S., COOK, Company I
Edgar, Warren Craig, PVT, Company H
Edsall, Franklin Grover, PVT, Company H
Edtards, Simpson Alexander, PVT, Company A
Edwards, Frank Lee, PVT, Headquarters Company
Edwards, Kenneth T., CPL, Headquarters Company
Effrof, Sol, PVT, Company G
Egnor, Harry Demitt, MECH, Company H
Eipper, Charles John, CPL, Company C
Eirich, Ludwig Mathews, CPL, Headquarters
  Company
Ekisiah, Harry Hagob, CPL, Company H, C
Elconick, David Hirsch, PVT, Company F
Elgin, David Andrew, PVT, Company G
Elledge, Bengomon, PVT, Company K
Elliott, Floyd M., CAPT, INF N.G., Company M
Elliott, Robert Thomas, PVT, Company C
Elliott, Strecklin Foster, PVT, Supply Company
Ellis, James Corbit, PVT, Company F
Ellis, Percy P., SGT, Company G
Ellsworth, William H., PVT, Company L
Elmer, John J., 1ST SGT, Company G
Emerson, Arthur H, 1LT, I.R.C., Company A
Enderly, Preston George, PVT, Company G
Endfield, Herbert R., PVT, Company B
Engelking, Edmund Fritz, SGT, Company F
Engle, Charles William, PVT, Company C
Engle, William Irwin, PVT, PVT1CL, Company I
Englert, Leonard, PVT, Company A
English, Patrick J., PVT, Company B
English, William, PVT, Company H
Enneser, Leo, PVT, Company E
Entrott, Winfield, CPL, Company M
Entwistle, Samuel, PVT, Company H
Eppley, Joseph Anthony, PVT, Company C
Epstein, Harry, PVT, Company A
Erger, George, PVT, Company K
Erickson, Andrew, PVT, Company H
Ermie, Angelo, PVT, Company A
Erody, Bernard Michael, PVT, Company K
Errico, Daniel A., PVT, Company B
Errico, Guiseppe, PVT, Company C
Erskine, Alfred Howard, PVT, Company F
Erttler, Fred, PVT, Medical Detachment
Ervin, James Francis, PVT, Company H
Esposito, Salvatore, PVT, Company D
Estep, John, PVT, Company G
Evans, Arthur Henry, PVT, Company A
Evans, Raymond James, PVT, Company A
Evans, William Henry, SGT, Company L
Evans, William, PVT, Company F
Ewsuk, Kostik, PVT, Company C
Ezercur, Max, PVT, Company H

Faas, John, COOK, Company D
Fabbro, Giovanni, PVT, Company C
Fabishak, Joseph, PVT, Company G, OC
Fagher, Frank Andrew, PVT, Company F, C
Faione, Dominick A., PVT, Company B
Falk, George, PVT, Company C
Falkiner, Robert Hayes, PVT, Company L
Fallone, Luigi, PVT, Company H
Fandry, Gust, PVT, Company F, C

Fanning, John Martin, PVT, Company K
Farley, James, CPL, Company H
Farrell, Edward William, PVT, Supply Company
Farrell, Harrold Leonard, CORP, PVT, Company E
Farrell, Harry J., PVT, Company B
Farrell, Thomas, PVT, Company B
Farrell, Thomas, PVT, Company L
Farrell, Thomas, PVT, Company 4, 4th Replacement
  Battalion, 51st Pioneer Inf, died overseas
Farrington, George Mathuel, CPL, Company C
Faryoski, Stanislaw, PVT, Company I
Fasano, Nicholas Joseph, PVT, Headquarters
  Company
Fasolicili, Alexandro, PVT, Company H
Fasolo, Sebastiano, PVT, Company E
Fassett, John Louis, PVT, Company D
Fassig, Charles Roberts, PVT, Company G
Fastenberg, Louis, PVT, Company L
Faull, Charles, PVT, Company F, C
Fay, Charles J., PVT, Company D
Feder, Nathan, PVT, Company I
Federici, Vito, PVT, Company L
Fedullo, Biagio, PVT, Headquarters Company
Feeney, George E., PVT CPL, Company H
Feifer, Solomon, PVT, Supply Company
Feil, William, PVT, Company M
Feiler, Charles J., PVT, Company B
Fein, Joseph H., PVT, Company I
Feinstein, Charles Matthew, PVT, Company H
Feisstl, Frank, PVT, Company C
Feist, Milton, PVT, Company L
Feldman, Louis, CPL, Company D
Felker, George H, PVT, Company E
Felli, Umberto V., PVT, Company K
Felton, Howard, PVT, Company F
Femreite, Olaf, PVT, Company K
Fenaughty, Francis Joseph, PVT, Company I
Fennelly, William Thomas, PVT, Company C
Feola, Luigi, PVT, Company K
Feoli, Archangelo, PVT, Company L
Ferguson, Frank Austin, PVT, Company H
Ferguson, George Graham, CORP, Company L
Ferrara, Alfio, PVT, Company B
Ferrara, Ferdinando, PVT, Headquarters Company
Ferrarini, Charles, PVT, Headquarters Company
Ferris, Arthur Boyd, PVT, Company I
Ferro, Alphonse, PVT 1CL, Company M
Ferrone, Filippo, PVT, Company H
Festa, John, PVT, Company B, C
Fiacco, Lumberto, PVT, Company H
Fialkowski, Thomas Henry, PVT, Company K
Fiammetta, Vincent, PVT, Company C
Fical, Leamon, PVT, Company H
Ficarrotta, Natale, PVT, Company F
Fickbohm, Robert John, PVT, Headquarters Company
Field, Stephen F., CORP, Company I
Fiesel, Peter Richard, PVT, Company K
Filkens, Lewis F., COOK, Supply Company
Finan, Victor, CPL, Supply Company
Finch, Joseph Andrew, PVT, Company G
Finch, Marvin Romain, CPL, Company C
Finckelstein, Louis, PVT, Company M
Findling, Max, PVT, Company D
Fink, Humboldt E., PVT, Company K
Finkle, Ferrell F., CPL, Company M
Finn, Abraham, PVT, Headquarters Company
Finn, Joseph W., COOK, Company D
Finnigan, Phillip, PVT, Company L, died in U.S.
Fiola, James, PVT, Company H
Fischbeck, Robert Anthony, CPL, Company D
Fischer, Lawrence, PVT, Company F

Fishbaugh, Charles, PVT, Company A
Fishbone, Meyer Benjaman, PVT, Company M
Fisher, George Frank, SGT, Company A
Fisher, William Victor, PVT, Company M
Fishman, Isidor, PVT, Headquarters Company, died
   overseas
Fitch, Gerald Eames, PVT, Supply Company
Fitzer, MCuffie, PVT, Company M
Fitzgerald, James A., CPL, Company K
Fitzgerald, Stanley MacFarland, PVT, Company D
Fitzgibbon, George, PVT, Headquarters Company
Fitzmorris, John, PVT, Company E
Fitzpatrick, James Aloysius, PVT 1CL, Company I
Fitzpatrick, James Francis, PVT, Company M
Fitzpatrick, Peter, PVT, Company G
Fitzpatrick, Robert, PVT, Company G
Fitzsimmons. Lawrence, PVT, Company M
Fitzsimons, James C., CORP, Company I
Flach, Walter C., PVT, Company B
Flanagan, John Joseph, PVT, Company M
Flanagan, Patrick Joseph Jr., PVT, Company D
Flarity, Harry D., CORP, Company B
Flatley, Richard, PVT, Company G
Fleiner, Joseph Henry, PVT, Company M
Fleischmann, Frederick Joseph, PVT, Company G
Fleming, David James, PVT, Company A
Fleming, Patrick H., 1LT, D.M.D. M.C.51.PI,
   Medical Detachment
Fleming, Sidney Thurman, PVT, Supply Company
Flemming, John Joseph, CPL, Company H
Fliegelman, Charles, PVT, Company A
Flood, John Joseph, PVT, Company H
Fogarty, William F., CPL, Company G
Follett, Frank Cuyler, PVT, Company M
Fontanazza, Guiseppe, PVT, Company K
Forbell, Elwood Lewis, CORP, Company A
Ford, Ambrose, PVT, Company D
Ford, Sidney H., PVT, Company G
Ford, William B., PVT, Company E
Formica, Joseph, PVT, Company F
Forsberg, Joseph, PVT, Company I OC
Forte, Joseph, PVT, Company C
Fortmann, Bernard, CORP, Company E, [Fortman]
Fortney, Clarence Daniel, PVT, Company F
Fosco, Vito, PVT, Company I, [Foseo]
Fossa, Emil, PVT, Company F
Foster, Emmett, PVT, Company A
Foster, Harry Frederick, PVT, Company F
Foster, Roland W., PVT, Headquarters Company
Fotiou, Charles John, PVT, Supply Company
Fountain, Frank, PVT 1CL, Company I
Fox, Alfred Irving, PVT, Company M
Fox, Arthus, SGT, Company M
Fox, Michael Gerald, PVT, Company A
Fraleigh, Alfred, CORP, Company K
Fraley, Jacob Peter, PVT, Company C
Franch, Frederick W., SGT, Company L
Franchini, Attilio, PVT, Supply Company
Francis, Raymond, PVT, Company F, C
Frank, Joseph Reuben, PVT, Company M
Frankel, Abraham, PVT, Supply Company
Frankel, Samuel, PVT, Company F
Frankl, Walter Howard, PVT, Company L
Frato, Salvatore, PVT, Supply Company
Fratturo, Liberatore, PVT, Company C
Frecentese, Felice, PVT, Company L
Fredenburgh, Earle A., SGT, Company A
Frederick, Valentine, PVT, Company I
Fredman, Albert C., 1LT, IRC, Company C
Freed, Charles, PVT, Company K
Freikor, Leo, PVT, Company A

Fremmer, William, PVT, Company A
French, John Charles, CPL, Company M
French, Joseph Harry, PVT, Company H
Frey, John Emil, SGT, Company C
Frey, Martin John, PVT, Company K
Fricschkorn, Louis, PVT, Company M
Fried, Henry Frank, PVT, Company L
Friedman, Harry, PVT, Company D
Friedman, Melvin, PVT, Company L
Friedman, Sam, PVT, Company E
Fritz, Adolph John, PVT, Headquarters Company,
   died overseas
Fritz, John F., SGT, Company I
Frohling, Frank Henry, PVT, Company E
Frost, Roswell William, BN SGT MJR, Headquarters
   Company
Fruehwirth, Charles Edward, PVT, Headquarters
   Company
Fucci, Salvatore, PVT, Company G
Fufford, Joseph, PVT, Headquarters Company
Fuhrer, William Ludwig, PVT 1CL, Company M
Fuller, Charles Ellison, PVT, Company K
Fuller, Charles M., PVT, Company G
Fuller, Harold, PVT, CORP, Company G, U
Funnell, Howard, PVT, Company G
Furia, Arnold, PVT, Company K
Furman, Benjamin Harrison, PVT, Company D

Gabler, Max, PVT, Company H
Gadinsky, Abraham, PVT, Company M
Gaige, Harry L., 2 CL MSN, Headquarters Company
Gaignet, Joseph Emil, PVT, Company A
Galante, Giuseppi, PVT, Company F
Galdi, Albert, PVT, PVT1CL, Company I
Galdi, Arthur, PVT, Company B
Galeota, Nicola, PVT, Company M
Gallagher, Edward Terrance, MCH, Company C
Gallagher, James Henry Jr., PVT, Company M
Gallagher, Leo Francis, PVT, Company D
Gallagher, Rodney B., SGT, Company A
Galli, Stephen A., PVT, Company K
Gallo, Luigi Di Vincenzo, PVT, Company D
Gallone, John, PVT, Company F
Galloway, Frank Abram, PVT, Company D
Galluccio, Amodio, PVT, Company I
Galphin, Eldridge McSwain, 2LT, INF R.C.,
   Company M
Galvin, James Joseph, PVT, Company C
Galvin, Peter, PVT, Company E
Galvin, Thomas J., CPL, Headquarters Company
Gambill, Ira Everett, PVT, Company F
Gamzon, Max, PVT, Company H
Gandoli, Carming, PVT, Company L
Ganley, Thomas, PVT, Company C
Gans, Harry Simon, PVT, PVT1CL, Company I
Garabedian, Souklas, PVT, Company M
Garceo, John, PVT, Supply Company
Gardiner, Ray Corliss, PVT, Company K
Gardner, Clyde Roger, PVT, Company C
Gareis, Joseph Raymond, PVT, Company D
Garey, Douglas George, PVT, Company C
Garner, Fate, PVT, Company H
Garrison, Clayton, PVT, Supply Company
Garrison, Leroy, SGT, Company F
Garrison, Paul R., CORP, Company E
Garrison, Sanford D., PVT, Company B
Garrison, Walter Thurman, PVT, Supply Company
Garrison, Wayne, CORP, PVT, Company E
Garry, James Joseph, PVT, Company H
Garuolo, Louis, PVT, Company K

Garvey, Edward Vincent, CORP, Company I, died
  overseas
Garvey, Jesse, PVT, Company E
Gary, Albert Horton, PVT, Company L
Gaskin, John James, CORP, Company E
Gaudino, Guiseppie, PVT, Company B
Geaney, Thomas, PVT, Company E
Geary, Amond C., PVT, Company L
Geide, William Phillip, PVT, Company M
Geiger, Rudolph, PVT, Company C
Genteel, Thomas, PVT, Company E
Gerard, Leo O., CORP, Company I
Gerkens, John Fredk., CORP, Supply Company
Geschwinder, Edward C., SUP SGT, Company M
Gettings, William Lawrence, PVT, Company G
Geurriero, Alexander, PVT, Supply Company
Giandomenico, Antonio, PVT, Company C
Gibbens, Frank, CPL, Company C
Gibbs, Merrill J., CPL, Company H
Gibney, James Joseph, PVT, Company C
Gibson, Edward, PVT, Company G, C
Gifford, Frank J. Jr., PVT, Company A
Gilbert, Chauncey MCL, LT, U.S.R. INF, Company G
Gilboy, George, CORP, PVT, Company E
Gilbreth, Joseph L., COL, INF, Regimental
  Headquarters
Gildersleeve, Charles Edward, PVT, Company L
Gilhooly, John Joseph, PVT, Company D
Gill, Thomas Emmett, PVT, Company L
Gilles, Harry, PVT, Company E
Gillespie, Hermond J., CPL, Headquarters Company
Gillespie, Joseph V., PVT, Company B
Gilliard, Edward John, PVT, Company G
Gilliland, Stephen, PVT, Company B
Gilman, Harry Bertram, CORP, Company A
Gingue, Joseph, PVT, Company L
Giordano, Alessandro, PVT, Company D
Giordano, Pasquale, PVT, Company C
Giovannelli, John, PVT, Company I
Gister, Stanley, PVT, Headquarters Company
Gladding, Charles Freeman, SGT, Company A
Glass, Wiley W., 1LT, IRC, Company L
Glasser, Benjamin Jacob, PVT, Company M
Gleason, Frank Peter, PVT, Company A
Glenn, James Lamar, PVT, Supply Company
Glenn, Thomas Andrew, PVT, Company L
Glennon, Daniel Vincent, PVT, Company E
Glennon, Hugh A., PVT, PVT1CL, Company E
Glicksman, Isidor, PVT, Company A
Glorioso, Angelo, PVT, Company K
Gluck, Irving, PVT, Company I, OC
Gminski, Stanley John, PVT, Headquarters Company
Goan, Augustin, PVT, Company B
Godfrey, George Clayton, PVT, Company H
Godwin, Harold Reginald, PVT, Company D
Goetz, Joseph, PVT, Company M
Gold, Joseph, PVT 1CL, Company I
Gold, Michael, PVT, PVT1CL, Company I
Goldberg, Abrahm Lincoln, PVT, Company G
Golden, Eugene Leviven, PVT, Company C
Golden, Eugene S, PVT, Company E
Goldman, Meyer, PVT, Company H
Goldsmith, Arthur, PVT, Company M
Goldsmith, Harry Gray, PVT, Company E
Goldsmith, Ira John, PVT, Company K
Goldstein, Alexander, PVT, Company M
Goldstein, Philip, PVT, Company L
Golub, Aaron, PVT, Company A
Gompper, Charles B., PVT, Company K
Gonsales, Lawrence, PVT, Company A
Goodison, James, PVT, Company I

Goodman, Lewis, PVT, Company H
Goodman, Philip, PVT, Headquarters Company
Goodman, Samuel, PVT 1CL, Company M, died
  overseas
Goodsell, Hiren A., PVT, Company B
Goodstein, Charles, PVT, Company F
Goodstein, Elliot M., PVT, Company B
Goodwin, Arthur J., SGT, Headquarters Company
Goodwin, Austin Cyril, PVT, Company A
Gordon, Abraham, PVT, Headquarters Company
Gordon, George William, PVT, Company D
Gordon, Howard Bradner, PVT, Company A
Gordon, Isidore, PVT, Company D
Gordon, Jacob, PVT, Company B
Gordon, Nathan, PVT, Company F, C
Gorgoni, August, PVT, Company F
Gormis, Joseph, PVT, Company H
Gorr, Herman Christaphor, PVT, Company D
Gorsky, Joseph, PVT, Company A
Gorsky, Stanley, PVT, Company A
Gosk, Joseph, PVT, Headquarters Company
Goth, Karl Augustus, PVT, Company F, Transferred
Gottlieb, Aaron, PVT, Headquarters Company
Gottschalk, Elmer, CPL, Company C
Grable, Carl Adolph, SGT, Company L
Grace, Joseph Aloysius, SGT, Company C
Grace, Kenneth, LT, U.S.R. INF, Company G
Grace, William Aloysius, PVT, Company F
Gradek, Felix, PVT, Company F
Graham, James Andrew, SGT, Company A
Graham, Michael Joseph, PVT, Headquarters
  Company
Gramm, Joseph H., PVT, Company B
Granati, Guilio, PVT, Company C
Grandinetti, Vincent, PVT, Company K
Grant, Frederick S., PVT, Company B
Grant, George, PVT, Company G
Grasea, Benjamin, PVT, Company B
Grask, Griffen, PVT, Company F
Grau, John Mariot, PVT, Company G
Graubart, Bernard, PVT, Company D
Grauer, William, PVT, Company M
Gray, Eugene Lansing, PVT, Company D
Gray, Ffarrington T., CORP, Company L
Grazioso, Alfonso, PVT, Company E
Greco, Guirino, CPL, Headquarters Company
Greco, Marcello, PVT, Headquarters Company
Greco, Santo, PVT, Company E
Grecorizzo, Vincenzo, PVT, Company M
Green, Henry Augustus, PVT, Company G
Green, Hughie Eugene, PVT, Company C
Greenbaum, Leo, PVT, Company D
Greenberg, Albert, PVT, Company C
Greenberg, Harry, PVT, Headquarters Company
Greenberg, Henry, PVT, Company E
Greenberg, Hyman David, PVT, Headquarters
  Company
Greenburg, Abe, PVT, Company C
Greene, Dennis E., PVT, Company B
Greene, George, PVT, Company M
Greenough, Clarence S., 1 CL MSN, Headquarters
  Company
Greenspan, Abraham, PVT, Company M
Greenwald, Phillip, PVT, Company G
Grefner, Nathan, PVT, Headquarters Company
Greggo, Angelo Basil, PVT, Company L
Griffin, George William, CPL, Company K
Griffin, Thomas Francis, PVT, Company C
Griffith, James Alfred, PVT, Company F
Griffith, William Fred, PVT, Company G
Griffiths, Waldo, PVT, Company L

Grobe, Leonard J., PVT, Company B
Gronowski, Walter Frank, CORP, Company F
Grosberger, Samuel, PVT, Company M
Gross, Charles, COOK, Company A, A.W.O.L
Gross, Frederick, PVT, Company H
Grote, Nicholas Napolean, COOK, Company A
Grotz, Frederick Francis, PVT, Company K
Groves, Adrian Darwood, CPL, Company H
Gruban, Samuel C., PVT, Medical Detachment
Gruler, Frederick Charles, PVT, Company E
Guckian, Paul Peter, PVT, Company H
Guest, William W., SGT, Headquarters Company
Guihan, Paul Francis, PVT, Company C
Guiliani, Frank, PVT, Company H
Guimettico, Lorenzo, PVT, Company C
Gumina, Biaggio, PVT, Company E
Gusrang, George Edward, PVT, Company I
Gustina, Peter, PVT, Company H, C
Gustina, James W., PVT, Company B
Gutfleisch, Joseph William, PVT 1CL, Company M
Guy, Hildon G., PVT, Company M
Guzman, Felix, PVT, Company L
Guzzett, Antonio, PVT, Supply Company

Haack, Ernest August, MECH, Company L
Haas, Charles, PVT, Company K
Haas, William, PVT, Company B
Hacker, David L., LT, N.A.INF, Company G
Hackett, George, MECH, Company G
Hackett, James Edward, PVT, Company E
Hafner, William, PVT, Company F
Hagen, Edwin J., PVT, Company K
Hagen, Ole, PVT, Company F
Hahn, Otto Paul, PVT, Company K
Haladjian, Yerwant, PVT, Company A
Halbritter, August F., BUG, Company D
Hall, Royal Campbell, PVT, Company A
Hallenbeck, Stanley C, PVT, Company B
Hallstein, John Charles, PVT, Company F
Hallugan, James, PVT, Company C
Halobowsky, Felix, PVT, Company B
Halstead, Irving Charles, PVT, Company G
Ham, Jesse, PVT, Company G
Hamm, Fred Jacob, CPL, Company M
Hammer, Carlos H., PVT, Company B
Hammer, John W., PVT, CORP, Company B
Hammes, Frank W., Capt, ING, Headquarters
  Company
Hamsing, Carl, PVT, Headquarters Company
Hanes, Albert Ezekiel, PVT, Company F
Hanley, Thomas Francis, PVT, Company I
Hanna, Erwin James, SGT, Company C
Hannan, Frank Tompkins, PVT, Company D
Hansen, Harry, PVT, Company F, C
Hansen, Paul Egeriis, PVT, Company G
Harboe, Christian J., PVT, Company B
Harder, George Hermance, CORP, Company F
Hargraves, Ellis, PVT, Company C
Harlow, Homer, PVT, Company G
Harmon. John B., PVT, Company A
Harnett, Francis Thomas, PVT, Company E
Harnischfeger, Charles Joseph, PVT, PVT1CL,
  Company I
Harper, Otis, PVT, Company G
Harr, Edward Joseph, PVT, Company E
Harring, Clifford Mastin, PVT, Company A
Harrington, Daniel Joseph, PVT, Company H, C
Harris, Dwight J., 1LT, I.R.C., Company K
Harris, Eugene T., MAJOR, INF NG, 1st Battalion
Harris, Fraank S., CAPT, I.N.G., Supply Company

Harris, Grover C., PVT, Company H
Harris, James John, PVT, Headquarters Company
Harris, Paul E., CPL, Headquarters Company
Harris, William Edward, SGT, Company H, H51,
  died overseas
Harrold, Wilbur, PVT, Medical Detachment
Hart, William Joseph, PVT, Company A, OC, died
  U.S.
Hartzman, Max, PVT, PVT1CL, Company I
Harvey, James F., PVT, Company B
Harvey, Joseph Howard, PVT, Company A
Harz, Christopher Jr., PVT, Company C
Harz, Fritz, PVT, Company C
Haskew, Walter Thomas, PVT, Supply Company
Hass, William, PVT, Mch., Company B
Hasselman, Charles Vernon, CORP, Company E
Hatfield, Levi A., PVT, Medical Detachment
Hathaway, Wesley, Company H, C
Hatounian, Haig, PVT, Company K, C, Co K 51 Pion
  Inf to Aug 8/18, discharged Feb 18/19 Alien
  Enemy
Hauber, Merlin Augustus, PVT, Company A
Haupt, William O., 3 CL MSN, Headquarters
  Company
Haussmann, William, PVT, Cpl., Company B
Havey, Phillips F., SGT, Company H
Havill, Reginald, 2LT, I.R.C., Company K
Havill, Reginald, 2LT, INF, Regimental
  Headquarters
Hawley, William Henry, PVT, Company G
Hawthorne, George, PVT, Company A
Hawver, Walter William, CORP, Company F
Hayes, Fred, PVT, Company B
Hayes, Homer Albert, PVT, Company K
Hayes, Joseph Patrick, PVT, Company C
Hayner, Ross Andrew, PVT, Company D
Haynes, Elwin, PVT, Company G
Healy, Daniel Steven, PVT, Company D
Healy, Edmund J., PVT, Company B
Healy, Timothy John, PVT, Company F
Hebel, Joseph, PVT, Company F
Heck, Howell H., 1LT, I.R.C., Company E
Heckert, Chester A., PVT, Company H
Hedrick, Walter Slingerland, MESS SGT, Company A
Hegarty, Leonard A., 1ST SGT, Company H
Hegarty, Leonard A., 2LT, INF, Regimental
  Headquarters
Hegarty, Thomas John, PVT, Company L
Heiges, Calvin Arthur, PVT, Company G
Heiman, Samuel, PVT, Company M
Hein, Henry Joseph, PVT, Company L
Heitel, Harry Joseph, PVT, Company E
Held, Charles Herman, PVT, Company F
Heller, John Joseph, PVT, Company A
Heller, Leroy Francis, PVT, Company C
Helmers, Henry August, PVT, Company H
Hemingway, Donald H., 2LT, I.R.C., Company H
Henahan, Francis B., PVT, Company H
Hendrick, James George, SGT, Company K
Hendricks, Simon S., PVT, Medical Detachment
Hengstenberg, Louis Henry, SERGT, Company E
Henion, Walter Byrne, PVT, Company L
Henk, Harry Fred, PVT, Company K
Henry, Michael, PVT, Company L
Henry, Thomas W., SUP SGT, Headquarters Company
Hensel, William August, PVT, Company F
Hensel, William Frederick, CORP, Company F
Hensley, Bascombe S., 1LT, INF, Regimental
  Headquarters
Hensley, Bascombe S., 2LT, I.R.C., Company I
Henzel, Aloysius J., CORP, Supply Company

Henzel, John W., SGT, PVT, Company B
Herald, Thomas A., SGT, Company G
Hermance, Edward, PVT 1CL, Company F
Hernandez, Manuel, PVT, Headquarters Company
Herr, John George, PVT, Company F
Herrick, Charles Henry, PVT, Company L
Herrick, William C., 1LT, I.N.G., Company A
Hertan, Albert, PVT, Company M
Hewitt, Reed Max, PVT 1ST CL, Supply Company
Heyman, Carl, PVT, Company G
Hiatt, John E., PVT, Company D
Hickey, Clarence Joseph, PVT, Company E
Hickey, Cornelius John, PVT, Company M
Hickey, John James, PVT, Company D
Hickey, Joseph Francis, PVT, Headquarters
  Company
Hicks, Edward, PVT, Company D, OC, died overseas
Hicks, James S., PVT, Company B
Hicks, William Joseph, PVT, Company C
Higby, Leonard George, CORP, Company A
Higgins, Edward, PVT, Company B
Higgins, Geradus Backman, PVT, Company F, died
  overseas
Higgins, Lawrence T., PVT, Company K
Higgs, Frank, PVT, Company G, Overseas Cs
Hildenbrandt, Louis, CPL, Company B
Hilgert, William, PVT, Company L
Hillje, Harry Hendrick, CORP, PVT, Company E
Hillman, Jacob, BUG, Company M
Hillyard, Richard Elmer, CORP, Company F
Hillygus, Leroy Benjamin, PVT, Company I
Hinck, Bernard George, PVT, Company K
Hindes, Addison Earl, PVT, Company F
Hinds, Julian Barton, SGT, Company K
Hinkley, Alva, PVT, Company E
Hinkley, Harry D., PVT 1CL, Company M
Hirschberg, Henry Lazarus, PVT, Company F
Hirschberg, Jermone Gustave, PVT, Company G
Hislop, Howard Douglas, PVT, Company I
Hitchcock, Frank, COOK, Company E, died overseas
Hitchcock, William B, Capt, NG, Regimental
  Headquarters
Hitt, Frank, PVT, Company G
Hobbs, Charles Finley, PVT, PVT1CL, Company I
Hobbs, John, PVT, Company C
Hobby, Alfred Louis, CORP, Company L
Hock, William, BN SGT MJR, Headquarters Company
Hocking, William John, PVT, Supply Company
Hodge, Francis George, PVT, Company C
Hodges, Leroy Spencer, PVT, Company K
Hodoly, George Michael, CORP, Company I
Hoefer, Gustave C. H., SGT, Company G
Hoffarth, Joseph F., BUG, Company G
Hoffenberg, Harry, PVT, Headquarters Company
Hofferberth, Leonard, PVT, Company F, C
Hoffman, Max, PVT, Supply Company
Hoffman, Paul Edward, COOK, Company F
Hoffman, William Richard, PVT, Company A
Hoffner, Newell, CPL, Company C
Hofmann, Otto, CPL, Company D
Hofmeister, Frank Joseph, PVT, Company K
Hogan, Arthur John, PVT 1ST CL, Supply Company
Hogan, Daniel Frances, SGT, Company H
Hogan, William John, PVT, Headquarters Company
Hogg, George, MECH, Company I
Hogg, Paris, PVT, Company F, C
Holcomb, William Harrison, PVT, Company C
Holden, James Joseph, PVT, Company C
Holevack, John, PVT, Company C
Holland, James William, PVT, Company C
Holland, Joseph John, PVT, Company F

Hollander, Morris, PVT, Company C
Hollenstein, John Peter, PVT, PVT1CL, Company I
Holleran, Martin Joseph, PVT, Company K
Holliday, Arthur, PVT, Company A
Holliman, John Fletcher, PVT, Company F
Holmbraker, Frank Wm., PVT, Company G
Holmes, Gus L., PVT, Company D
Holzer, John, CPL, Headquarters Company
Holzwasser, Herman, PVT, Supply Company
Honsberger Clare, PVT, Company B
Hoolahan, George A., CORP, Company I
Hopkins, Charles V., SERGT, Company E
Hopper, Harry, PVT, Headquarters Company
Horman, Frederick Charles, PVT, Company H
Hornbeck, Percy, PVT, Company E, died overseas
Hornung, William, CORP, Company I
Horowitz, Henry, PVT, Company M
Horowitz, Saul, PVT, Company F
Horrevoets, George James, PVT, Company G
Horswell, John F., SGT, Company B
Horton, Gail Borden, PVT, Company G
Horton, Thaddeus, Jr., PVT, Company D
Hotaling, Merritt James, PVT, Company A
Houck, Henry John, PVT, Company H
Houmpavlis, George Aristis, PVT, Company G
Hourigan, Michael John, PVT, Company C
Howard, Harry, CPL, Company G
Howard, James R., SGT, Company M
Howden, Chester, PVT, Company C
Howe, Thomas, PVT, Company G
Howell, Alvin, CPL, Company C
Howland, Glenn Devoe, PVT, Company K
Hoyler, Henry C., PVT, Company B
Hubbard, George Henry, PVT, Company I
Hudson, Edward Peter, PVT, Company M
Hudson, Howard Farley, PVT, Company H
Hughes, Edward A., CPL, Headquarters Company
Hughes, Frank Joseph, PVT, Company L
Hulce, William, PVT, Company D
Hummel, Charles William, PVT, Company F, C
Hummer, William, PVT, Company M
Humphrey, Harry C., PVT, Company G, Cas
Humphreys, James, PVT, Company A
Hungerbuhler, Arnold George, PVT, Company H
Hunley, Thomas F, Company I
Hunt, Howard Porter, PVT, Company E
Hunt, William M., 1LT, IRC, 2nd Battalion
Hunter, Charles Elmer, PVT, Supply Company
Hurd, William, PVT, Company E
Hurlbut, Roy Edward, PVT, Company G
Hurley, Edward Joseph, PVT, Company E
Hurr, James Francis, PVT, Company A
Hushen, John Joseph, PVT, Company L
Hust, Floyd Dean, PVT, Company D
Hutcheson, William, PVT, Company E
Hyatt, Allen T., SUP SGT RGT, Supply Company
Hyatt, James L. Jr., SUP SGT RGT, Supply Company

Ianniello, Nicola, PVT, Company D
Igneri, Joseph, PVT, Company G
Immediato, Joseph, PVT, Company C
Immite, Andrea, PVT, Company I
Imparato, Joseph, PVT, Company I
Improta, Agusta, PVT, Company C
Ingerham, Arthur, PVT, Company D
Ingram, John Taylor, PVT, Medical Detachment
Ingram, William Francis, PVT, Company F
Innello, Andrew, PVT, Company L
Iorio, Peter Antonio, PVT, Company A
Ippolito, Vito, PVT, Company G

Irby, Pierce B., LT, U.S.R. INF, Company G
Ireland, Thomas Howard, PVT, Company H
Irving, Frederick Gordon, PVT, Company A
Irving, Monson Alanzo, SGT, Headquarters Company
Iseman, Robert, BND CPL, Headquarters Company
Isenecker, Ambrose Lawrence, PVT, Company H
Isenhart, Jacob William, PVT, BUGL, Company F,
   died overseas
Isenhart, Worthington H., 2 CL MSN, Headquarters
   Company
Israel, Udell, PVT 1CL, Company M
Izzo, Joseph Mike, PVT, Company C

Jackowski, Wladyslaw, PVT, Company C
Jackson, Austin Edward, PVT, Company E
Jackson, Floyde E., PVT, Company H
Jackson, Francis L., SGT, Company B
Jacobs, Michael J., PVT, Company G
Jacobs, William, PVT, Company B
Jacobson, Elias Meyer, PVT, Company L
Jacobson, Hilding Ali, PVT, Company M
Jacoby, Jerome Julius, CORP, Company I
Jagels, Henry Joseph, PVT, Company G
Jagger, Frank Anthony, PVT, Company F
Jamieson, William, PVT, Company C
Janicke, Stanley, PVT, Company E
Jansen, Cornelius, COOK, Company L
Jarmakowski, Frank Alozys, PVT, Company F
Jarnagin, Jerry Overton, PVT, Supply Company
Jaskiewicz, Peter, PVT, Headquarters Company
Jefferson, Albert B., WAG, Supply Company
Jenkins, Harold Elliott, PVT, Company K
Jenkins, William Wellington, CORP, PVT, Company E
Jennings, Harold Cordrope, PVT, Company D
Jennings, Leonard, PVT, Company K
Jensch, Sidney Howard, PVT, Company A
Jensen, Christian, CORP, Company L
Jensen, Jens Peter W., MCH, Company B
Jobes, Mount Jr., PVT, Company M
Johns, Hiram Jack, PVT, Company M
Johnson, Benjamin Francis, PVT, Company K
Johnson, Charles Spenser, PVT, Company L
Johnson, Herbert, PVT, Headquarters Company
Johnson, Herman T., PVT, Headquarters Company
Johnson, Hollis Wesley, PVT, Company A
Johnson, James Henry, PVT, Company F
Johnson, Nils Hugo, PVT, Company F
Johnson, Robert Berger, PVT, Company E
Johnson, William, PVT, Company F
Johnston, Millard, PVT, Company B
Joines, Paul, PVT, Company F
Jolls, Mark E., CPL, Company B
Jonas, Augustus, ASST BND LDR, Headquarters
   Company
Jones, Arthur, PVT, Supply Company
Jones, Ben. Jr., PVT, Company F, died overseas,
   SOTGW War Vol I - Kentucky
Jones, Floyd Leon, CPL, Company H
Jones, James Fenton, PVT, Company A
Jones, Melville R., MCH, Company B
Jones, Oscar Eugene, PVT, Company M
Jones, Ralph Alexander, PVT, Company K
Jones, Raymond Thomas, MESS SGT, Supply Company
Jones, Sidney B., 2LT, INF, Regimental
   Headquarters
Jones, Sidney B., 2LT, IRC, Company L
Jordan, Anthony, PVT, Company G
Jordan, William Francis, COOK, Company A
Jorgensen, Jonas Christian, PVT, Company M
Joyce, Thomas Aloysius, PVT, Company K

Juba, Michael Francis, PVT, Company C
Julian, Charles C., 2LT, I.R.C., Company F
Jurkowitz, Isidore, PVT, Company I

Kaczmarek, Maryon, PVT, Company F
Kager, Edward G., PVT, Company B
Kahn, Benjamin, PVT, Company L
Kain, Thomas Francis, PVT, Company G
Kalfakis, James Emanuel, PVT, Company D
Kalogris, James Peter, PVT, Company K
Kamenetsky, Alex, PVT, Supply Company
Kamermayer, Julius, CORP, Company F
Kanner, Harry, PVT, Supply Company
Kantorowski, Stefan, PVT, Company M
Kantz, Macey, PVT, Company E
Kantz, Macey, PVT, Medical Detachment
Kaplen, Leo, PVT, Supply Company
Kaplis, Joseph, PVT, Headquarters Company
Karcszwski, Andrew, PVT, Headquarters Company
Karg, William Jr., PVT, Company M
Karpinski, John, PVT, Company K
Karsten, Charles, PVT, Supply Company
Kasch, Herman Frederick William, PVT, Supply
   Company
Kasper, Anthony, PVT, Company E
Kaszmarek, Walter, PVT, Headquarters Company
Kaufman, Charles, PVT, Company F
Kaufman, Samuel, PVT 1CL, Company M
Kaufmann, Gustave Frederick, PVT, Company E
Kavanaugh, Patrick, PVT, Company C
Kayton, Charles, PVT, Company F
Keane, Harry Michael, PVT, Company I
Keane, Lawrence, PVT, Company A
Kearns, Frank X., CAPT, I.N.G., Company K
Keating, Michael Joseph, PVT, Company L
Keating, William John, PVT, Company F
Keck, John, PVT, Company D
Keefe, Edward Verdy, PVT, Company K
Keefe, William Henry, PVT, Company C
Keegan, Patrick Joseph, PVT, Company G
Kehoe, Robert Emmett, PVT, Company C
Kehran, Cornelius, PVT, Company L
Keith, Taylor, PVT, Company F
Keleher, Cornelius P., SGT, Company B
Kellam, Almer Slee, PVT, Company G
Kelleher, Cornelius, CORP, PVT, Company E
Kelleher, Thomas Francis, PVT, Company G
Keller, Henry H., PVT, Company L
Kelly, Francis A., Chaplain, Promoted to 27th
   Division Chaplain
Kelley, John Maurice, PVT, Headquarters Company
Kelley, John, PVT, Headquarters Company
Kellner, Henry Joseph, PVT, Company D, OC
Kelly, Francis, PVT, Company G
Kelly, Henry Joseph, PVT 1CL, Company K
Kelly, Joseph, PVT, Company H
Kelly, Thomas A., PVT, Company K
Kelsey, Erwin H., CPL, PVT, Company B
Kendall, Frank David, PVT, Company K
Kenna, Joseph Patrick, PVT, Company C
Kennedy, Dale, CPL, Company M
Kennedy, Daniel F, RGT SGT MJR, Headquarters
   Company
Kennedy, Patrick Joseph, PVT, Company K
Kennedy, Thomas Joseph, PVT, Company A
Kennedy, Thomas P., CORP, Company B
Kenney, Edward Thomas, PVT, Supply Company
Kenney, John Patrick, BUG, Company D
Kenny, John Patrick, PVT, Company A
Keogh, John Joseph, PVT, Company L

Keresesman, Peter Jr., PVT, Company F
Kern, Walter W., PVT, Company D
Kerr, Chaarles, PVT, Company M
Kerr, Frederick H., MESS SERGT, Company E
Ketcham, Lyman Frank, PVT, Company I
Keteltas, John Samuel Jr., PVT, Company C
Kevelson, Abraham, PVT, Headquarters Company
Keyser, Walter S., PVT, CPL, Company B
Kidd, Colin Rankin, SGT, Company H
Kidd, Ninian S., CPL, Company G
Kiernan, William Joseph, PVT, Company G
Kiersted, Aaron B., CPL, Company M
Kieser, Frederick Louis, CORP, Company E
Kiley, Matthew J., 1LT, INF R.C., Company M
Kilhenney, James, PVT, Company C
Killeen, John Joseph, PVT, Company C
Kindler, William H., PVT, Company B
Kiney, Patrick, PVT, Company B
King, Arthur K., MECH, Company I
King, Herbert T., PVT, Company D
King, James, PVT, Company L
King, John J., SGT, Company B
King, Joseph Aloysius, PVT, Company L
King, Leo Leonard, PVT, Headquarters Company
King, Roger T., SGT, Company H
Kingston, Fred David, CPL, Company C
Kinnunen, William August, PVT, Company E
Kipling, Alfred Richard, PVT, Company I, died
  overseas
Kircher, Joseph Peter, PVT, Company K
Kiser, Arthur J., PVT, Company E, (Kieser), E
Klapmeyer, William, PVT, Company H
Klausman, Charles, PVT, Company K
Klein, George Magnus, 1ST SGT, Company F
Klein, John, PVT, Company I
Klein, Joseph, PVT, Company A
Kleinberg, Abraham, PVT, Company F
Kleindienst, Gustave Andew, PVT, Company E
Kline, Harry Leonard, CPL, Company C
Kline, John F, Colonel, Regimental Headquarters
  (10th NYNG)
Klopp, James Kent, PVT, Company H
Knapp, Charles A., PVT, Company B
Knapp, Herbert E., SERGT, Company E
Kneale, Hollis Ray, PVT, Company K
Kneib, Frank, PVT, Supply Company
Knibbs, George Harrison, PVT, Company A
Knilans, Robert Harry, PVT, Company K
Knoblauch, George Edward, PVT, Company A
Knott, John J. Jr., PVT, Company B
Knowles, Chas. J., COOK, Company B
Knowles, Frederick, PVT, Company I
Kober, Frank Phillip, PVT, Company C
Kobernuss, Henry Edward, PVT, Company K
Kochenburg, Frederick William, SGT, Company C
Koeberich, Theodore Julius, PVT, Company F
Koehler, Frederick, PVT, Company A
Koehler, Jacob Solon, PVT, Company K
Koenig, Albert Alexander, PVT, Company H, C
Koenig, Fred Christian, PVT, Company L
Koerner, Theodore, PVT, Company I
Kohout, John Otto, PVT, Company I
Kolobuchowski, John, PVT, Headquarters Company
Koltun, Louis, PVT, Company I [Kolten]
Konight, Banjamin, PVT, Company H
Kontos, Kleomenes, PVT, Company C
Koop, Charles Raymond, PVT, Company D
Koop, John Frederick, PVT, Company I
Korc, John, PVT, Company F
Korwan, William S., SGT, Company I, [Korivan]
Kosteski, Frank, PVT, Company E

Kosticki, Frank, PVT, Company K
Kostrzychi, Leo, PVT, Company F
Kotenberg, Eibert E., PVT, Company K
Kovnat, David, PVT, Company E
Kowal, Joseph, CPL, Headquarters Company
Kraft, Conrad Christian, PVT, Company C
Kramer, Joseph John, PVT, Company F
Kramer, Philip, PVT, Company L
Kraus, Bernard, PVT, Headquarters Company
Kraus, John Jr, PVT, Company A
Krause, Frederick, PVT, Company A
Kravetz, Max, PVT, Company M
Kravitz, Hyman, PVT, Headquarters Company
Kreimeyer, John Michael, PVT, Company C
Kreslein, Adolph E, PVT, Company E, died U.S.
Kretzschmar, Victor Jr, PVT, Company I
Kroepke, Fredrick, PVT, Supply Company
Kroger, Earl Marcus, PVT, Company A
Krolak, Andrew, PVT, Company F
Kronick, Michael, PVT, Company F
Kroop, Frank Ferdinand, PVT, Company A
Krzyzycki, Walter, PVT, Company C
Krzyzykowski, John, PVT, Headquarters Company,
  51 PIR HQ CO to Apr 8/19
Kucharski, Casimir Joseph, PVT, Headquarters
  Company
Kuhn, John W., PVT, Cpl., Company B
Kujawa, John, PVT, Company A
Kukuck, Raymond Phelps, PVT 1ST CL, CORP, Supply
  Company [Kuckuck]
Kunnunen, William A, PVT, Company E
Kunze, George Adolph Jr., PVT, Company I
Kureloff, Nathan, PVT, Company B
Kurtz, John Henry, PVT, Company M
Kuster, John Frank, PVT, Headquarters Company
Kusz, Joseph Frank, CPL, Headquarters Company

Lacy, Walter G., PVT, Supply Company
Laffin, Joseph Francis, CPL, Company K
Lafountain, Frank Marshall, PVT, Company M
Lagana, Vincent, PVT, Company K
Lahl, Albert Charles, PVT, Company F
Laiho, Vincent, PVT, Company A
Lake, Edward Maltby, SGT, Company L
Lalone, Fred, PVT, Company L
Lalor, Thomas Francis, PVT, Company M
Lamb, Walter B, SUP SGT RGT, Supply Company
Lamorte, Michael, PVT, Company F
Lamprecht, Sterling Power, CPL, Company K
Landau, Herman N., PVT, Company B
Lane, John Andrew, PVT, Company A
Lang, Charles Claar, PVT, Company L
Lang, Reuben, PVT, Company E
Langan, James, PVT, Company G
Langan, John Francis, PVT, Company I
Langan, John William, PVT, Company G
Langan, William J, PVT, Company E
Lange, Robert, PVT, Company I
Langer, Charles Jacob, PVT, Company G
Langlos, Victor, PVT, Company A, PVT 1CL, Sept
  10/18
Lannone, John, PVT, Company M
Lapaglia, Agatino, PVT, Company K
Lapidius, Norman, PVT, Company G
Laporta, Enrico, PVT, Supply Company
Lappman, Henry, PVT, Cpl., Company B [Lappeman]
Large, William A., PVT, Company B
Laschinsky, Asher, PVT, Supply Company
Laskoski, John, PVT, Company F
Lasner, John H., SGT, Medical Detachment

Latini, Pancrazio, PVT, Company A
Laughlin, Roy Oliver, PVT, Company L
Laughlin, Thomas Francis, PVT, Company L
Lauricella, Angelo William, PVT, Company C
Lauro, Ferdinando, PVT, Headquarters Company
Lawson, William Frederick, PVT, Company E, U
Lawyer, Eugene J., PVT, Company E
Lax, Harry William, PVT, Company D
Lay, Edwin Thorne, PVT, Company E
Leander, Joshua E., 1LT, IRC, Company L
Leavitt, Henry Sheldon, CPL, Company M
Leckey, James, PVT, Company G
Lefevre, George Hawkins, PVT, Company G
Lehane, James, CK, Company G
Lehman, Charles, CPL, Company D
Lehr, Paul C., 1ST SGT, Company L
Leibrock, Alfred George, PVT, Company K
Lembeck, Bernard, PVT, Headquarters Company
Lemke, Julius W., PVT, Company K
Lemon, Lincoln Lee, CORP, Company F
Lenihan, Leo Vincent, PVT, Company F
Lennick, Joseph, PVT, Company F
Lenoci, Frank, PVT, Company H
Leonard, Francis Bartholomew, PVT, Company K
Leonard, Joseph John, PVT, Company K
Leonardi, Charles G., PVT, Company B
Leone, Joseph, PVT, Company E
Leonetti, Peter Anthony, PVT, Company L
Leparulo, Frank, PVT, Company I
Leprell, Lawrence John, PVT, Company F
LeRoy, Walter Mynard, SUP SGT, Company K
Leslie, George Arthur, PVT, Company A
Leszczynski, Alexander, PVT, Headquarters
   Company
Levanduski, Andrew Joseph, PVT, Company E
Levanduski, Joseph, PVT, Company E
LeVey, Maximilian George, PVT, Company A
Levine, Morris, PVT, Company H
Levis, James Taylor, CPL, Company M
Levy, Charles, PVT, Company D
Levy, Joseph, CPL, Company D
Levy, Joseph, WAG, Supply Company
Levy, Thomas Edward, PVT, Company K
Lewin, Aaron, PVT 1CL, Company M
Lewis, Chester A., SGT, Headquarters Company
Lewis, Edward E., SGT, Company I
Lewis, George A., PVT, Company E
Lewis, George Dawson, PVT, Company A
Lewis, Oswald, PVT, Headquarters Company
Lewis, Samuel James, PVT, Supply Company
Lewis, Sydney Sherman, PVT, Company L
Liberio, Alexandro, PVT, Company G
Liconti, Louis, PVT, Headquarters Company
Liddie, William Elliott, PVT, Company I
Liecinski, John, PVT, Company C
Lightman, Albert Simpson, PVT 1CL, Company I
Liguori, Angelo A., PVT, Company B
Lilga, Sigurd Oskar, PVT, Company A
Lilly, David Clair, PVT, Company L
Linacre, George H., WAG, Supply Company
Lindberg, Arthur Leo, PVT 1ST CL, Supply Company
Linder, Young S., PVT, Company E
Linehan, Nicholas P, SGT, Company G
Linger, Edgar B., PVT, Company K
Linnane, Patrick Joseph, PVT, Company E
Lipe, L.G., PVT, Company A
Lipiec, John George, PVT, Headquarters Company
Lipka, Stanley, PVT, Company K
Lipshutz, Woolf, PVT, Company B
Livingston, John E., CORP, Company I
Livingston, Samuel Maurice, PVT, Company L

Lloyd, Jacob E., PVT, Medical Detachment
Lobel, Leon, PVT, Company E
Locicero, Joseph, PVT, Company C
Lockwood, George T., SGT, Medical Detachment
Loercher, Walter William, PVT, Company H
Lofthouse, Merrill Ernest, PVT, Company G
Login, William, PVT, Company K
Lohiser, Howard W., PVT, Company K
Lombardi, Phill, PVT 1CL, Company K
Lomonaco, Pietro, PVT, Company G
Long, Frank W., 1LT, I.R.C., Company F
Long, John Verdell, PVT, Company F
Longeill, Sylvester, PVT, Company L
Longely, William George, PVT, Company D
Longo, Francesco, PVT, Company F
Longyear, Charles P., SGT, Company L
Lopez, Brigido, PVT, Company A
Lord, Nathan, PVT, Company A
Loudon, Joseph Parker, PVT 1CL, Company M
Loughlin, Thomas Gerard, PVT, Company H
Louis, Nicholas Walsh, PVT, Company L
Loux, Adelbert H., 3 CL MSN, Headquarters
   Company
Lovaglia, Frank, PVT, Company F
Love, Nathan Stedmon, PVT, Company L
Lovejoy, Francis, PVT, Company C
Lowe, Frank C., PVT, Company H
Lowery, William James, PVT, Company H
Lubecky, John J., PVT, Company L
Lucia, Louis, PVT, Company D
Luciano, John, PVT, Headquarters Company
Lucklow, Philip, PVT, Company F, C
Lucy, Joseph, PVT, Company G
Ludlow, James Patrick, PVT, Company A
Lueders, Harry, PVT, Company B
Luft, Carl H., PVT, Company H
Luglio, Vincenzo, PVT, Company E
Luisi, Louis, PVT, Company M
Lundberg, Lawrence Carl, PVT, Company L
Lupardi, Joseph, PVT, Company E
Luscher, Oscar, PVT, Supply Company
Lustig, Arthur, PVT, Company M
Luyten, Alfonse Theodore, PVT, Company G
Lyall, Cleo Glen, PVT, Company L
Lybolt, Harold, PVT, Supply Company
Lyke, Charles Alexander, PVT, Company L
Lynch, James A., PVT, Company E
Lynch, John W., 1ST CL PVT, Company L
Lynch, Raymond Victor, PVT, Company K
Lyons, Joseph Francis, PVT, Company C
Lyons, Patrick James, PVT, Headquarters Company

Mabie, Louis P., SERGT, PVT1CL, Company E
MacAuley, Arthur, SERG, Supply Company
Maccarroni, Carmelo, PVT, Company A
MacEachern, John Jr., PVT, Company K
Mack, Frank K., MECH, Company H
Mack, John, SGT, Company B
Mackey, Joseph Hasbrock, PVT, Company E
Mackey, Oscar Rudolph, PVT, Company M
Mackie, Joseph, PVT, Company K
MacLane, Ira E. Jr., CPL, Headquarters Company
Macpherson, Charles Wesley, PVT, PVT1CL, I
Macrigiankis, Mike, PVT, Company I,
   [Macregeankis]
Macy, Frank Joseph, PVT, Company H, C
Macy, Harold Edward, SGT, Company F
Maddalena, Cavio, PVT, Company I
Madden, Michael Joseph, PVT, Company C
Madill, Robert William, PVT, Company K

Magee, Joseph Albert, PVT, Company E
Magin, John J.H., ORDERLY SGT, Headquarters
  Company
Magner, William L., PVT, Company I
Maguire, Fancis J., PVT, Medical Detachment
Maguire, Michael, PVT, Supply Company
Maharay, Thomas Ransdell, PVT, Company C
Mahary, Fred Gillies, PVT, Company G
Maher, Michael Francis, PVT, Supply Company
Maher, William Stephen, PVT, Supply Company
Mahoney, Joseph James, PVT, Company K
Mahoney, Thomas M., SGT, Company G
Maibaum, William, PVT, Company I OC
Mailinger, Gustav, PVT, Headquarters Company
Maines, Charles F., SGT, Company M
Maisenhelder, Harry G., BND CPL, Headquarters
  Company
Makely, George A., PVT, Company B
Malak, Joseph E., MECH, Headquarters Company
Malkiewicz, Wladyslow, PVT, Company A
Mallick, John A., CORP, Company E
Malloney, Daniel C., COOK, Company B [Maloney]
Malloy, John T., PVT, Company E
Malloy, John W., PVT, SGT, Company B
Maloney, Denis W., 1LT, I.R.C., Company H
Maloney, James A., PVT, Company B
Maloney, John Henry, PVT, Company F
Manahan, Hugh Francis, PVT, Company L
Mancari, Joseph, PVT, Company F
Mancuso, Francisco, PVT, Company G
Mancuso, Leonardo, PVT, Supply Company
Mandalto, Paul, PVT, Company I [Madalto]
Mandarino, Enrico, PVT, Company K
Mangan, Raymond W., SGT, Company H
Mangogna, Liborio, PVT, Company G
Manino, Rosario, PVT, Company H
Manley, William Joseph, PVT, PVT1CL, Company I
Manley, William Patrick, PVT, Company L
Mannain, John Neil, SGT, Company K
Manniello, James, PVT, Co. M 51st Pion Inf,
  6 Cas Co, died U.S.
Manning, George John, CPL, Company D
Manning, William J., PVT, Company B
Manno, Giacomo, PVT, Company K
Mansfield, James A., CPL, Company K
Mansfield, John G., 1ST SGT, Company B, U
Mansfield, Richard R., BUG, Company G
Manuel, Rowland P., 1LT, INF R.C., Company M
Manzari, Vito, PVT, Company A
Mapes, Clifton, PVT, Company D
Mapes, Ralph Howard, PVT, Supply Company
Marano, Tony, PVT, Company B
Marco, Louis, PVT, Company F
Marcoux, Alfred, PVT, Headquarters Company
Marcus, Isidore, PVT 1CL, Company M
Maresca, Benjamin, PVT, Company F
Margolin, Louis, PVT, Headquarters Company
Marino, Angelo, PVT, Company E
Marino, Benedetti, PVT, Company D
Mark, Lawrence, MCH, Company C
Markle, Leroy, SGT, Company M
Marks, Harry J., CPL, Company D
Marleau, Thomas Joseph, PVT, Company H
Marmion, Brander, CORP, PVT, Company E
Marmon, Garold G., PVT, Supply Company
Marquer, Alfred, PVT, Headquarters Company
Marquis, Albert Louis, PVT, Company L
Marrone, Antonio, PVT, Company C
Marrone, Frank, PVT, Company K
Marsden, William H., CPL, Company G
Marsh, Eldred Aaron, CORP, PVT, Company E

Marsh, Theodore, PVT, Company H
Marshall, Barton H., 1LT, IRC, Company C
Marshall, Raymond Earl, PVT, Company A
Marsicano, Umberto, PVT, Company L
Marsolais, Raoul Oscar, PVT, Company D
Martell, James Corrigan, PVT, Company M
Martin, Dallas K., PVT, Company B
Martin, Edward Aloysius, MCH, Company C
Martin, Henry W., 1ST SGT, Company I
Martin, Joseph, PVT, Company F
Martin, Lettie A., PVT, Company K
Martin, Nathan, PVT, Company D
Martin, Nicholas James, PVT, Company H
Martindale, Kenneth Charles, SGT, Company A
Martino, Cornelius, PVT, Company C
Marvin, William Augustus, CK, Company C
Marzulli, Antonio, PVT, Supply Company
Mascaro, Luiggi, PVT, Company H
Maselanis, Charles, PVT, Company E
Mashora, Faustin, PVT, Company K
Massey, John J., PVT, Company L
Massey, William John, PVT, Company K
Mastin, Edward C. Rookston, PVT, Company G
Masucci, Americo, CPL, Company H
Matarrese, Vito Nicolo, PVT, Company H
Mateyoke, Paul, PVT, Company G
Matthews, Louis G., PVT, Company E
Matthews, Michael Joseph, PVT, Company H
Matthews, William S., 1LT, I.N.A., Company F
Matthews, William S., CAPT, INF, Regimental
  Headquarters
Mattice, Paul B., 1LT, I.NA, Company B
Mattison, Milton J., PVT, Company K
Matweenko, George, PVT, Company F
Mautone, Pantaleo, PVT, Company D
Maxfield, Chester R., PVT, Company G
Maxwell, John Joseph, PVT, Company M
May, Charles Anton, PVT, Company I
Mayone, Louis, CORP, PVT, Company E
Mayr, Charles John, PVT, Company F
Mayrer, George Andrew, PVT, Company D
Mazzarella, Nicholas Henry, PVT, Company M
Mazzola, Arasmo, PVT, Company B
Mazzone, Frank, PVT, Company H
Mcauley, James W., PVT, Medical Detachment
McAvoy, Frank Joseph Jr., PVT, Headquarters
  Company
McBurnie, William John, PVT, Company L
McCabe, Frank Edward, PVT, Company L
McCaffrey, John Edward, PVT, Company F
McCall, Frank George, PVT, PVT1CL, Company I
McCall, Leroy Stevens, PVT, Supply Company
McCann, Daniel James, CPL, Company C
McCann, James J. Jr., SGT, Company D
McCarroll, John Francis, PVT, Company L
McCarthy, Cornelius Thomas, PVT, Company G
McCarthy, John J., PVT, BUG, Company I
McCarthy, Joseph Patrick, PVT, Company C
McCauley, Charles J, CPL, Company G
McCauley, James, PVT, Company L
McCaw, Albert Clement, CPL, Company C
McClair, Hugh J., CPL, Company H
McClellan, George R., PVT, Company K
McClelland, Duncan Eber, PVT, Company A
McClelland, John Andrew, PVT, Company M
McClure, Willard Morse, CPL, Company C
McColgan, David Branfel, PVT, Company E
McCoppin, Howard, CORP, Company K
McCord, David John, PVT, Company D
McCormack, Hugh, PVT, Company C, died overseas
McCormick, James, PVT, Company E

McCracken, Elmer Milton, SGT, Company L
McCravey, Louis Steele, CPL, Company D
McCreery, John, PVT, Company A
McCullough, Frank, PVT, Company F
McCullough, George J., SGT, Company M
MConald, John James, PVT, Company L
MConald, John R., 2LT, INF, Regimental
    Headquarters
MConald, John, PVT, Company K
MConald, Roy, PVT, Company C
MConald, Walter Daniel, PVT, Company G
MConough, Walter Patrick, CPL, Company D
McElveney, George A., CPL, Company D
McEneaney, Edward Patrick, PVT, Company G, died
    overseas
Mcevany, Thomas Joseph, CPL, Company D
McFarland, Arthur W., 1LT, I.R.C., Company K
McGarl, Edward Francis, PVT, Company G
McGarr, William, PVT, Company G
McGee, William G., PVT, SGT, Company B
McGinley, John Joseph, PVT, Company A
McGinn, Edward, PVT, Company G
McGinn, James Aloysius, PVT, Company H
McGinty, James Francis, PVT, Headquarters
    Company
McGirr, Walter Thomas, PVT, Headquarters Company
McGloin, Eugene, PVT, Company D
McGloin, Thomas Francis, PVT, Company C
McGoldrick, Paul Arthur, PVT, Company F
McGowan, Thomas J., CPL, SGT, Company B
McGrath, Timothy Joseph, PVT, Company G,
    Stockade Camp Merritt
McGraw, Herbert August, PVT, Company D
McGraw, Willard John, CPL, Company K, died
    overseas
McGrury, John C., PVT, Company B
McGuinness, Joseph H., 1LT, I.R.C., Company H
McGuire, Michael, PVT, Company I
McGunnigle, Harold, CPL, Headquarters Company,
    to May 9/18
McHugh, Herbert Bertie, CORP, PVT, Company E
McHugh, James Francis, PVT, Company D
McIntee, William, PVT, Company G
McIntosh, Norman McLeod, PVT, Company K
McIntyre, Charles M., PVT, CPL, Company B
McIntyre, Harold W., PVT, CPL, Company B
McKee, Pierce, PVT, Company G
McKenna, Bernard J., PVT, Company E
McKenna, Corneluis Bernard, PVT, Headquarters
    Company
McKeon, James Edward, PVT, Company H
McKeown, James Aloysious, SGT, Company K
McKernan, William J., PVT, Company E,
    Headquarters Company 51 Pion Inf to July 29/18;
    Company E 51 Pion Inf to disch
McKiernan, Michael, PVT, Company G, C
McKillen, Daniel Joseph, CPL, Company D
McKillen, Neil Patrick, PVT, Company D
McKillop, Hugh R., PVT, Company E
McKinstry, Harold John, CPL, Company C
McKlevis, Vincent, PVT, Company K
McKnight, George, PVT, Headquarters Company
McLafferty, Joseph, PVT, Company M
McLaughlin, John W., PVT, Company E
McLaughlin, William Francis, PVT, Company C
McLean, William, CORP, Company I
McLeod, Norman W., 1ST SGT, Supply Company
McLoughlin, John Patrick, PVT, Company F
McMacken, Robert, PVT, Supply Company
McMahon, Joseph F., PVT, PVT1CL, Company B
    [McMahan]

McMahon, Leroy Andrew, PVT, Company H
McManus, Hugh Patrick, PVT, Company H
McManus, Michael Frances, PVT, Company H, C
McMaster, Carroll T., SGT, Company L
McMillin, James, PVT, Company L
McNally, Francis J., SERGT, CORP, Company E
McNamara, Richard B., PVT, Company B
McNamara, Thomas Joseph, PVT, Company C
McNamee, Richard J., PVT, Company E
McNece, Wellington Kinsley, PVT, Company L
McNelly, Oscar, PVT, Company H
McNicholas, Thomas, PVT, Company A
McNiff, John, CORP, Company E
McNulty, James Joseph, CPL, Company C
McQuillan, Peter Joseph, SGT, Company C
McSharry, Patrick, PVT, Company K
McTamney, Frank Leo, PVT, Company K
McTernan, Miles, PVT, Company E
McVeigh, Allie, PVT, Company A
McWhite, Edwin, COOK, Headquarters Company
Mead, Addision Peter, BUG, Company L
Meadows, Bernard Ford, PVT, Company L
Meaney, Thomas F., 1LT, I. RC, Company B
Means, Victor A., 2LT, I. N. A., Company K
Mehal, John D., PVT, PVT1CL, Company I
Mehrmann, George, PVT, Company I, (Mebrivan)
Mei, Guiseppe, PVT, Company D
Meier, Francis Xavier Jr., CORP, PVT, E
Meisel, Herman, PVT, Company G
Mekul, Max, PVT, Headquarters Company
Melick, Albert, PVT, Company E
Melville, Christopher Patrick, PVT, Company K
Melvin, Valentine A., PVT, Company G
Melvin, Walter Thomas, PVT, Company L
Mercier, Charles E. Jr., WAG, Supply Company
Merck, Edward, PVT, Company D
Merel, Robert F., PVT, Company B
Merking, Christian Philip, PVT 1CL, Company M
Merrick, Leo Jerome, WAG, Supply Company
Merrigan, John T., SUP SGT, Supply Company
Merritt, Frederick M., MESS SGT, Company H
Merritt, George Everett, PVT, Company C
Merritt, Percy Oscar, CORP, Company A
Merz, Carl, PVT, CPL, Company B
Messina, Antonio, PVT, Company I, died overseas
Messinger, Alfred G., CPL, Company M
Messino, Petro, PVT, Company H
Methven, Harry, MECH, Company I
Metress, John Joseph, PVT, Company A
Meyer, Arthur Frank, PVT, Company L
Meyer, Henry Harry, PVT, Supply Company
Meyer, Peter Lepold, PVT, Company G
Meyer, William, PVT, Company L
Meyers, Charles H., PVT, Company K
Miceli, Joe, PVT, Company I
Michael, William Henry, SGT, Company K
Michalski, John, PVT, Company K
Michels, Oakey, PVT, Company H
Michelsen, William, PVT, PVT1CL, Company I
Michnal, Herman Joe, PVT, Company L
Mignoli, Dominick, PVT, Company L
Mikul, Julius, PVT, Headquarters Company
Milano, Harry, CORP, Company H
Milbauer, Murry Ruby, PVT, Supply Company
Milburn, Harry G., PVT, Medical Detachment
Miletello, Giovanni, PVT, Company F
Miley, Michael Emmett, PVT, Company M
Milgate, Harold William, MECH, Company L
Millar, Willim, PVT, Company K
Miller, Charles Fred, PVT, Company A
Miller, Clyde R., PVT, Company A

Miller, Edward, CPL, Company H
Miller, Edward, PVT, Company L
Miller, Frank O., PVT, Medical Detachment
Miller, Frank S., 1LT, I.N.A., Company I
Miller, Frederick Albert, PVT, Company E
Miller, Frederick George, SGT, Company A
Miller, George Thomas, PVT, Company E
Miller, Guy Emmon, PVT, Company L
Miller, John Anthony, PVT, Company A
Miller, John E., BND CPL, Headquarters Company
Miller, John Henry Jr., PVT, Company E
Miller, Michael, PVT, Medical Detachment
Miller, William Francis, PVT, PVT1CL, Company I
Miller, William H., PVT, Medical Detachment,
Miller, William Puckey, PVT, Supply Company
Mills, Charles William, PVT, Company A
Mills, Winfield G., PVT, Company B
Minch, William Philip, PVT, Company H
Miner, Everard, PVT, Company L
Mineriro, Eugenio, PVT, Headquarters Company
Minibayzo, Nicholas, PVT, Company F
Minkler, Ray, PVT, Company E
Minkoff, Harry, PVT, Company B
Minore, Vincenzo, PVT, Company D
Mirchin, Frank, PVT, Headquarters Company
Mirra, Americo, PVT, Company C
Mocciaro, Cataldo, PVT, Company D, OC
Moeller, Frederick, PVT, Company A
Moffett, Lancelot, PVT, Company C
Moggio, Silvio, PVT, Company D
Mohan, Peter Joseph, PVT, Company A
Mohme, Frank, PVT, Headquarters Company
Molinari, John J., CORP, Company I
Moll, George, PVT, Company L
Mollott, Jacob, BND CPL, Headquarters Company
Monaghan, Edward Michael, PVT, Headquarters
  Company
Monahan, James Joseph, PVT, Company A
Mones, Jacob, PVT, Company M
Mongan, Edwin Paul, PVT, Company A
Mongan, James Gerald, PVT 1CL, Company M
Mongin, Andrew Francis, PVT, Company A
Monro, Charles, PVT, Company I, Mouro, Charles
Monroe, Douglas L., PVT, Medical Detachment,
Monzi, Vincenzo, PVT, Company E
Moonan, Francis J., MECH, Company I
Mooney, Edward Nelson, PVT, Company C
Mooney, John Edward, PVT, PVT1CL, Company I
Mooney, Martin Michael, PVT, Company F
Moore, Benjamin T., 2LT, I.R.C., Company H
Moore, Edward Joseph, PVT, PVT1CL, Company I
Moore, Edward W., MECH, Company H
Moore, Robert, PVT, Company L, died overseas
Moore, Thomas C., 1ST SGT, Company D
Moore, William B., SGT, Company I
Mooshy, Milton Eremia, PVT, Company A
Mooshy, Milton Frenia, PVT, Company G, C
Moran, Matthew P., PVT, Company B
Moran, William Aloysius, PVT, Company M
Moree, Bennie, PVT, Company M
Morgan, Jay Lester, PVT, Company H
Morgan, Richard, PVT, Company E
Morgenroth, Nathan, PVT, Company C
Morgin, Joseph A, CPL, SGT, Company B
Moriarty, John H., 1LT, IRC, Company L
Morini, Magno, PVT, Company C
Morris, Robert E., PVT, Medical Detachment,
Morris, Thomas, PVT, Company L
Morris, Walter, CORP, Company I
Morrisey, Edward Leo, CK, Company C
Morrison, Wallace G., 2LT, ING, Headquarters

Company
Morse, Homer Martel, PVT, Company G
Morse, Paul J., SGT, Company B
Mosbroker, John, PVT, Company L
Moses. Joe, PVT, Company F
Moshbaugh, Andrew A., PVT, Company K
Mosinka, Charles, PVT, Company K
Moss, Bartow Patrick, PVT, Company A
Moustakos, Peter, PVT, Company E
Moyer, Clayton Myrl, PVT, Company L
Mrugalski, Joseph Francis, PVT, Company E
Mueller, Charles Frederick William, PVT,
  Company G
Mulcahey, Robert F., PVT, Company G
Mulhall, Edward Francis, PVT, Company G
Mulhern, Edward Thomas, PVT, Company C
Mullaney, Harold A., PVT, CPL, Company B
Mullaney, James Francis, COOK, Company L
Muller, Carl Leon, PVT, Headquarters Company
Muller, John Frederick, PVT, Company A
Muller, Konrad, CORP, Company F
Mullins, Edward, CPL, Company M
Mulloy, Ralph Aloysius, PVT, Company K
Mulready, Thomas M., SGT, Company I
Munch, Edward Francis, PVT, Company M
Munda, Edward, CORP, Company I
Muni, Antonio, PVT, Company K
Munschauer, Irville William, PVT, Company K
Murphey, Lester Allen, PVT, Company D
Murphy, Bernard, PVT, Company D
Murphy, Clyde M., PVT, Company L
Murphy, Frances Stephen, PVT, Supply Company
Murphy, George Washington, PVT, Company A
Murphy, James Arthur, PVT, Headquarters Company
Murphy, John Francis, PVT, Company D
Murphy, John Joseph, PVT, Company D
Murphy, Joseph John, PVT, Company L
Murphy, Joseph P., MESS SGT, Company D
Murphy, Joseph Thomas, PVT, PVT1CL, Company I
Murphy, Levi Wickham, PVT, Company A
Murphy, Michael Anthony, PVT, Company C
Murphy, Michael Francis, PVT, Company I
Murphy, Timothy Dennis, PVT, Company G
Murphy, William H., PVT, Company K
Murray, Harry Lawrence, PVT, Supply Company
Murray, James Emmett, PVT, Company H
Murray, John Joseph, PVT, Company D
Murray, John Patrick, CPL, Company M
Murray, Michael, PVT, Supply Company
Murry, John T., PVT, Company B [Murray]
Musella, Frank, PVT, Company B
Musier, William H., PVT, Company B [Musior]
Muszynski, Joseph, PVT, Company F
Muzzy, Franklin G., 1LT, I.R.C., Company E
Mynk, Herbert, PVT, Company M

Nadel, Harry Aaron, PVT, Company A
Nanna, John, PVT, Company C
Napoli, Angelo, PVT, Company E, OK
Narrone, Antonio, PVT, Company C
Narun, Max Israel, PVT, Headquarters Company
Nash, Joseph Francis, PVT, Company L
Natale, Salvatore, PVT, Company H
Naughten, Malachy, PVT, Company H
Neale, Joseph Buckley, CORP, Company A
Neilans, Thomas, PVT, Company K
Nellis, Henry Jay, PVT, Company A
Nellis, J. Howard, CORP, Company A
Nelson, Guy V., PVT, Company K
Nelson, Hardin C., 1LT, I.R.C., Supply Company

Nelson, Nils H., PVT, Company A
Nelson, Samuel, PVT, Company F
Nemeroff, Harry L., PVT, Company B, died
   overseas
Nenzian, John, BUGL, Company E
Nerenberg, Jack, PVT, Company F
Neri, Rosario, PVT, Company L
Nettekoven, Herman, CPL, Company D
Nettekoven, John, PVT, Company D
Netter. Martin F., 2LT, I.N.G., Supply Company
Neu, Arthur Charlie, PVT, Company M
Neuberger, Henry Rosevelt, PVT, Company D, died
   overseas
Newbanks. John H., PVT, Company K
Newman, Gilbert T., 2LT, I. RC, Company B
Newman, Isidor, PVT, Company L
Newman, Jacob, PVT, PVT1CL, Company I
Newman, Joseph Nowicki, PVT, Company H
Newt, Ray McKinley, PVT, Company L
Nicholas, Nick K., PVT, Company G
Nickel, August Wilhelm, PVT, Company L
Nicoletti, Charles P., PVT, Headquarters Company
Nicoletti, Francesco, PVT, Company B
Nidds, Edward, PVT, Company I
Nikitin, Waiselle, PVT, Company I
Niles, Edgar C., CAPT, I.N.G., Company D
Nimtz, Emil Carl, PVT, Company E
Nitcy, Kenneth C., PVT, Company M
Noble, William D., PVT, Company B
Noell, James B., 1LT, I.R.C., Company D
Nolan, Frank, PVT, Headquarters Company
Nolan, William B., PVT, Company B
Nolde, Arnold, CPL, Company C
Noller, William Theodore, PVT, Company A
Noonan, James, PVT, Company I
Norfleet, Edgar P., 1LT, D.M.D. MRC.51PI, Medical
Detachment
Normandeau, Louis Alfred, PVT, Company L
Norswell, John, SGT, Company B
Norton, Peter W., CPL, Company M
Norton, Robert A., CORP, PVT, Company E
Novak, John Edward, PVT, Company F
Nover, Aaron, CORP, Company F
Novotny, Charles James, PVT, Company L
Nuccio, Tony, PVT, Company I
Nugent, Patrick, PVT, Company A
Nurse, Arden Roy, PVT, Company C
Nusbaum, Abraham, PVT, Company F, C
Nutini, Mario Alfred, PVT, Company H
Nyderek, John, PVT, Company G

Oaksford, Bernhard Ralph, PVT, Company A
Oathout, William H., PVT, Company B
Obermeyer, Jacob, PVT, Company A
O'Brien, Edward Francis, PVT, Company E
O'Brien, James A., CORP, Company H
O'Brien, James Francis, SGT, Company C
O'Brien, John Joseph, MECH, Company A
O'Brien, Peter, PVT, Company H
O'Bryan, Sherwood F., BUGL, Company B
Ochs, Conrad Jr., PVT, Supply Company
O'Clair, Lawrence, PVT, PVT1CL, Company I
O'Connell, August Aloysius, PVT, Company M
O'Connell, John James, PVT, Headquarters Company
O'Connell, John Joseph, PVT, Company K
O'Connell, William S., PVT, Company E
O'Conner, Dennis, PVT, Company L
O'Connor, Dennis Patrick, PVT, Company G
O'Connor, James Edward, PVT, Company F
Oddo, Edward, PVT, Company K

O'Dell, Albert George, PVT, Company M
O'Dell, Edward Clifton, PVT, Supply Company
Odgen, Ernest Benjamin, PVT, Company A
O'Donnell, Albert Alious, PVT, Company A
O'Donnell, Alexander, PVT, Company F
O'Donnell, Edward Joseph, PVT, Headquarters
   Company
O'Donnell, John Francis, PVT, Headquarters
   Company
O'Dwyer, Marion B., PVT, Company I
Offhouse, Douglas John, SGT, Company K
O'Hare Joseph Anthony, PVT, Company F
O'Keefe, David F., COOK, Company L
O'Keefe, Patrick, PVT, Company L
Oldfield, Walter Dignam, PVT, Company E
Olivieri, Areamo, PVT, Company A
Olkowski, Joseph, PVT, Company K
Olsen, Alfred, PVT, Company C
Olson, Edward Emanuel, PVT, Company M
O'Malley, Leo James, PVT, Company K
O'Meara, Walter Joseph, SGT, BN SGT MJR, 2LT,
Company B, Headquarters Company
O'Neil, Francis John, PVT, Company D
O'Neil, John Daniel Jr., PVT, Company L
O'Neill, John Andrew, PVT, Company L
O'Neill, Patrick Joseph, PVT, Company D
O'Neill, Walter John, PVT, Company I
Oppenheim, Ralph, PVT, Company F
O'Reilly, Robert Mawhinny, CPL, Company K
Orenstein, Abraham, PVT, Company G
Ornstein, Robert, CPL, Headquarters Company
O'Rourke, James Benard, PVT, Company C
Orphan, Geo. Nicholas, PVT, Company G
Ortell, Frank John, CORP, Company A
Osborn, Louis, PVT, Company H
Osborne, Albert William, PVT, Headquarters
   Company, died overseas
O'Shea, John Joseph, PVT, Company K
Ostrander, Frank Lewis, PVT, Company A
Ostrander, Frank, CPL, Company M
Ostrom, Albert J., PVT, Company M
Ostrom, Alvin, PVT, Company A
Ostrowski, Leonard, PVT, Headquarters Company
Ott, Charles F, CPL, Company D
Ott, Harry Agust, PVT, Company A
Otto, William A., MECH, Company L
Overhultz, Charlie Hamilton, PVT, Company M
Owens, Shelvia, PVT, Company M
Oyrowski, Adam, PVT, Company L

Pabody, John H., ORD SGT EOC, Supply Company
Pachlew, Samuel, PVT, Company B
Padluk, Mike, PVT, Company H
Page, Ivan Hamilton, PVT, PVT1CL, Company I
Page, William Charles, PVT, Headquarters Company
Painter, George Buckter, PVT, Headquarters
   Company
Paldin, George Walton, CORP, Company L
Palkovic, Stephen Thomas Jr., PVT, Company A
Palmateer, Elmer, PVT, Company A
Palmer, Frank P., COOK, Company G, died overseas
Palmieri, Asparo, PVT, Company G, C
Pangburn, Howard S., 3 CL MSN, Headquarters
   Company
Pansky, Frank W. Jr., PVT, Company E
Pantley, Edwin, PVT, Company D
Pantony, Vincent, PVT, Company B
Papacostas, John, PVT, Company K
Papadopoulos, Christos, PVT, Company L
Paratore, Peter, COOK, Company H

Parcelli, Joseph, PVT, Company G
Parfitt, William Samuel, CPL, Company K
Parini, Joseph Nino, PVT, Company E
Parke, Francis W., SGT, Company F
Parker, James, PVT, Company I
Parker, William J., COOK, Company I
Parks, William E., CORP, Company L
Parrott, Henry C., PVT, Company K
Parry, John R., PVT, Company L
Parson, Edgar Burnside, CORP, Company I
Parsons, Guy Charles, CORP, PVT, Company E
Parsons, Samuel Gordon, PVT, Supply Company
Pasciucca, Nicola, PVT, Company E
Patmore, Arthur Coventry, PVT, Supply Company
Patnode, Henry, PVT, Company G
Patsy, Thomas, PVT, Company K
Paul, Adam M., COOK, Company H
Paulsen, Edgar Peter, PVT, Headquarters Company
Pauly, Charles, SUPPLY SERGT, Company E
Pavlakon, Stephen, PVT, Company H
Pawelec, Walter, PVT, Company K
Pawling, Jesse R., 1LT, D.M.D. M.C.51.PI., Medical Detachment
Paxton, Thomas, PVT, Company I
Pazar, Stavros John, PVT, Company G
Pearlman, Herman, PVT, Company B
Pearlstein, William, PVT, PVT1CL, Company I
Pearson, Charles Edward, PVT, Company L
Pearson, Nils Eric, PVT, Company M
Peck, Lloyd L., PVT, Company B
Peddie, Edgar Cecil, CPL, Company H
Pegg, Charles R., PVT, Company L
Peiffer, Henry Peter, PVT, Company F
Peillegrin, David Benjamin, PVT, Company F [Pellegrini]
Pellino, Michele, PVT, Company A
Pelsang, Elmer Ellsworth, PVT, Company L
Pemberg, Max, PVT, Company B
Penney, William Henry Jr., PVT, Company M
Pensabene, Francesco, PVT, Company F
Peppard, Nathaniel G., PVT, Company B
Perdelwita, Edgar William, PVT, Company L
Perkins, Arthur Selah, PVT, Company F
Perry, Christopher J., COOK, Company M
Perry, Edward J., SGT, Company M
Perry, Joseph, PVT, Company C
Perry, Raymond J., PVT, Company I
Perry, Soul, PVT, Company H
Peters, Frederick, CORP, Company I
Peters, Henry Christopher, PVT, Company I
Peterson, George F., PVT, Company B
Petrino, Carmine, PVT, Company D
Petschke, Arthur Jr., BUGL, PVT, Company E
Petti, Matthew, Company E
Petti, Matthew, PVT, Company E
Pettit, Barnie Sims, PVT, Company C
Petty, Addison H., PVT, Company E
Peyser, Morell, CPL, Company D
Pfleiger, William F, PVT, CRP, Company B
Philip, William M., CPL, Company G
Phillips, Albert C., CPL, Company G
Phillips, Isidor, CPL, Company M
Phillips, Jerome Semon, PVT, Company M
Phillips, Joseph F., PVT, Company B
Phillips, Percival Abram, COOK, Company K
Phillips, William, PVT, Company B
Philpot, Eugene A., 2LT, I.R.C., Company A
Piazza, Salvatore, PVT, Company I
Pierce, Crawford, PVT, Company A
Piernik, Leo, PVT, Company F
Piersante, Pasquale, PVT, Headquarters Company

Pike, John Angel, PVT, Company K
Pindar, Egbert Washington, PVT, Company C
Pine, Burt Frank, PVT, Company I
Pinto, Rezaro, PVT, Company F
Pirozzi, Raffaele, PVT, Company D
Pisano, Frank, PVT, Company G, C
Piskac, Anthony, PVT, Headquarters Company
Piskorski, Zygmunt, PVT, Company K
Pitz, Joseph, PVT, Company D
Pizza, Nicholas, PVT, Company G
Pizzuto, John Baptist, PVT, PVT 1CL, Headquarters Company
Place, Harry L., BND SGT, Headquarters Company
Pladal, John J., CPL, SGT, Company B
Poach, Peter Joseph, PVT, Company G, died overseas
Pold, Leo, PVT, Company E
Polidoro, Vittorio, PVT, Company H
Polinske, Charles Ernet Emil, PVT, Headquarters Company, PVT1CL May 24/19
Pollio, Louis, PVT, Company M
Polowy, John, PVT, Company K
Poltorak, Wladyslaw Anthony, PVT, Company K
Polzella, Antonio, PVT, Company G
Porgaro, Frank Joseph, PVT, Company F
Portiera, Sante, PVT, Company H
Portley, Daniel, PVT, Company E
Portz, Ed Charles, PVT, Company D
Portz, John Jacon, PVT, Company D
Potter, Rayburn S., 1LT, I.R.C., Company D
Poulon, John D., PVT, Company B
Poulsen, Ove Helmuth, PVT, Company L
Pousant, Philip J., SERGT, CORP, E
Povenmire, Harlo M., CAPT, NG, Company L
Powell, Wesley S., SUP SGT, Supply Company
Powers, John Joseph, PVT, Company C
Powles, Harry, PVT, Company C
Pozner, Joseph, PVT, Company B, Headquarters Company
Prashker, Joseph, PVT, Company E
Prater, Robert, PVT, Company F
Prats, Desiderio Vincent, PVT, Headquarters Company
Pratt, Arthur C., PVT, Company K
Pratt, Leonard E., SERGT, Company E
Pratt, Percy Samuel, PVT, Company F
Preston, Eugene E., Capt, NG, Regimental Headquarters
Price, Frederick C., PVT, Company D
Price, John Worden, PVT, Company A
Price, Peter, PVT, Company H
Principe, Frank, PVT, Company G
Prisco, Giuseppe, PVT, Company I
Pritchard, Charles Summer, PVT, Company M
Probst, Charles Paul, PVT, Company I
Proctor, Joseph Henry Jr., CORP, Company F
Proechel, Harry, PVT, Company G
Proper, Howard, PVT, Company L
Protono, Antonio, PVT, Company C
Pryne, Raymond C., PVT, Company E
Pucillo, Ralph, PVT, Supply Company
Puntoriero, Domenck, PVT, Company F
Purcherelli, Frank, PVT, Company F
Purdy, Sylvanus, MAJ, D.M.D. M.C.51.PI., Medical Detachment
Pursell, Harry Edgar, PVT, PVT1CL, Company I

Quackenbush, Roy Leo, PVT, Company D
Quick, Ernest, PVT, Company B
Quick, George Girard, PVT, Company E

Quick, Rockwell, PVT, Company G
Quick, Werter Ward, PVT, Medical Detachment
Quinn, George W., PVT, Company B
Quinn, Leonard William, PVT, Company L, died
  overseas
Quinn, Patrick Joseph, PVT, Company K
Quinn, Philip F., CORP, Company I

Rabiego, Leo Martin, PVT, Company I
Rachlew, Sam'l, PVT, Company B
Racine, Fred. N., PVT, Company B
Rader, Carl Henry, PVT, Company L
Raffaldi, Ettore Torineo, PVT, Company F
Rahtjen, Edwin, PVT, Company L
Raikes, Louis, PVT, Company I
Rakowski, Casimier, PVT, Company K
Rakowski, Martin Henry, PVT, Company K
Raldires, Manuel, PVT, Headquarters Company
Rampe, Albert Eugene, MCH, Company D
Randolph, Bruno Warren, PVT, Company L
Rank, Willard, COOK, Company H
Rankin, Ollie W, PVT, Company L
Rant, Francis Walter, PVT, Headquarters Company
Ranucci, Antonio, PVT, Supply Company, died U.S.
Raper, William C., PVT, Company H
Raponi, Guiseppe, PVT, Company C
Rasback, Myron E., PVT, Company H
Rascoe, James Barnes, PVT, Company F
Rash, Bennett Flournoy, PVT, Company L
Rasulo, Andrew, PVT, Company B
Rathgeb, William I., SGT, Company G
Rau, George Anthony, PVT, Company L
Rauch, Otto, BUG, Company B
Rauer, Joseph Anton, PVT, Company A
Ray, Allen Leon, PVT, Company K
Raymond, William, PVT, Company M
Reap, Charles A., 2LT, IRC, Company L
Reddington, Frank Edward, PVT, Company A
Redfern, Gilbert, CORP, Company L
Redmond, James Bernard, PVT, Company I
Redner, William, PVT, Company E
Redon, Joseph Sidney, PVT, Company A
Reed, Harvey Raymond, CPL, Company K
Reed, Henry Joseph, PVT, Company A
Reed, Paul Vernon, PVT, Company F
Regan, John Joseph, PVT, Company I
Regan [Reagan], Pierre J., SGT, Company B
Regas, Antonio John, PVT, Company C
Rehfeldt, George Earl, PVT, Company L
Rehling, William George, PVT, PVT1CL, Company I
Rehn, Fred N, PVT, Company E
Reichenbach, Joseph Charles, PVT 1CL, Company M
Reid, George Patrick, PVT, Company L
Reid, John Furney, PVT, Company D
Reid, Raymond Bennett, PVT, Company C
Reilley, James, PVT, Company G
Reilly, Alphonsus, PVT, Company D
Reilly, Frank, PVT, Company I
Reilly, Patrick, PVT, Company G
Reimer, Frank C. G., SGT, Headquarters Company
Reinbold, Charles Joseph, PVT, Company L
Reinhart, Harold Edward, PVT, Company C
Reis, John W., SGT, Company M
Relyea, Edmund D., 2LT, INF, Regimental
  Headquarters
Relyea, Edmund D., SGT, Company M
Relyea, Ward, CPL, Company M
Rembe, Watson Dewey, PVT, Company H
Remson, Maurice, PVT, Company M, C
Reohr, Joseph Harry, MCH, Company D

Reschke, Edward, PVT, Company B
Retter, Martin J., 3 CL MSN, Headquarters
  Company
Reuss, Leonard George, PVT, Company H
Reydel, Louis, PVT, Supply Company
Reynolds, Charles Raymond, BGL, Company C
Reynolds, William E, PVT, Company E
Rhinehart, Walter Joseph, PVT, Company E, died
  overseas
Ribak, Samuel D., PVT, Company B
Ribsamen, Charles, PVT, Company E, died overseas
Rice, Charles Michael, PVT, Company L
Rice, Homer Nelson, PVT, Supply Company
Rice, Robert L., MESS SGT, Company M
Rich, Grover Cleveland, PVT, Company C
Richardson, Earle Raymond, PVT, Headquarters
  Company
Richardson, George M., 2LT, I.R.C., Company F
Richman, Samuel, PVT, Company C
Rickes, Valentine Gilbert, BUG, Company K
Ridgway, Kirkham William, PVT, Company A
Riding, Walter Arnold, CPL, Headquarters Company
Ridner, John R., PVT, Company I
Riess, Frank J., PVT, Company B
Rigg, Ollie C., PVT, Company H
Riggs, George B., PVT, Company D
Rightmire, Burt Williaam, PVT, Company K
Rilee, Robert L., PVT, Company K
Riley, John Edward, PVT, Company C
Riley, Thomas Harold, PVT, Company M
Riley, William G., CPL. SGT, Company B [Riely]
Rinaldi, Arthur, PVT, Company D
Rincione, Castrenze, PVT, Company M
Ringwood, Pierce Ignatious, SGT, Company K
Rivera, Manuel Hipolito, CORP, Company L
Rizzatti, Timothy, CPL, Company H
Rizzo, Baldassare, PVT, Company M
Robb, James Joseph, PVT, Company I
Robbins, William Edwards, PVT, Company A
Roberson, Frank Ramont, PVT, Company G
Roberts, James H., PVT, Company E
Roberts, Jess G, CPL, Company G
Roberts, Thomas Hugh Jr., CPL, Company C
Robinson, George Keeler, PVT, Company L, died
  overseas
Robinson, George Womrath, 1ST SGT, Company A
Robinson, George, SGT, Company D
Robinson, Percy B., PVT, Company B
Robinson, William Henry, PVT, Company K
Robinson, Winthrop, CPL, Headquarters Company
Rochford, Joseph Daniel, PVT, Company D
Rochlitz, Leo Benjamin, OVT, Company C
Rock, Samuel, PVT, Company A
Rocker, John, PVT, Company I
Rodd, Frederick John, PVT, Company K
Rode, George Lewis, PVT, Company G
Rodiguez, Emanuel Antonio, PVT, PVT1CL,Company I
Roe, Percy H., COOK, Company E
Roemer, William John, PVT, Company D
Rogers, James F., CORP, Company I
Rogers, John J., SGT, Company I
Rogers, John Jerome, CORP, Company L
Rogers, Max, BND SGT, Headquarters Company
Rogers, Nat, PVT, Company K
Rolandelli, Gaspers Albert, PVT, Company H
Roller, Nathan Jr., PVT, Company L
Rollet, Albert Jean, COOK, Company H
Rolli, Cesare, PVT, Company C
Romer, George Henry, PVT, Company A
Romiti, Vincenzo, PVT, Company C
Ronan, Leo Joseph, PVT, PVT1CL, Company I

Ronanowskie, Simon, PVT, Company H
Rooney, Edward Francis, PVT, Company A
Rooney, James, PVT, Company E
Roosa, Carlton Egbert, SUP SGT, Company F
Rosch, Francis Clifford, SGT, Company L
Rose, George Vencent, PVT, Company C
Rose, Joshua Raymond, SGT, Company K
Rosen, Isadore, PVT, Company K
Rosen, Samuel, PVT, Company B
Rosenau, Henry, PVT, Company E
Rosenberg, Edward Hull, PVT, Company G
Rosenberg, Julius, PVT, Company B
Rosenberg, Michael, PVT, Company I
Rosenfeld, Henry, PVT 1CL, Company M
Rosenoff, Harry, PVT, Headquarters Company
Rosenthal, George Gustav, PVT, Company M
Rosenthal, Hyman, PVT, Company I
Rosenthal, Maurice, PVT, Company B
Rosenzweig, Harry, BUG, Company M
Ross, John, PVT, Supply Company
Ross, Lloyd E., PVT, Medical Detachment
Rossiter, Edward A., PVT, Company B
Rosso, Tony, PVT, Medical Detachment
Rosst, Willaim E., CORP, Company I
Roth, Emil, PVT, Company F
Roth, John Leo, PVT, Company E
Rothenberg, William, PVT, Company M
Rothstein, Benjamin, PVT, Company M, C
Rouss, Edward Adrian, PVT, Company C
Rowe, Edward E., WAG, Supply Company
Rowe, George Adelbert, BUG, Company L
Roy, Louis Pierre, 1ST SGT, Company C
Royce, Julius H., PVT, Company B
Roylance, Herbert, PVT, Company D, Headquarters
  Company
Rozmyslowicz, Czeslaw, PVT, Company F
Rubin, Nathan, PVT, Headquarters Company
Rubino, Frank, PVT, Medical Detachment
Rucci, Guiseppi, PVT, Company C
Ruch, George Chester, SGT, Company C
Rudd, Everett C., SGT, Company H
Rudnick, Jack, PVT, Company K
Rudnick, Leo Frank, CPL, Company K
Ruehl, William Peter, PVT, Company L
Rulfs, Herman, PVT, Company E
Rumsey, Leonard George, PVT, Company D
Runge, Paul, SGT, Company C
Rupert, Elmer Hollenbeck, PVT, Company A
Rusack, Albrecht F., PVT, Company B
Rusch, Albert H., PVT, Medical Detachment
Rushe, James Joseph, PVT, Company L
Rusinak, Wladistaw, PVT, Company K
Ruso, Charles E., COOK, Company D, OC
Ruso, George Wesley, SGT, Company A
Russell, Earl Theodore, PVT, Headquarters
  Company
Russell, Hunt, 1LT, Company B
Russell, Ralph Luce, PVT, Company L
Russell, Thomas Joseph, PVT, PVT1CL, Company I
Russo, Antonio, PVT, Company E
Russo, John, PVT, Company F
Russo, John, PVT, Headquarters Company
Russo, Joseph, PVT, Company C
Russo, Joseph, PVT, Company K
Russo, Leo G., PVT, Headquarters Company
Russo, Vito, PVT, Company F
Russos, Alexander George, PVT, Supply Company
Ruzzelle, Nicola, PVT, Company G
Ryan, Archie Ernest, PVT, Company K
Ryan, James Edwin, PVT, Company G
Ryan, James, PVT, Company L

Ryan, Mark Anthony, CPL, Company M
Ryan, Norman H., WAG, Supply Company
Ryan, Timothy Francis, PVT, Company D
Ryan, William John, CORP, Company A
Ryan, William John, PVT, Company D, died
  overseas
Rybaltowski, Vincent, PVT, Company E
Ryder, Clarence Knight, PVT, Supply Company
Rzeszot, Marcel, PVT, Company K

Sabatino, Michael, PVT, Company A, OC
Sabetto, Angelo, PVT, Company D
Sadigur, Harry, PVT, Company L
Safranek, William Jr., PVT, PVT1CL, Company I
Salamone, Gerlando, PVT, Company H
Saltsman, Everett Jeremiah, PVT, Company H
Salzberg, Jacob, PVT, Company G
Sametzki, Alfred Joseph, CPL, Company D, OC
Sammon, Thomas Joseph, PVT, Company E
Samuelson, Herbert Wm., PVT, Company G
Samules, Lester Jacobs, PVT, Company G
Sandahl, Abel. P. M., 1LT, D.M.D. MRC.51PI,
  Medical Detachment
Sanders, Douglas C., 2LT, INF, Regimental
  Headquarters
Sandwick, George B., PVT, Company B
Sanford, Harold A., SGT, Company M
Sansone, Frank, PVT, Company M
Sansoni, Frank, PVT, Company H
Santacroce, Guiseppe, PVT, Company B
Santarpia, Aniello, PVT, Company D
Santieri, Alphonzo, PVT, Company C
Santimassimo, Adolph Puolo, PVT 1CL, Company K
Santo, Michael, PVT, Company D, OC
Sapio, Felice Antonio, PVT, PVT1CL, Company I
Sapp, William, CPL, Company M
Sargent, Nick, PVT 1CL, Company I
Sargol, August, PVT, Company D
Sarrafian, Osdanig John, PVT, Company L
Sass, Frank, CPL, Company M
Sassano, Gerre, PVT, Company K
Sasso, Irving Jacob, PVT, Company M
Sauer, Edward George, PVT, Company H
Sauer, George William, PVT, Company D
Saulpaugh, Albert, LT Colonel, NG, Regimental
  Headquarters
Saulpaugh, Milton Vincent, SGT, Company F
Sault, Edward, PVT, Company B
Savino, Paulo, PVT, Company A
Sbarro, Dominick, PVT, Company C
Scalero, Anthony, PVT, Company F
Scannalla, Sam, PVT, PVT1CL, Company I
Scanpone, Anthony, PVT, Company L
Scarongella, Pasquale, PVT, Company H
Scavonie, Joseph J., 1 CL MSN, Headquarters
  Company
Scelsi, William Angelo, PVT, Company M
Schaefer, Albert, PVT, Headquarters Company
Schafer, Herman, PVT 1CL, Company I
Schauman, Hubert Francis, PVT, Company E
Schaumann, Carl, MCH, Company D
Scheffel, Jacob, PVT, Company E
Schenfield, Raymond Louis, PVT, Company A
Schermer, David, PVT, Company M
Schermerhorn, Ray Allen, PVT, Company D
Schickler, Frederick Charles, PVT, Company L
Schimilevitz, Robert, PVT, Company M
Schinzel, George P, PVT, Company E
Schipp, Francis A., SGT, Company M
Schittone, Vincenzo, PVT, Company M

Schloimovitz, Solomon, PVT, Company F
Schmid, Joseph George, PVT, Company L
Schmidlapp, Carl Jacob, CORP, Company A
Schmidt, Henry George, PVT, Company K
Schmidt, Henry John, PVT 1CL, Company M
Schmidt, Herman, COOK, Company F
Schmidt, Otto Christopher, PVT, Company E
Schmidt, Walter L., PVT, Company K
Schmidt. William, PVT, Company M
Schmidtlein, Adam F., PVT, Company B
Schmidtt, Otto J., PVT, Company B
Schmitt, Joseph Carl, PVT 1CL, Company M
Schnackenberg, Franklyn John, PVT 1ST CL, Supply
    Company
Schneider, Gustav, PVT, Headquarters Company
Schneider, Percival Clarence, CORP, Company L
Schnitzer, Michael, PVT, Company G
Schoenberg, Joseph, PVT, Headquarters Company
Schon, Louis, CPL, Company M
Schonau, Harry William, CORP, Company I, [Schonan]
Schoonmaker, Calvin, PVT, Company G
Schoonmaker, Raymond Leslie, PVT, Company F
Schoonmaker, William, PVT, Company B
Schramka, Anthony John, PVT, Company K
Schreckinger, Harry, PVT, Headquarters Company
Schroder, Thomas G., PVT, Company K
Schroedel, Charles, PVT, Company A
Schroeder, Louis, PVT, Company M
Schuberg, Theodore, COOK, Company M
Schubring, Alexander, CORP, Company E
Schuehler, Gustav, PVT, Company D
Schulman, Phillip, PVT, Headquarters Company
Schultz, Charles Max, PVT, Company H
Schultz, Harry H., PVT, Medical Detachment
Schultz, Wallace, PVT, Company A
Schupp, Anthony M., MECH, Company M
Schutt, James G., PVT, Company B
Schutzman, Morris, PVT, Headquarters Company
Schwab, David, PVT, Company M
Schwartz, Jacob, PVT, Company A
Schwartz, James Brewster, PVT, Company C
Schwartz, Samuel, PVT, Company D
Schwarz, Adam Frank, PVT 1CL, Company M
Schwarz, Herbert, PVT, PVT1CL, Company I
Schwarz, Victor William, PVT, Company D
Schwenker, Arthur Victor Hugo, PVT, Company C
Schwere, William, CPL, Headquarters Company
Schwimmer, Alexander Sandor, PVT, Company L
Scott, William J., FIRST SERGT, Company E
Scoville, Casper M., PVT, Company L
Scruggs, Malcomb Everett, PVT, Company E
Sealy, James Ward Pell, PVT, Headquarters
    Company
Searles, Leonard P., SERGT, Company E
Sears, Chauncey Leo, CORP, Company A
Sears, John Whitfield, PVT, Company F
Sebesta, Louis, PVT, Company M
Sechrest, Lewis A., PVT, Headquarters Company
Segelman, Abe, PVT, Company D
Seidlecky, Frank John, PVT, Company A
Seipel, Claude K., SGT, Company F
Selby, John A., 1LT, I.R.C., Company H
Seligmann, George, PVT, Company M
Selke, Frank Charles, BGL, Company C
Sementor, George, PVT, Company K, C
Semmler, Edward Herman, CPL, Company K
Sendner, Arthur, PVT, Company E
Sennewald, Curt Rudolph, PVT, Company M
Sentenat, Meliton Perez, PVT, Company A, C
Sepe, Paolo, PVT, Company H
Serra, Joseph P., PVT, Company K

Settle, William Russell, PVT, Supply Company
Seymour, Harry M., CORP, Company E
Seymour, Henry Charles, PVT, Company F
Shabshelowitz, Morris, CORP, Company F
Shackles, Alfred P. T., PVT, Headquarters
    Company
Shahbegian, Harry Kachadoor, PVT, Company L
Shanahan, Thomas Francis, CORP, PVT, Company E
Shannahan, Patrick Joseph, PVT, Company I
Shapiro, Benjamin, PVT, Company F
Shapiro, Louis, PVT, Company D
Shapiro, Louis, PVT, Company E
Shapiro, Meyer, PVT, Company L
Shaver, Carl, PVT, Company B
Shaw, John, PVT, Company G
Shea, Lawrence P., SGT, Company G
Shea, Michael J., PVT, Headquarters Company
Shea, Timothy, PVT, Company H
Shear, Elmer Vanderzee Jr., CORP, Company A
Shear, Wendell, PVT, Company E
Sheedy, John Joseph, PVT, Company G
Sheehan, Patrick J., PVT, Company D
Sheehy, Joseph F., PVT 1CL, Corp, Company I
Sheeley, William Charles, PVT, Company D
Sheeran, John J., PVT, Company B
Sheil, William, PVT, Company I
Shelford, William, PVT, Company D
Shepard, Grover Franklin, PVT, Company C
Sheridan, Edward Albert Jr., PVT, Company A
Sheridan, Patrick, PVT, Company G
Sherman, Charles, PVT, Company B, died overseas
Sherwood, Forest Walter, PVT, Company D
Shields, Francis Luke, PVT, Company D
Shields, Joe Lee, PVT, Company H
Shiers, Fred Sylvester, PVT, Company D
Short, Claude Donald, PVT, Company D
Short, Raymond, CPL, Company M
Short, William, CPL, Company D
Shufelt, Wallace Jerry, SGT, Company F
Shutter, Irving Lawson, PVT, Company D
Sickels, William E., PVT, Company M
Sickler, Lynn M., PVT, Company A
Sickles, James Pender, SGT, Company A
Sidenio, Natale, PVT, Company I
Siebert, Leo Paul, PVT, Company C
Siegel, Herman, PVT, Company D
Siegel, Morris, PVT, Company I
Siegfried, Milton Aaron, PVT, Company C
Sienkevc, Joseph, PVT 1CL, Company I [Sienkeve]
Sievert, Herman Rudolph, MECH, Headquarters
    Company
Sifacakis, Peter J., PVT, Company B
Signori, Elvero Anthony, PVT, Company F
Silberberg, Herbert, PVT, Headquarters Company
Silleck, John B., PVT, Company B
Silver, Samuel, PVT, Company L
Silverman, Isador, PVT, Company M
Silverstein, Henry, CPL, Headquarters Company
Silverstein, Herman, 2LT, BND LDR, Headquarters
    Company, died overseas
Simmons, Gerald W., 2LT, INF, Regimental
    Headquarters
Simmons, Gerald W., SERGT, Company E
Simmons, John H., CORP, Company I
Simmons, Sheldon M., PVT, Medical Detachment
Simons, Carl L., CPL, Company B
Simpson, Frank, PVT, Company K
Simpson, Royal Walter, PVT, Company M
Sinopoli, Joseph, PVT, Company H
Sirago, John, PVT, Company I
Sjambelluri, Francesco, PVT, Company B

Skaggs, James, PVT, Company G
Skampneski, Stanislaus, PVT, Company F
Skannel, Harold W., CPL, Company H
Skelig, Carl Louis, PVT, Company D
Skennion, Bernard Thomas, PVT, Company A
Skorupka, Henry, PVT, Company F
Skowrenski, Antonio, PVT, Company E
Slater, Bernard M., SGT, Company G
Slattery, Robert Augustine, CPL, Company D, died overseas
Slavik, Alexander Frank, CPL, Company K
Slavik, Frank, PVT, Company I
Slavin, Edward E., SGT, Company I
Slawsky, Robert P., SGT, Company D
Sleeper, Clarence E., PVT, Company E, died overseas
Sliverstein, Julius, PVT, Company A
Sloan, Graham M., 2LT, IRC, Company C
Slomka, John, PVT, Company K
Slonim, Joseph, PVT, Headquarters Company
Slutsky, Meyer, PVT, Company M
Smalley, Reuben R., PVT, Company B
Smith, Albert R., PVT, Company B
Smith, Alexander Raymond, PVT, Company K
Smith, Alexander W., PVT, Company B
Smith, Arthur W., PVT, Company B
Smith, Charles F., PVT, Company D
Smith, Charles H., PVT, Company B
Smith, Daniel Austin, PVT, Company A
Smith, Delmar B., PVT, Company B
Smith, Edward F., PVT, COOK, Company B
Smith, Edward P., PVT, Company E
Smith, Fred, MCH, Company D
Smith, George Woolsey, PVT, Company H
Smith, Grover Cleveland, PVT, Company L
Smith, Guy, PVT, Company D
Smith, Henry V. D., SERGT, Company E
Smith, Jerred, SGT, Company F
Smith, Myles F., 2LT, I.R.C., Company E
Smith, Robert C., PVT, Company G
Smith, Robert Chester, PVT, PVT1CL, Company I
Smith, Terence Philip, PVT, Company H
Smith, Victor F., PVT, Company B
Smythe, Edward Vincent, PVT, Company E
Snapp, Sherman R., PVT, CRP, Company B
Sneed, Walter Evan, PVT, Company L
Snell, Clifford James, PVT, Company A
Soderland, Arthur, PVT, Company A
Soin, Max Phillip, PVT, Company D
Sokalmer, Benjamin, PVT, Company F, C
Soloman, Abraham, PVT, Headquarters Company
Solomon, Henry Walter, PVT, Company M
Solomon, Monroe, PVT, Company L
Sorge, Charles August, CORP, PVT, Company E
Soth, Carl Augustus, PVT, Company A
Sottong, Victor George, PVT, Company L
Spagnuolo, Pietro, PVT 1CL, Company I
Spano, Charles, PVT, Company I
Sparkman, Acie, PVT, Company L, died overseas, SOTGW Vol II - Missouri
Sparling, Ralph, PVT, Company F
Specht, Edward, PVT, Company L
Sperl, Floyd Grover, PVT, Company E
Spezzano, Frank Leonard, PVT, Company D
Spillane, John Valentine, PVT, Company M
Spinella, Alfred, PVT, Company A
Spiniello, Carmine, PVT, Company E
Spiropoulos, Peter, PVT, Company B
Spitaler, Harry B., PVT, Company G
Spoerner, Henry E., PVT, Company M
Sponenberg, Barney J., PVT, Company A

Spree, Herbert Theodore, PVT, Supply Company
Springer, Daniel, WAG, Supply Company
Squazzo, Fred, SGT, Company G
Squillante, Nicola, PVT, Company H
Srenkay, George, PVT, Company M
St. Amour, James A., PVT, Company D
St. John, Eugene F., WAG, Supply Company
Stabile, Christopher, PVT, Supply Company
Stachnik, Frank J., PVT, Company K
Stafford, Dan, PVT, Supply Company
Staiger, Fred George, PVT, Company G
Stanich, John Joseph, PVT, Headquarters Company
Stankewinz, John, PVT, Company L
Stanton, Haskell Milton, CPL, Headquarters Company
Stapleton, John Aloyious, CPL, Company D
Stapleton, John, PVT, Company G
Stapleton, William Joseph, PVT, Company D
Starbuck, John Phillips, PVT, Company H
Stark, John R., PVT, Company I
Starr, Walter P., 3 CL MSN, Headquarters Company
Starr, William J., 2LT, I.R.C., Company D
Stauffer, Russell S., 2LT, I.R.C., Company D
Stavros, Dukas, PVT, Supply Company
Stearns, Joseph Asa Jr., CPL, Company K
Steel, Charles, PVT, Company K
Steelman, George N., CPL, Company B
Stefinelli, Nicola, PVT, Company B
Stein, Harold August, PVT, Company C
Steiner, Herbert, PVT, Company L
Steinman, Hyman, PVT, PVT1CL, Company I, I
Steinman, Isaac, PVT, Company F
Stelter, Otto A., PVT, Company M
Stern, Arthur Jerome, PVT, Headquarters Company
Stern, Samuel Samson, PVT, Company E
Stern. Samuel Paul, PVT, Company I
Sterr, William Vincent, PVT, Company L
Stevens, Charles, COOK, Supply Company
Stevens, James Gilford, PVT, Company H
Stever, Edward Newell, PVT, Company C
Stewart, Edward M., BUGL, PVT, Company B
Stidham, Henry H., PVT, Company D
Stiller, Frank Paul, PVT, Company F
Stiso, Francesco, PVT, Company A
Stockman, Charles, PVT, Company I
Stockenberg, Robert, PVT, Company B
Stoessel, Jacob, PVT, Company D
Stokem, Francis William, PVT, Company M
Stokem, John Westley, PVT, Company M
Stollmack George, PVT, Company B
Stone, Albert, PVT, Company M
Stone, Elmore B., CPL, Company B
Stout, Ernest Holwell, CORP, PVT, Company E
Stowell, Hugh H., PVT, Company B
Strachen, Roy J., PVT, CRP, Company B, [Strachon]
Strait, Max, PVT, Company D
Straite, Walter L., PVT 1ST CL, Supply Company
Stratman, William F., PVT, Company M
Strauss, Christian, PVT, CRP, Company B
Streng, Leo Herman, PVT, Supply Company
Strickland, William J., PVT, Company I
Strippoli, Pasquale, PVT, Company L
Strunk, Fleece, PVT, Company L
Strusienski, Peter Paul, PVT, Headquarters Company
Stuart, Harry, PVT, Company L
Stuart, Thomas Clark, SGT, Company K
Stubley, Herman, PVT, Company H
Sturgis, Daniel Clinton, PVT, Company D
Sturla, Charles J., SGT MESS, Company I
Sturm, Paul Hine, PVT, Company D

Styles, Charles, CPL, Company M
Suits, Melvin, PVT, Company A
Sullivan, Arthur, PVT, Headquarters Company
Sullivan, Daniel Lawrence, PVT, Supply Company
Sullivan, Daniel, PVT, Company D
Sullivan, Dennis James, PVT, Company L
Sullivan, Joseph Vincent, PVT, Company M
Sullivan, Patrick John, PVT, Company G
Sullivan, Thomas Joseph, PVT, Company C
Sundheimer, William Albert, CORP, PVT, Company E
Suppa, Vincent Costandino, PVT, Headquarters
   Company
Supper, William Gustave Jr, PVT, Headquarters
   Company
Suresky, Joseph, PVT, Supply Company
Susskind, George, PVT, Company G
Sutherland, Alfred Roy, CPL, Company D
Sutkin, Isidore, PVT, Company C
Swager, Harry Martin D.V., PVT, Company C
Swann, Yager H., PVT, Company B
Swart, Clifton Walter, PVT, Company E
Swartout, Harry J., PVT, Medical Detachment
Swarts, John Joseph, PVT, Company C
Sweeney, John Francis, PVT, Company G
Sweeney, Miles E., PVT, Company G
Sweeney, William Aloysius, SGT, Company L
Swenson, Sven Edwin, PVT, Company E
Swindell, Charles Edward, PVT, Company M
Swint, Charles, PVT, Company E
Swint, Charles, PVT, Company E
Sylvester, Alexander, CORP, PVT, Company E
Symonds, Lowell D., SERGT, Company E
Szkudlarek, Michael, PVT, Headquarters Company
Szymanski, Frank, PVT, Company C

Tabacco, Pado, PVT, Company A
Tabachow, Morris, PVT, Company D
Taccxino, Rocco, PVT, Company A
Taepke, Walter August, PVT, Company L
Tanfield, Howard Winfred, PVT, Company E
Tanner, Carl F., 2 CL MSN, Headquarters Company
Tashjian, Minas Harouton, PVT, Company L
Taubenhaus, Benjamin, BUGL, PVT, Company I
Tavolacci, Joseph, PVT, Headquarters Company
Taylor, Allen R., SGT, Company G
Taylor, Charles Robert, PVT, Company D
Taylor, Dee Daniel, PVT, Company D
Teal, Raymond, PVT, Company B
Teator, Courtney Lee, MESS SGT, Company K
Teator, George Dewey, SGT, Company F
Tebbutt, Marshall, SGT, Headquarters Company
Tegiacchi, Virgilio, PVT, Company B
Teidman, Otto, PVT, Company B
Templeton, James Oliver, PVT, Supply Company
Tenant, Robery Corry, PVT, Company C
Tesoro, John T. Jr., WAG, Supply Company
Testa, Valentino, PVT, Company H
Tetelman, Michael Martin, PVT 1CL, Company M
Tetro, Mauro, PVT, Headquarters Company
Tevlin, John, PVT, Company A
Thatford, Charles Joseph, PVT, Company I
Thayer, Charles A., SGT 1CL, DMD 51 PI, Medical
   Detachment
Thayer, Frank Curtis, PVT, Company C
Themopoulos, Thomas, PVT, Company E
Thiel, William Carl, PVT, Company H
Thomas, Columbus Sylvester, PVT, Company L
Thomas, Frederick J, PVT, Company E
Thomas, Herbert H., CPL, Headquarters Company
Thompson, Eugene F., 1LT, D.M.D. MRC.51PI,
   Medical Detachment
Thompson, Frederick Stanislau, PVT, Company I
Thompson, Leo Joseph, PVT, Company D
Thompson, Muller Bennet, PVT, Company L
Thorn, Ernest Hall, PVT, Company G
Thorne, Edward R., CAPT, I.N.G., Company B
Thorne, Fred Philip, CORP, Company H
Thornton, Elmer Ray, PVT, PVT1CL, Company I
Thornton, James, PVT, Company B
Thurston, Benjamin T., PVT, Company K
Tiedman, Otto A., PVT, Company B
Tieman, George, BUG, Company H
Tierney, Michael Francis, PVT, Company L
Tiffany, Stephen R., CAPT, I.N.G., Company F
Tillery, Eddie, PVT, Company L
Timothy, Nicholas Joseph, PVT, Company A
Timothy, William, PVT, Company A
Tingley, Homer H., PVT, Company E
Tinken, John Henry, PVT, Company H
Tinschert, Frank, PVT, PVT1CL, Company I
Tischler, Wendilen Andrew, PVT, Company L
Tobin, Harry, PVT, Company B
Tobin, Thomas Ernest, PVT, Company G
Toksvig, Fred A., STBLE SGT, Headquarters
   Company
Tolley, Harry B., PVT, Company H
Tomasi, Giuseppe, PVT, Company G
Tomassi, Vincent, PVT, Company A
Tompkins, Daniel Davis, CORP, Company F
Tompkins, Harold, PVT, Supply Company
Tompkins, Lance, PVT, Company B
Tompkins, Victor B., PVT, Company B
Tompkins, Vincent, PVT, Company D
Tooker, Alfred J., COL SGT, Headquarters Company
Toolan, Edward James, PVT, Company C
Toolan, Thomas Joseph, PVT, Company L
Topp, William H., PVT, Company K
Toscano, Rocco, PVT, Company I
Townsend, Charles H., PVT, Company D
Townsend, Reynold K, CAPT, I.N.G., Company A
Tracy, Patrick Thomas, PVT, Supply Company
Trader, Berkely, PVT, Company I
Travis, John Frederick, CPL, Company K
Treanor, Patrick, PVT, Company G
Trenholm, Taliaferro T., PVT, PVT1CL, Company I
Treuhaft, Benjamine, PVT, Company C
Triebert, John, PVT, Company A
Triller, Charles, SGT, Company K
Triscari, Sebastiano, PVT, Company A, Co. A 51
   Pion Inf to Aug 18/18
Trischitta, Salvatore, PVT, Company D
Tropea, Salvatore, PVT, Company B
Troy, Hugh Aloysius, CPL, Company K
Tsanos, James, PVT, Company K
Tsatsos, Gustave B., PVT, Company L
Tsoskolos, Charles, PVT, Company K
Tucker, Edgar Townsend, SGT, Company L
Tucker, Herbert, PVT, Company D
Tufts, Sydney Arthur, PVT, Headquarters Company
Tully, Harry Alexander, PVT, Supply Company
Tummolo, Antonio, PVT, Company E, Co E Pion Inf
   to July 25/18; Co C 160 Inf to Sept 9/18; Co I
   127 to disch
Tunno, Guiseppi, PVT, Company C
Turck, Charles Francis, PVT, Company I
Turley, James Christoper, PVT, Supply Company
Turner, Charles Boughton, PVT, Company C
Turner, Clifton, 1LT, I.R.C., Company A
Turner, George, PVT, Company I
Turner, Henry Joseph, PVT, Company E
Turner, Otis Oscar, PVT, Company M

Turner, Walter High, PVT, Company L
Turnier, Andrew, PVT, Company B
Turpin, Lambert Marshall, PVT, Supply Company
Tushinsky, Aaron Zolman, PVT, Headquarters
  Company
Tushkesvich, John, PVT, Company D
Tuthill, Eldred G., PVT, Company B
Tweed, John James, PVT, Company C
Tyndall, John Joseph, PVT, Company H

Uebelacker, Matthew M., CPL, Company G
Uhlendorf, Charles Herman, PVT, Company M
Uhrdin, Arthur, MECH, Company A
Ulrich, Samuel, PVT, Company L
Underhill, Robert W., CORP, Company L
Ungar, Phillip, PVT 1CL, Company M
Utter, Harry Elmer, PVT, Supply Company

Vacca, Rosario, PVT, Headquarters Company
Vadney, William T., PVT, Medical Detachment
Vail, Otis, PVT 1ST CL, Supply Company
Valavan, James, PVT, Company M
Valk, James Fred, PVT, Company E
VanDeMark, Alfred, PVT, Supply Company
Vanderhoef, Frank, PVT, Company M
Vanderhoff, Frank Rutherford, PVT, Company A
Vanderpoel, Lester Minor, PVT, Company E
Vanderpoel, Ralph, CPL, PVT, Company B
Vandervoort, Charles Edwin, RGT SGT MJR,
  Headquarters Company
VandeWater, Arthur M., MECH, Supply Company
VanDuzer, Henry Jarrold, PVT, Supply Company
VanEtsen, Anthony Gilbert, PVT, Company L
VanEtten, Charles A., MECH, Company M
VanEtten, Floyd Lester, PVT, Company E
Vanhorn, Clyde, PVT, Medical Detachment,
VanHouten, Alexander, PVT, Company H
VanKleeck, Gordon, PVT, Company F
VanRiper, Bert W., PVT, Company D
VanRiper, Cleon Henry, PVT, Company E
Vanslet, Joseph Francis, CK, Company C
VanSlyke, Webster, PVT, Company B
VanSlyke, William, PVT, Company D, OC
VanValkenburg, Otis D., PVT, Company B
VanWert, James Ward, PVT, Headquarters Company
Varin, Adolph Joseph, PVT, Company H
Vasilakos, Ganyokos, PVT, Medical Detachment
Vaughan, Wallace, PVT 1CL, Company I
Vaughan, William P., PVT, Medical Detachment
Veitch, James, PVT, Company G
Vella, Joseph, PVT, Company G
Ventero, Arthur, PVT, Medical Detachment
Venticinque, Nicholas, PVT, Company A
Verge, James Andrew, PVT, Company C
Vergis, Peter, PVT, Company I
Verity, Walter Ignatius Thomas, PVT, Company M
Verneau, Charles Albert, PVT, Company C
VerValen, Charles, MECH, Company H
Vilie, George W., PVT, Company B
Vinci, Toney, PVT, Company C
Vipond, Walter, PVT, Company L
Vitale, Dominic Joseph, PVT, Company L
Vogel, Abraham, PVT, Company M
Volk, Joseph John, PVT, Company L
Vollmer, August, PVT, Company E
VonSchoppe, Charles F., PVT, Company H
VonWahl, Hubert Bismark, PVT 1CL, Company M
Vorel, Charles, PVT, Company M
Vose, John C., 1LT, INF, Regimental Headquarters

Vose, John C., 2LT, I.N.G., Company A
Vossler, Charles, 1ST SGT, Company K
Vought, Charles, PVT, Medical Detachment

Wadsworth, Charles Wesley, PVT, Company A
Wagel, Jacob Raymond, PVT, Company G
Wagenbaugh, William G., MECH, Company E
Wager, David Collis, CORP, Company L
Wagner, Arthur, PVT, Company F
Wagner, Charles Adrian, PVT, Company E
Wagner, Charles Anthony, PVT, Company D
Waigate, Stanley Edward, PVT, Company K
Wald, David, PVT, Company E
Wald, Joe, PVT, Company A
Waldorfer, Leo, PVT, Company F
Walgate, Harvey Walter, PVT, Company K
Walker, John, PVT, Company G
Walker, Robert, PVT, Company A
Walker, Walter Henry, PVT, Company D
Wall, Fred, CK, Company G
Wallace, George E., MCH, PVT, Company B
Walsh, Charles E., CPL, Company D
Walsh, David H., 1LT, I.N.A., Supply Company
Walsh, Martin, PVT, Company H
Walsh, Robert D. P., SGT, Company I
Walsh, William Thomas, PVT, Company C
Waltermire, Homer George, CORP, Company F
Wanamaker, Otis Douglas, CPL, Company H
Ward, Herman, PVT, Company H
Ward, Richard E., PVT, Company E
Wardrop. Benjamin Francis, PVT, Company K
Warner, Demerritt Alvah, CPL, Company C
Warren, Blaine, PVT, Company G, C
Warshauer, Morris, PVT, Company A
Wase, Ernest M., PVT, Company B
Wasilewski, Joseph, PVT, Company F
Wassung, George Arthur, PVT, Company A
Waters, David Ernest, PVT, Company E
Waters, Sanford Otis, PVT, Company H
Waters, Saul H., PVT, Company B
Watson, Donald Ives, PVT, Company K
Weaver, Henry Ross, PVT, Company G
Webber, William Russell, CPL, Company K
Weber, David J., CPL, Company H
Weber, Martin Henry, PVT, Company L
Webster, Henry, PVT, Company D
Webster, John A., 2LT, ING, Headquarters Company
Webster, Steacy E., 2ND LT, IRR, Company C
Weed, Charles E., 2 CL MSN, Headquarters Company
Weekes, Floyd S., CORP, Company I, (Weckes)
Weeks, Frank Eugene, SGT, Company H
Weinberger, Emanuel William, PVT, Headquarters
  Company
Weinberger, Milton, PVT, Company B
Weingartner, William John, PVT, Company E
Weinsheimer, Edward Theron, CPL, Company K
Weireter, Paul Casper Joseph, PVT, Company L
Weiser, Edward Joseph, PVT, Company A
Weiss, Charles, PVT, Company M
Weiss, David, CK, Company G
Weiss, Hyman, PVT, Company K
Weiss, Julius, PVT, Company M
Weiss, Max, PVT, Company M
Weissman, Paul, PVT, Headquarters Company
Welch, Eddie, PVT, Company A
Welch, Roy G., 1LT, I.R.C., Company F
Welch, Stanley Merritt, PVT, Company F
Wellbrock, Arthur Christian, CORP, Company A
Wellbrock, Arthur Christian, CPL, Company K,
  transferred to Co. A Pioneer Reg

Welling, Frank Myers, PVT, Company A
Wells, Arthur, PVT, Headquarters Company
Weltman, Aaron, PVT, Company H
Wener, Bernard Charles, PVT, Company M
Wentz, Richard F., CPL, Company K
Weppler, Thomas Andrew, PVT, Company H
Wereley, Alonzo Stanley, SGT, Company D
Wesley, Vanderbilt William, CORP, Company F
Wessels, John, PVT, Company D, OC
Wessely, Rudolph, PVT, PVT1CL, Company I, I
West, Abbot, PVT, Company E
West, Allie G., PVT, Company B
West, James Leroy, CORP, Company F
Westcott, Lester, PVT, Company C
Wetzig, George, PVT, Company I
Weymouth, Merle McCausland, 1LT, INF N.A.,
  Company M
Whalen, Michael Francis, PVT, Company D, OC,
  died overseas
Whalen, William James, CPL, Company C
Wheatley, Frederick George, PVT, Headquarters
  Company
Wheeler, Clarence Henry, 1CL PVT, Company K
Wheeler, Edward, CORP, SGT, Company F, died
  overseas
Wheeler, Eugene, PVT, Company A
Wheeler, John Selem, CORP, Company F
Wheeler, Orville C., PVT, Company I
Whikehart, Charles Edward Jr., PVT, Company M
Whipple, Ralph Emerson, PVT, Company L
Whitaker, James E., PVT, Company K
White, Frank Edward, PVT, Company L
White, John James, PVT, Company D
White, Locke, 1LT, NG, Regimental Headquarters
White, Roland Eldred, CPL, Company C
White, Victor, PVT, Company E
White, William P., 2 CL MSN, Headquarters
  Company
Whitehead, Ira Whaley, PVT, Supply Company
Whitesides, Anderson, PVT, Company B
Whitman, Fred J., PVT, Headquarters Company
Whitney, George Orlando, PVT, Company A
Whitson, Robert Ludlow Jr., PVT, Company K
Whittaker, Arthur, PVT, Company C
Wible, Charles Mck., PVT, Company B
Wickham, Richard E., PVT, Company D
Wiemann, Richard Frederick, PVT, Company K
Wier [Weir], Emmet C., 2LT, I. RC, Company B
Wiesenberg, Samuel, PVT, Company F
Wilcox, Leon Horace, CPL, Company K, U
Wiljakainen, Hjalman, PVT, Company E
Willey, Earl T., PVT, Company I
Williams, Archie Griffith, PVT, Headquarters
  Company
Williams, Carl C., PVT, Company K
Williams, Charles H., COOK, Supply Company
Williams, Edwin P., COOK, Company E
Williams, Frank, PVT, Company A
Williams, Louis Broadhead, PVT, Company C
Williams, Michael, PVT, Company A
Williams, Reese Edgar, PVT, Company M
Williams, Seymour Elwin, PVT, Company A
Williams, Theodore Scott, PVT, Company C
Williams, William, PVT, Company C
Williamson, Sim, PVT, Company K
Willis, Richard H., PVT, Company B
Wilsey, W. Clyde, PVT, Company H
Wilson, Alfred Alexander, CORP, Company I
Wilson, Edward L., PVT, Company B
Wilson, Fred, PVT, Company F
Wilson, Harry George, PVT, Company I

Wilson, Richard Edgar, PVT, Headquarters Company
Wilson, Walter Joseph, PVT, Company G
Windisch, August, PVT, Headquarters Company
Windrum, Ray Alton, CORP, Company F
Winegar, Daniel Chester, PVT, Company M
Wing, Charles Neill, PVT, Company D
Winner, Harry E., PVT, Company B
Winner, Rosewell C., PVT, Company B
Winters, Francis Jr., PVT, Company E
Winters, Thomas Anthony, PVT, Company A
Wise, William Harvey, PVT, Company E
Wisely, John J., SGT, Company B
Wishnack, Phillip R., PVT, Company B
Wisneski, Joseph James, PVT, Company F
Wisniewski, Brownie, PVT, Headquarters Company
Witkoski, Bernard Franklin, PVT, Company E
Witkowski, Leo Eddie, PVT, Company K
Witowicz, William, PVT, Company M
Witt, Henry B., PVT, Company A
Wittam, Harold G., 3 CL MSN, Headquarters
  Company
Wittlief, William Fred Jr., PVT, Company K
Wodowski, Harry, PVT, Company L
Woehrel, Louis Theophile, SGT, Company C
Woerner, William, PVT, Company F
Wolfe, John, PVT, Company E
Wolfersheim, Herman, COOK, Company M
Wolff, Charles Abraham, PVT, Company M
Wolz, August, PVT, Company F
Wood, Joseph Francis, SGT, Company C
Wood, Owen Jasper, PVT, Company L
Wood, Walter G., SGT, Headquarters Company, U
Woodhull, Fred Ralph, PVT, Company C
Woodruff, Everett, SERGT, CORP, Company E
Woodson, Hylan H., 1LT, D.M.D. MRC.51PI, Medical
  Detachment, sailing with Co. A 51st P. Inf
Woodson, Hylan H., 2LT, M.R.C., Company A
Worker, Charles, PVT, Company A
Worpenburg, Charles J., PVT, Company B
Worthington, Gwilym R., CORP, Company L
Wozniak, Joseph, PVT, Headquarters Company
Wright, Everett W., CORP, Company I
Wright, Frank, PVT, Headquarters Company
Wroblewski, Michael, PVT, Company E
Wronke, Alexander, PVT, Headquarters Company
Wudowsky, Benjamin, PVT, Supply Company
Wunderlich, Daniel Joseph, PVT, Company E
Wyant, Leroy Earl, PVT, Company A

Yaeger, George Aaron, PVT, Company G
Yarter, Leo, PVT, Company D
Yates, Harry Rodney, PVT, Company C
Yauch, George, PVT, Company F
Yeghoian, Egia Sahag, PVT, Company I
Yetzer, Carl Anton, SGT, Company K
Youker, Fred John, CORP, Company A
Youlio, Lawrence C., PVT, Company D
Young, Alfred Joseph, PVT, Company H, severely
  wounded 21 Sept 1918
Young, Ike, PVT, Company K
Young, Julius, PVT, Company B
Young, Lawyer Sidney, SUP SGT, Company A
Young, Percy N., SUP SGT, Company H
Young, William, PVT, Company A
Young, William E., PVT, Company I, died overseas

Zadina, Frank William, PVT, Headquarters Company
Zager, Harry, PVT, Company D
Zalewski, Frank Stanley, PVT, Company G
Zampini, Joseph, PVT, Company H

```
Zannella, Michael, PVT, Company F, C        Zelvin, Karl, PVT, Company F
Zannis, Nicholas, PVT, Company K            Ziegler, John Ernest, PVT, Company F
Zapentis, William, PVT, Company L           Zierow, William Frederick, PVT, Company E
Zastrow, Fred W., PVT, Company M            Zietz, August Louis, PVT, Company D, OC
Zavhary, Robert Y., LT, U.S.R. INF, Company G    Zinn, Louis Agustus, PVT, Company I
Zazzarino, Francesco, PVT, Company L         Zorn, Warren Henry, PVT, Company H
Zelimer, Philip George, CORP, Company F      Zullo, Luciano, PVT, Company D
Zellner, John Samuel, PVT, Company F
```

Sources

Farrow, Edward S. "A Dictionary of Military Terms", Thomas Y. Cromwell Company, New York, Revised Edition, 1918.

Lerwil, Leonard L. "The Personnel Replacement in the United States Army", CMH_Pub_104-9, August 1954.

New York State Military Museum and Veterans Research Center. "Roll of honor: Citizens of the State of New York who died while in the service of the United States during World War I" https://dmna.ny.gov/historic/reghist/wwi/HonorList, accessed 5 Jan 2018.

COMPANY B

The following is from the diary kept by SGT John G. Mansfield of Company B. He was with NYNG 10th Infantry before the war. His notes and scrapbook pages are located at the USAHEC, and has been transrribed, combined and condensed by the author. When there was a conflict between his notepad and his compiled movement notes, I assumed that the notebook carried with him during the war was correct.

3 Feb 1917. Diplomatic relations broken with Germany.

4 Feb 1917. Called into service.

7 Feb 1917. Left Albany to do guard duty at N.Y. waterworks Catskill Mts. Spend the first night at Brown's Station, hiked to Davis corners Feb.8th, from there to Atwood NY patrols covering 1 ½ miles north, 2 miles south.

6 Apr 1917. War Declared on Germany

6 Apr 1917. We left the water works arrived in Albany in the afternoon, went on guard at the State Capital Gov.'s mansion and power house.

June 1917. Summer in Albany.

15 July 1917. Mustered into Federal Service.

11 Aug 1917. left Albany for Harrisburg, PA, for guard duty on Penn RR lines around Harrisburg.

12 Aug 1917. Arrived in Harrisburg. Co. B Headquarters LeMoyne, PA. At Harrisburg then had target practice and Saturday morning inspection

14 Aug 1917. Left Harrisburg for Maine Forge, PA, with 6 men to guard bridge 10 ft high 100 yards long. Boarded at farm house.

24 Oct, 1917. Left Mailie Forge for Harrisburg. Formed Company from outpost along Penn RR Bridges.

26 Oct., 1917. Company left Harrisburg for Camp Wadsworth, Spartanburg, SC.

29 Oct. 1917. 6 a.m. arrived Camp Wadsworth, Spartanburg, S.C.

24 Dec 1917. Company Skeletonized. Men transferred to outfits in 27 Division, only non-com left for duty until 27 May 1918.

27 May 1918. Company B filled up to war strength May 27, '18 with draft men.

Until 15 July 1918. Trained in Camp Wadsworth.

51st Pioneer Infantry Camp at Camp Wadsworth, SC,
Mansfield Diary, USAHEC.

General View of the 51st PIR (X marks Co. B Street),
Mansfield Diary, USAHEC

Mack the Company B mascot, Mansfield Diary,
USAHEC.

Ball Team Going to a Game, Mansfield Diary,
USAHEC.

Co M Mascot, Mansfield Diary, USAHEC

Knott, Raney, Mansfield, Norswell, Beerle & Ross, Mansfield Diary, USAHEC.

51st Pioneer Ball Team, Mansfield Diary, USAHEC.

17 July 1918. We left Camp Wadsworth, SC, at 11 A.M.. Entrained for Camp Merritt, NJ.

19 July 1918. Arrived at Camp Merritt, NJ, at 10:15 A.M.

Received our overseas equipment. Received Twenty-four hour pass, went to Albany and returned back to camp five and a half hours late came very near being left behind.

26 July 1918. Left Camp Merritt at 1 A.M. Marched to Alpine Landing. Piled on ferry boat and sailed down the Hudson River or North River to Hoboken, NJ. Embarked on the U.S.S. Kroonland sailed and left pier at 3:30 PM.

Sailed on U.S.S. Kroonland, joined the fleet had a very pleasant trip good eats. No rough weather, slept down in hole below water line.

First night on guard the rest of the trip slept on deck every night

6 Aug 1918. Arrived in Brest, France at 6:00 P.M.

7 Aug 1918. Disembarked at noon. Marched to Rest Camp near Pontanezen Barracks (Napoleons Old Headquarters) at Rest Camp we worked day and night building barracks and unloading ships. Hiked to rest camp, near Brest, for recuperation and bath.

14 Aug 1918. At 2 a.m. entrained in French day coaches (2nd and 3rd Class) eight men to a compartment, canned goods and hard tack and hard hash were thrown into us and doors closed.

17 Aug 1918. After riding in these stuffy cars three days and three nights we arrived at Maron, a small French Village. Billeted in hay lofts with chickens and rabbits. The French Government have all houses and stables labeled for a certain number of horses and men, the owners, receiving one cent a day per man.

21 Aug 1918. Left Maron at noon. Marched on Toul a distance of 8 miles to Toul spent the night in Marshal Nez Barracks. Arrived at 12:30 A.M.

22 Aug 1918. Left Toul at 11 A.M. Hiked to Pagny Sur Muese. 7 miles again. Arrived at 6 P.M. Billeted in lofts, barns where everyone received the itch. It was a case of work all day building wire entanglements and scratch all night.

30 Aug 1918. first casualties of the 51st Pioneer Inf from Co. M. three men killed were wounded from shrapnel. [Amitrano, George, PVT, Co. M; Boggio, Remo, PVT 1CL, Co. M]

2 Sept 1918. 9:30 P.M. Left Pagny Sur Muese at 9 P.M. Marched to Bautzen Barracks outside of Toul arriving at 12:30 A.M. at this place.

3 Sept 1918. At these barracks large details were sent out detailed to different divisions near the line.

10 Sept. 1918. Left Toul for McCormack's Dump. At 4 P.M. were loaded on auto trucks and taken to woods near Manders close to the front attached to the 1st Engineers of the 1st Division rained all the trip and while in the woods mud was knee deep. Arrived 11:30 P.M. to woods arr. 2:30 A.M. [McCormack's Dump might have been named for flight leader Vaughan McCormack who died in a crash while trying to land.]

12 Sept 1918. At 1 A.M. Germans began shelling the woods. Marched from McCormack's Dump to St. Baussant (participating in the first American drive). At 2 A.M. company was formed, at 3:30 A.M. we left the woods, advancing (marching) under heavy shell fire. Marched through Beaumont to Seicheprey the American line. Arrived at front at 5 A.M. just in time to see the first wave of our troops go over the top. Across from St. Baussant the German line. We started right in to repair roads and bridges, destroyed by the German shell fire, so that the supplies and artillery could follow up the infantry advance. At this place we began to realize what war really was, wounded being brought as we were repairing one bridge four men were killed about twenty feet away from us by shell fire.

Night of 12 Sept 1918. At 6 P.M. we arrived in what was Saint Baussant it was completely destroyed. We slept in the ruins of what was a church. At daybreak we started to work again to repair the roads.

Night of 13 Sept 1918. we slept in what was a German dugout two nights before under a convent. No blankets or overcoat and raining most all the time. In all this time we ate canned salmon receiving only one cooked meal in 48 hours. 48 hours on the roads getting to us. It was a warmed over affair but it tasted mighty good.

14 Sept 1918. At 5:30 P.M. left St. Baussant for Wood Le Foux Bois, Nouginsard. Started on forced march passing through Essey and Mousard. Also Hendicourt arriving in woods just outside of Nousard near Montsec at 11 P.M. spent Saturday and Sunday in the woods with the 1st Engineers. Some eats and a good bunch of fellows.

16 Sept 1918. Loaded into auto trucks at noon rode 15 miles to Royaumeix 8 P.M. Billeted in big barn with cots. Clean + cots very comfortable.

18 Sept 1918. Left our billet moved to old YMCA Building mile & half away

19 Sept 1918. Moved from YMCA to Barracks one hundred yards away. We were supposed to be in rest camp at this time after coming from the front, but instead we are unloading, from freight cars, eight and nine inches shell. Were loading narrow gauge rail road cars with 8 and 10 inch shells.

7 PM Loaded into auto trucks. Rode from Royaumeix back to Bautzen Barracks outside of Toul arriving at 9 P.M.

20 Sept 1918. Paid for July + Aug $210 Francs.

27 Sept 1918. Had hot bath at Red Cross Rest House near Toul.

29 Sept 1918. Went to mass held in one of the one of the barracks, said by French Chaplain.

6 Oct 1918. Walked 2 miles to church no Mass. Mass only on the Sunday that the priest can get away from the front.

9 Oct 1918 Received pay for Sept. 143.50 Francs sent $50.00 or 177.50 Francs.

15 Oct 1918 Left Bautzen Barracks At 6PM for Army Candidate School.

17 Oct 1918. 9 a.m. Arrived at La Valbonne.

Postcard of Camp LA VALBONNE (Ain)
"Where we spend about seven hours a day at drill"

18 Oct 1918. Assigned to 5th Company 2nd Bat. All of the 51st men in same company.

21 Oct 1918. Started with real work. Rush as squads right + left, school of soldiers + physical exercises. Also took notes on hand grenades.

22 Oct 1918. Tuesday. Drill in throwing hand grenades other work about the same as day before.

23 Oct 1918. Wed. Work same as day before. Brigadier General Smith spoke to the candidates for a half hour.

24 Oct 1918. Did not drill. Rifles were issued to men who did not have one.

26 Oct 1918. Inspection of rifles from 7:30 AM to 8:30 AM Inspection of quarters 8:30 to 9:00 then rolled packs and hiked from 9:30 to 11:30 No drill or formations in afternoon.

30 Oct 1918. Took up new AEF formation for as skirmishes Had practice in throwing live hand grenades Mess has been the best I have. Bread and coffee without milk and sausages for breakfast Dinner stew using little meat coffee without milk. Supper tomatoes and cabbage most all water coffee bread. Seven hours drill a day

2 Nov 1918. Passed inspection OK again. Entire company confined to barracks for having dirty barracks, until further notice. Bought razor for 97.75

3 Nov 1918. Mess improving. Two weeks of courses gone and so far everything OK. Honorable mention for not having canteen hung in proper place under bunk about 1 1/2 out of the way. first call since school began

6 Nov 1918. Thursday. Rumors that peace had been declared carried great joy. Lots of noise and big parade

8 Nov 1918. Friday Inspection this morning from 7:30 to 8:30 AM. 3rd inspection and everything O.K. Eve Show given by Company at YMCA very good

9 Nov 1918. Sat hike of about four miles

12 Nov 1918. Day declared holiday on account of the Germans signing.

28 Nov 1918. Thanksgiving. No drill. Dinner mashed potatoes, beef, bread, coffee.

30 Nov 1918. (Saturday) Company had Thanksgiving dinner. Big affair. Had good time. Turkey, potatoes, Brussel sprout, raddish, bread, candy, nuts, jams, salad lettuce, pumpkin pie, ? pie, dressing, cigars, ? good ?

6 Dec 1918. Left OLS Valbonne at 2 PM in freight cars 40 men to a car. 0 men out of the 3rd Co 1400 men out of camp. Breaking up of camp.

8 Dec 1918. Arrived Le Mans.

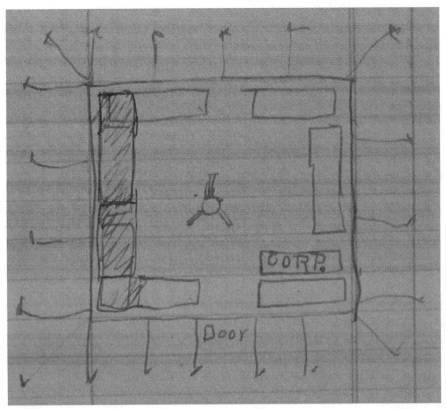

Set up of enlisted bunks in their tent. (Note the tent pegs and ropes.), Mansfield Diary, USAHEC.

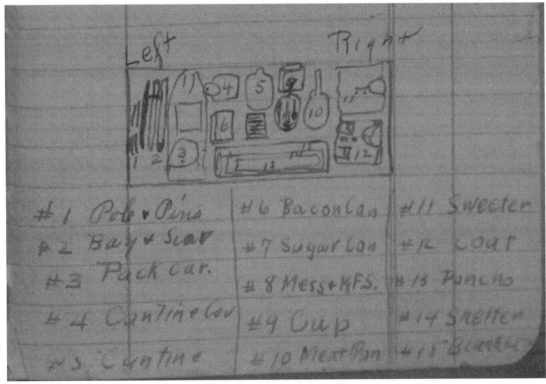

Layout of individual kit for inspection, Mansfield Diary, USAHEC.

Entanglements in No Man's Land, Mansfield Diary, USAHEC.

Albany Men of Company B 51st in Germany, Mansfield Diary, USAHEC.

Arrived in Lyon 3:10 PM Left Lyon 3:30 PM

Arrived at Bourges **Sat 7 1918** at 8:30 AM Arrived at Le Mans midnight

Dec 7 1918 Detrained Sunday morning

Dec 8 1918 at 7:30 AM Marched to French Barracks about mile. This evening all men were issued whatever new clothing they needed. Rumors are very strong to the effect we're going right back to the States.

Old 5th Squad
Segt. Dittus Kingston M 10th
Pvt Green Newbury L 1st
Pvt Turner Buffalo L 74th
Segt Mansfield Albany B 10th
Segt Porter Niagara Falls E 3rd
L Corp Yund Amsterdam H 2nd
1st Segt Ormston Watertown C 1st
Corp Doyle Tonawanda K 74th

5th Squad
        Co Regt
No 1F Yund Corp H 2nd Amerstam
No 2R Green Fred Pvt L 1st Newberg
No 3F Ormiston L.R. 1st Segt C 1st Watertown
No 4F Mansfield J.G. Segt B 10th Albany
No 1R Sapp F. Y. Segt C 10th Albany
No 2R Turner J. PVT L 74th Buffalo
No 3R Roberts E. M. 1st Segt M 3rd Auburn
No 4R Hickey A.M. Segt K 2nd Glensfalls

Entrenching Tools
No. 1 – 2 – 3 Front Carry Shovels
Corp Gun Cleaners
No. 1 Rear Pick
No. 2 Rear Wire Cutters
No. 3 Rear Bolo and Scabbard
No. 4 Rear Nothing

COMPANY F

World War I Journal of Gordon Van Kleeck, Company F

This chapter contains the journal of Corp Gordon Van Kleeck (1894 - 1977), of Company F of the 51st Pioneer Infantry Regiment. This material has been graciously supplied by his great niece, Roxy Triebel. The journal begins in 1918 and follows through until 1919, when the 51st Pioneer Infantry returned to the United States. The journal that Gordon kept as the historian for his unit was written in a small spiral pocket notebook. Most spelling etc. has been left as he wrote it in the original. (Roxy transcribed this diary and there are words that were illegible.)

Some of the people mentioned in the journal: Genevieve was probably Genevieve Winne, the woman Gordon would marry in 1923. Everett and Freeman were his brothers. Roxy, Vera, Elta, and Dot were his sisters. Gordon also mentions exchanging letters with someone named "Alice", but I'm not sure who she was. A "Ralph" is also mentioned - this is probably Ralph Sparling. Gordon mentions a buddy named "Charlie Mays" several times. [Note: there was a Charles May in Company I]

Note: The 51st Pioneer Infantry Regiment traveled to France on two ships, and also returned from France on two ships.

Part 1 training at Camp Wadsworth, SC and Camp Merritt, NJ. July 15 to July 25, 1918.

July 15, 1918. Camp Wadsworth, S.C. I have (been) in the U.S. service about seven weeks now and while it would not suit me for a permanent job I can stand it as long as the war lasts I guess. We have been packing our things and getting ready to move all day. We are going out sometime tonight I think. None of us know where we are going but think it will be Camp Merritt. As that is only a short distance from home I am hoping for a pass. It will be some trip.

July 16. Camp Wadsworth, S.C. We are still at Wadsworth but as our stuff has been sent to the station we will probably go in the morning. Was just over to Jack's Restaurant and had a feed as the grub was not up to the usual standard. We are looking forward to a long trip tomorrow.

July 19. Camp Merritt, N.J. I am at Camp Merritt at last. It is Friday and we left Wadsworth Wednesday morning. Arrived here yesterday morning and had a fine trip although we could not leave the car or send any mail along the way. This is a much nicer place than Camp Wadsworth and I hope we can stay here a couple of weeks before going over. The officers are inspecting our clothing and equipment today and we get mostly new before going. Most of us think we can get (off) after the inspection and our new uniforms are given out. I would enjoy a few days in Coldbrook or even a few hours.

July 21. Camp Merritt N.J. I had inspection today and a lot of stuff was rejected. The way our equipment was tested the officers would pull and try to rip the things. Anything that did not rip was passed. Most everything ripped. I have received part of my new equipment and will probably get more tomorrow. There were a large number of visitors in camp but I did not see anyone I know. Charlie Mays and I went to Merritt Hall for a little supper tonight. We are hearing all kinds of stories about when we go. This is sure a nice camp and we would all like to stay here for a couple of weeks.

July 25 Camp Merritt. Well we are going for sure I guess. We have got our little Overseas caps and our large hiking shoes. Adams, Cahill, Mays and I were over to Merritt Hall for supper tonight. That was probably our last good meal in this country for some time. Received letter from Hilda Mae today. We were promised passes home for today and some of us had hired a car to take us to Kingston. This morning we received orders to get ready to leave. I sent telegrams home telling the folks I could not come. Roxy phoned yesterday and wanted to come down but I told her I would be home in a day or two. I sure was fooled. Everything is packed up tonight and I am sitting on a mattress writing. The fellows are raising the Devil around me. No one seems to be very down hearted. I surely am not. The folks at home sent me money but it came in camp so late that I could not get it.

Part 2 aboard the U.S.S. Kroonland en route to France, first entry from Brest, France. July 26 to August 7, 1918.

July 26, 1918. U.S.S. Kroonland. We are on board the transport Kroonland. This is our first day. I am quartered near the bottom of the ship three floors down. It is a little hot but not bad. The bunks are made of steel frame and wire netting. They are built three high and I have a bottom bunk. We left camp about three o'clock this morning and hiked about five miles over a rather rough and hilly road. Some of the fellows had to fall out and were picked up by ambulance. The ferry Cincinnati took us to the transport. I laid down in my bunk and never knew when we left. We ate our first meal in about twenty-four hours tonight. It was the largest I have ever seen fed to troops. Every one reported more than he could eat. Sparling and I with a bunch of other fellows were the last ones fed and we were held to clean up in the kitchen. It was quite a job. Seven or eight war vessels are in sight at all times and a couple of aeroplanes followed us out to sea. I am not sick yet but have lots of time for that. We are all assigned to a certain raft and had our first raft drill tonight. The ship that used to be the Vaterland was in port when we left. She certainly is a large vessel and ought to carry a large number of troops.

July 27. U.S.S. Kroonland. We were called for raft drill this morning about four o'clock, before daylight. This is the first (time) I have been able to count our convoy. We have seven transports, one cruiser and 2 destroyers. I am enjoying myself alright except when we are sent below. The band has been playing for us and now we have to turn out the lights and get in our bunks. We are wearing our overalls all the time now instead of uniforms and life jackets must be worn over them even when we sleep.

July 28. U.S.S. Kroonland. We were given a bath today. The regular baths are to(o) small for the bunch so we had to undress and go on deck where some of the sailors (turned) a hose on us. It was fine. Are (Our) sleeping quarters are very hot and I can hardly stand it to stay there.

July 26. U.S.S. Kroonland. Last night one of the ships lost a man over board and turned back aways to look for him. I don't think he was found as they did not lower any boats. He must have had his life jacket off for the ocean was very smooth. The men climb upon the rail and it is a wonder more don't fall overboard. Mays is working in the canteen and got me some cake and chocolate today. It is opened only a couple of hours each day and is a popular place. The fellows line up hours before it opens. We were given another salt water shower bath today. I am detailed to go on guard tonight. The weather is damp and foggy now.

Aug 1. U.S.S. Kroonland. Have been feeling sick for a couple of days and can't even bear the smell of food. Have only eaten some candy and crackers for two days now. My guard post is a water can and have to see that no water is wasted and allow canteens to be filled only certain hours. I am to allow no lights of any kind on deck at night. Even the luminous dials on wrist watches must be kept under cover. I am on post from eight to twelve o'clock morning and night. When not sleeping I get some chance to read for there are plenty of good books on board. I am commencing to feel better now.

Aug 2. U.S.S. Kroonland. Am feeling very good now and have eaten two meals today. The weather is nice and we are making good time.

Aug 3. U.S.S. Kroonland. Wrote a letter to Roxy last night. We are not allowed to say much but I did the best I could. I don't like the chow we are getting now and as I am nearly broke I can't buy much at the canteen. The Finland had engine trouble last night and fell behind. One of the destroyers staid with her. I think she is alright now for she is coming up close again. The Finland is a sister ship to the Kroonland. We have a couple ships in the convoy that I think are Italian. Their camouflage coloring is different. All the ships look strange when the lights first strike them in the morning. We still have to get up before day light and stand by our rafts until the sun is up. Early morning is the most dangerous time for submarines they say. That is the time I am sleeping best. Once I never heard the alarm and slept right through.

Aug. 5. U.S.S. Kroonland. We are getting close to France. The cruiser and destroyers turned back today and we were joined by nine small submarines and an observation balloon attached to one of them. They are very small, long and low. It looks nice to see a line of them on each side of the convoy. It is Sunday and so foggy that I can only see a short distance. I think we will soon reach land and I will sure be glad.

Aug. 7. Brest, France. I am in France. The last day was quite rough weather. Last night someone reported a man overboard and one of the destroyers used a search light for half an hour looking for him. Later we found it was a false alarm. We landed at Brest and it is a very pretty city. All the buildings are stone. We are camped four or five miles from the city in our pup tents and a detail has gone to get rations for the regiment. It has commenced to rain and supper will taste good for we only had an early breakfast this morning. I am going on guard and can see a rather poor night ahead of me. It is getting dark and some of the men are just getting in. They will have to hustle or get wet before they get their tents up.

Part 3 Brest, France. August 8 to August 13, 1918.

Aug. 8. Brest, France. It rained all last night and half today. We had two meals today and are feeling fine. Orders have been given for us not to leave camp or buy anything of the peasants. I am broke so that does not bother me.

Aug. 9. Brest, France. We all from Co. F had to go to the dock today and carry railroad rails. Our dinner was given us there and we were sent back in auto trucks. I am tired out and will have to rest. That was the hardest job I ever saw.

Aug. 10. Brest, France. We went to the docks early this morning. It was an easy day for we only had to sweep the dock and most of us only worked a couple of hours. At dinner I got in line twice and had enough for the first (time) since I came here. This afternoon we found a place to wash up and it was great. At camp water is scarce and we are allowed only one canteen full a day for all uses. Coming back we rode through the business section of the city and it was fine. I hope to get a chance to visit it. One of the officers took a bunch for a walk tonight but they are not allowed to stop anywhere and my feet are sore so I am staying in camp.

Aug. 11. Brest, France. Half of the Co. went to the dock today but I was one of those who stayed in camp. This morning some of us were put on water detail. We had to go quite aways for it and there was no hurry about it so we made several trips and walked around the country. This afternoon I wrote a letter home but have not sent it yet as I can't get an envelope. After supper Lieut. Julian took between two or three hundred men over to the barracks for a shower bath. It sure did us good and I for one feel like a new person. I have been having trouble to keep warm nights so tonight I am making a sleeping bag of my blankets with some safety pins in my comfort. I think it will be better.

Aug. 12. Brest, France. My sleeping bag was fine last night and I will use it all the time now. We did not go out to work but were in camp all day. Had some exercise in the Manual of Arms and foot inspection. This afternoon went were taken to a place where we could wash our clothes. I had quite a lot of it to do. It was only a ditch but I managed to get them partly clean. We have orders to be ready to move any minute and may go yet tonight or early in the morning. We were given an extra amount of supper.

Aug. 13. Brest, France. Did not do much today but at night sixteen men including myself were given orders to pack up and went with Lieut. Matthews down to the dock. There we worked all night getting out rations for our battalion on the trip from Brest. I only got an hour's sleep about morning.

Part 4 aboard train and Sexey-aux-Forges, France. August 14 to August 24, 1918.

Aug. 14. Railroad train France. Got on train and started early this morning. It is made up of third class cars and we have nine men in our compartment. There is some nice scenery along the way but I am suffering from cramps and can't enjoy it very much. At St. Brieut (St. Brieuc) we were given coffee. We have food in each compartment. Ours is hard tack, corned beef, beans and jam. I think the trip will be about four days. We are going southeast. I see plenty of German prisoners and at one station there was a trainload of slightly wounded Germans. The prisoners are working on the railroad. None of them seem very unhappy.

Aug. 17 Sexey-au(x)-Forges, France. We have arrived. It was some trip taking nearly four days. There seemed to be American camps and barracks everywhere and near Bourges we saw an aeroplane station and about twenty planes in the air. Some of them came near us. At one station there were a lot of peaches in boxes and we swiped some of them. Then the officers had guards posted at each car whenever we stopped and we could not even get off. I am sorry I did not take more peaches. After passing Verizon (probably "Vierzon") a man named Doberstien went on the step while the train was running and was knocked off by something. By the time we could get the train stopped it had left him several miles behind. Word was sent back but it does not seem as if he could be alive. At Dijon we got our gas masks and helmets after dark. Today we detrained somewhere near Toul. Were given dinner on the bank of a canal and are now billeted in a nearby town. I with nineteen others are quartered in the loft of a barn. We have cots with a bed sack filled with straw on each. It is very dark and dusty and I hope we will be sent to some other place soon. Anyhow there is plenty of water here and we can wash. Water has been a valuable thing for the last ten days.

Aug. 19. Sexey-au(x)-Forges, France. We are still at Sexey. The first night Ray, Charlie and I went out for a walk and tried a bottle of wine that France is so famous for. I don't want any more of it for it is sour and made me dizzy. Some of the fellows drank to(o) much of it and the sergeant in charge of the place where I sleep came in last night so drunk he could hardly walk. I see plenty of aeroplanes and sometimes we can hear guns. We must be close to the front. The 18th was Sunday but it made no difference to us. Tomorrow we have field inspection and yesterday afternoon we did our first drilling in about four weeks. I had to take my squad out and drill it myself. We don't get any bread here only hard tack but plenty of that.

Aug. 20 Sexey-au(x)-Forges, France. Had field inspection today and this afternoon drill. We are getting plenty of open order drill. This evening a battalion of field artillery and a supply or quartermasters corps passed through the town towards the front. They said more were on the way.

Aug. 20. Sexey-au(x)-Forges, France. Last night we were kept awake by aeroplanes overhead. They were fighting and by the sound we think they must have dropped some bombs. Machine guns could be heard and some fellows went out and said they could see the flashes in the air. I was too tired to even get up and look. Am hoping it will be quiet tonight for I need some sleep. Had drill all day. We are getting gas mask drill now. Ray and I went down to the canal tonight and took a bath. A little different from our old shower baths but alright at that. I saw fifteen or twenty aeroplanes today. They are getting old to me.

Aug. 22. Sexey-au(x)-Forges, France. We had drill in the morning as usual. Last night was quiet and we heard no aeroplanes. Saw a Boche plane go over today. Some battery fired on it but did not make any hits. In the afternoon we had a sham battle in the woods and hills near here.

Aug. 23. Sexey-au(x)-Forges, France. We had a pretty hard day today. Plenty of drill in the morning and a sham battle in the afternoon. Otherwise things were the same as usual.

Aug. 24. Sexey-au(x)-Forges, France. We had the regular Saturday inspection of rifles this morning. In the afternoon Ray, Charlie and I went for a walk. We found a plum orchard with lots of blue plums on the ground. Had more than we could eat.

Part 5 Ropage, France. August 25 to September 17, 1918. Ropage is about a mile east of Toul.

Aug. 25 Ropage, France. Last night we got orders to pack and move at once. We left here about eleven o'clock and was on the road all night and half of the next day. I am now with a detail of twenty-five men in an old concrete fort about twelve or fifteen miles from the front. It is called Ropage and was built in 1897 I think. It is part of a system of defense for Toul and the wo(o)ds here are full of concrete and earthworks. We relieved some French soldiers who were there. It was some hike and my feet are sore. This is a pretty place and I hope we stay for a while.

Aug. 26 Ropage, France. Today this has been a sort of picnic. Our rations were a little short and we got some vegetables of the Frenchman in charge of the place. Red went out on a foraging trip and swiped a small bag full of some kind of peas and potatoes. We had a fine stew. About night a cook was sent up and Bundy who was sick and stayed behind came too.

Aug 27 Ropage, France. Most of us went down to where the rest of the platoon is last night and brought up more rations on a cart. This morning some of us went for a walk to a French Y.M.C.A. near here and bought hot chocolate and bars. In the afternoon we went down and got 120 rounds of ammunition per man. At night Ray and I went to the Y.M.C.A. again and saw a French movie. We did not care much for it but can't expect to see much better here. The Y.M.C.A. is for American soldiers too and an American girl is there in charge of that part of it.

Aug. 29. Ropage, France. Not much doing for a couple of days. We received a stove for our kitchens and wood. Last night O'Hare, Ray and I went to the American Aviation Station near here and was in the Y.M.C.A. there. The American had a couple of observation balloons shot down by the Germans within sight of our fort on the 28th but others were put up in place of them at once. We think the American Army is making plans for a big drive in a few days. We expect it about the tenth of next month. Hundreds of guns are going to (the) front through this section.

Aug. 30 Ropage. We had a few minutes drill with bayonet this morning and I wrote a letter to Roxy. Received one from Alice yesterday. Lieut. Richardson and Capt. Tiffany were here and took dinner with us. This afternoon we have been tearing (down) an old wooden barrack in the woods to make a kitchen and mess hall for ourselves. It is some job. We signed the pay roll a couple of days ago and I hope we get the money soon.

Aug. 31. Ropage, France. Have our kitchen about half finished. Last night was pretty noisy around here for the artillery was busy along the front. The Germans got one of our ammunition depots with shell fire and the explosions and flames could be seen nearly all night. One of the mechanics from the Aviation Station was here last night. We hear that the people in Toul have been ordered to move out. This will soon be a lively place I think.

Sept. 1. Ropage, France. I was over to the French Y.M.C.A. last night and found a picture of the drafted boys marching away from Kingston to the train. It was in a French magazine called *Le Miroir*. I was surprised to find it over here. Today was Sunday and our cook treated us to flapjacks and syrup for breakfast. They were great we thought.

Sept. 2. Ropage, France. I was to the French and Aviators Y.M.C.A. both last night. A German plane came over later and the guns kept us awake for a while shooting at it. The sergeant and corporal were away part of the day and I had to drill the men the for a couple of hours. It is some job. Did not go out tonight but wrote a letter instead. It is clear weather so I suppose Fritz will be over to keep us awake tonight.

Sept. 3. Ropage, France. Things were rather quiet last night and we only had a little drill during the day. Had a little practice in taking down and assembling a St. Etienne machine gun.

Sept. 5. Ropage, France. Things were a little quiet for a couple of days. A Hun came over on the 4th at night and the American guns turned loose for a while. One of the Huns got an observation balloon and we saw it go down. A bunch of Marines are in the woods waiting for the big drive on Metz.

Sept. 7. Ropage, France. The Marines are still here. They are the same ones who did so well in the first part of the war and are quite sure they can repeat their other successes. We have to put guards around the place now and I was corporal of the guard last night.

Sept. 8. Ropage, France. All was quiet last night except it rained very hard and is still raining. I stayed in all day and wrote a letter to Everett.

Sept. 13. Ropage, France. There was not much doing for a few days but now the Marines have left for the front and we had some job looking over the place where they camped. It seemed as if they had left half of their equipment behind them. We found everything from rifles to papers of pins. Some of the boys found stuff very useful and a few German souvenirs that the Marines had brought from some other place. The section of front near hear has been very lively for a couple of days now. The drive has started on Metz and the Americans have made an advance of nine kilometres the first day. They captured a bunch of Germans and had only a small loss compared to the Germans. The aeroplanes have been busy too but I don't know what success they had. Just heard the ace Putnam was killed. He had about twenty planes to his credit.

Ropage, France. Sept. 17. We had a couple of clear days for a wonder but today it rained again. An ammunition train stayed in the woods here yesterday as they only travel by night. Some of our aeroplanes have been lost lately and things are rather quiet on this front I guess. We can't seem to get any papers. Austria is asking for peace we hear and all are hoping the war will be over soon. I have received letters from Mother, Roxy and Genevieve. Wrote one to Mother today. I was over to the Aviation Station Sunday night and saw an aeroplanes that was shot full of holes and came in all right. Had supper there with some of the mechanics. They have several Liberty planes there and say they are fine.

Part 6 Toul, France to Fey en Haye, France. September 18 to October 7, 1918

Sept. 18. Toul, France. I went to the Aviation (Station) again last night and saw a plane that had fallen down near there. Have a piece of one wing for a souvenir. When I got back about eight o'clock and found everyone was nearly packed up as we had orders to move at once. Our barrack bags went on a truck but did not start until about ten o'clock. Now we are in Toul in barracks and all of the other companies are here too. I don't know what we are going to do but am certain we won't stay long. This is the replacement camp for the 4th Army Corps and we must be attached to that.

Sept. 20. Toul, France. We have had two days here and I think are going to start away this afternoon. It has been raining most of the time lately. We were given a list of things to keep and the rest was put in our barrack bags and turned over to the Quarter Master. Also we were paid this morning and many of the fellows are drunk already. It has been some fun to watch them for they have been reeling around all over the place. I drew 28½ francs for two months. There is a Red Cross Station near here and I have been there several times and bought hot chocolate and doughnuts.

Sept. 22. Puvenelle Woods or Forêt de Puvenelle. We left Toul about eight o'clock on the 20th and hiked all night until 5 A.M. when we stopped in a small village named Saizerais. Our kitchen was there and our extra equipment. We had breakfast and dinner and at 3 P.M. started out again. Are now in a little wooden barracks in the woods near the front. On the hike at night we were on the wrong road and went up a long hill through a woods. The mud was very deep and a lot of the fellows had to fall out. We only had about one hundred left when we stopped. All are here now except three or four.

Sept. 23. Fey en Haye. It is Sunday today but not much like the Sundays in the States. We got up this morning and had to hide again. My platoon was away from the rest of the Co and by the time we heard anything about breakfast it was all over. I swiped some bread and syrup and ate some of my reserve rations. It is late in the afternoon now and we are in our shelter tents in a woods near the front on ground formerly occupied by the Germans. A truck is here with our kitchen and we will probably get something to eat soon. I am fixing my tent to get a good rest for I think we hike again in the morning or some time tonight.

Sept. 26. Fey en Haye. I have found out what the Pioneers are for. We are a working crew. For the last three days we have been working with pick and shovel on a new road the engineers are putting in to the front. The dirt has to be dug out and the road is filled in with rock brought from a village near here that has been destroyed by artillery fire. We are in range of the German guns all the while and shells often go through the woods we are camped in. And along the road they are quite plenty. We are fast learning how to duck when we hear them whistle. One fell this morning about twenty yards from a group of fellows I was in. And lots of others further away. Our artillery fired a few shots over and all is quiet now. We saw an aerial battle this morning. One of the machines landed a short distance from here and I was told the aviator was wounded. It was a French machine. We have to keep very busy on the job from morning to night. I am writing this noontime as we are not allowed to have any lights at nights on account of Boche planes. Water is scarce. I have not had enough to wash my face or hands for three days. The Red Cross has a station in an old house near camp and some of us go there every night and get hot chocolate and eat hard tack. Rations are not very large here now. It has been clear weather for two days but the ground is still damp and I have caught a bad cold. Well this is war and we do the best we can.

Sept. 28. Fey en Haye. This is my first chance to write anything again. I had a candle burning a while one night and started a letter to Roxy but have not been able to finish it. Mail came yesterday and the day before I got six letters. Two were from home and one was a notice from a bank in Paris that Everett had sent me one hundred and nine francs. I have most of my pay left and no place to spend it. Don't know what I will do with it all. I am sick today and have not been out to work.

Fey en Haye. I was out to work on the road again yesterday. The Germans threw a lot of shells over but as usual they did no damage. The Americans made an attack a couple days ago and a large number of wounded have been brought in over this road. The papers state they have made a big advance near Verdun and captured eight thousand prisoners. Last night's papers said Bulgaria was asking for a separate peace. I am sick again today and am staying in my tent. It is only a bad cold and sore throat but the doctor is treating it and the weather is too cold and windy for me to go out much. I fail to see why this country is called Sunny France.

Oct. 3. Fey en Haye. We are still working on the road and things are the same as before. It is shelled every day as usual. Yesterday fourteen shells came over in about ten minutes and only one exploded. It was lucky the rest did not for some of them fell right where a bunch of the boys were getting out stone in the ruined village today and once this morning got orders to go in dugouts when shelling was a little heavy. Just now we have the same orders and I am sitting in an old trench writing this. A trench is a much pleasanter place than a dug out although it may not be so safe. I mailed a letter to Roxy through the Red Cross a couple days ago but don't know when I will get a chance to write another. We are all glad to hear Bulgaria has surrendered. It brings us a little nearer home we think. Most of us have an idea Turkey will be next. In fact we expect to have Turkey for Thanksgiving.

Oct. 7. Fey en Haye. Yesterday was Sunday and we had the day off. Ray, Charlie and I went to Mamey where there was a Y.M.C.A. and bought cake, chocolate and jam. Last night the Germans threw a few shells pretty close to us an(d) some of the boys spent the most of the night in a trench. I was on gas watch the latter half of the night but the first half my blankets felt to(o) good for me to leave them no matter how many shells came over. I did not know if my tent would stop the shells or not but took a chance and came through alright. Today we got paid and I got one hundred and forty-five francs. I have about three hundred and seventy-five francs on hand besides the money in Paris the folks sent me. We move today and I am nearly all packed up. I don't know where we go.

Part 7 Bois du Four, France to Xivray France. October 10 to about October 21, 1918.

Oct, 10. Bois du Four. We left the place we were in Monday afternoon. I found out that the town we were working in was Fey en Haye. Our Co. is now encamped in another woods in dugouts and iron huts. I think the name of this place is the Bois du Four. Meyr, Adams and myself are in a hut built on the side of a bank of corrugated iron. We are working on another road about a mile from here. There is not much shelling in this place but Boche planes come over every day. We saw a battle between Boche and American planes today and one of the Boche planes came down in flames. It has been rainy here lately but today was clear. We are hearing a lot about the Central Powers asking for peace. Everyone is hoping it is so but we can't seem to get any newspapers here.

Oct. 12. Bois du Four. We are still working on the road and are having nice weather. Mays found a small charcoal burner in a German trench and we got some charcoal and have a little fire nights. Last night we made coffee and had that with hard tack and jam before going to bed. The coffee was so strong we could not sleep good that night. We have not heard much about peace for a couple of days although we got a few newspapers.

Oct. 14. Bois Xivray, France. We moved again Sunday morning. This time we did not hike but had trucks and went about twenty miles I think. We are in another ruined town and are living in old houses and dug outs. Mays, Adams and myself have a very good dugout with bunks and a concrete floor. We had about four hours work cleaning it up before it was fit to live in. Now we have a good stove and have found a Salvation Army near here where they have lots of things to sell. I bought a lot of chocolate and an Ingersoll watch. I have a letter with my Xmas coupon in it ready to send home and must send it today or tomorrow. We hear Germany has agreed to all of the Allies terms and are leaving French territory. Darn good news I call it.

Oct. 15. Xivray, France. This town is Xivray I found out today. Our Captain and Lieutenants Julian and Long were in a railroad accident today. Long was killed and the Captain and Julian were injured. I don't know how bad for they are in some hospital. Lieutenant Matthews is in charge of us now and we all like him very much. Some of the sergeants are leaving to go to officers training school. Both the sergeants of our platoon are gone. They are Saulpaugh and Dickinson. Our food is getting better every day now. We are hearing a lot of rumors about the peace question but have not seen any papers lately. I think the story about the Germans giving up is untrue. We were repairing the road through the town today.

Oct. 18. Xivray, France. We are still working on the road but outside of the town. We all signed the payroll this morning. Some changes have been made in this company and I am a first class private now. Ralph Sparling is in the dugout with us now and all the bunks are filled.

Oct. 20. Xivray, France. It is Sunday today and of course has to rain. Ralph, Ray and I went walking today for about five hours and got pretty wet. We went to a mountain near here called Mount Sec and explored some German dugouts. They are a great piece of work. Some of them go all the way through the mountain. Coming back we were in a thick woods and saw a lot of dug outs and houses built by the German soldiers. Some of the houses were very nice. They were built on a rustic style and in nice shape. We stopped at the Salvation Army and bought chocolate and jam. Had to stand in line to get them. When we got back Mays had a good hot fire and we were able to dry our clothes by it. The stove has been a fine thing for us. Nearly every night we get some stuff and fix up a feed before going to bed. Have found out that even corned willy is good if fixed right. With the things we get at the Salvation Army and manage to beg, borrow or steal elsewhere we get along fine. Mays is the cook and sometimes we eat so much that we can not sleep good at night.

Xivray, France. Started to work this morning and were recalled and told to clean up as we were going to leave next morning. I went down with Mays to Bouconville where the Salvation Army is and I got a brass candle holder in a ruined church there for a souvenir. The church had been shelled but the steeple was still there and we were up in it looking at the bells there. Got back for supper and was told to pack up as we were going to leave that night. We packed and are waiting for the trucks to take us.

Part 8 Forêt de Puvenelle, France. October 12 to November 9, 1918

Oct. 12. Puvenelle Woods or Forêt de Puvenelle. We waited until nine o'clock and our officers told us to go to bed as even if the trucks came we would not leave until morning. Some other fellows had moved into our bunks and we slept on the concrete floor. This morning our cooks and kitchen had gone so we had to feed ourselves. Us four in the dugout made coffee and toasted some bread that we had. Besides we managed to capture a can of jam and that went good with some crackers from the Salvation Army. So we did not go hungry. All our trucks did not come so we loaded our packs and rifles in one truck and started to hike. After a couple of hours the trucks caught us and we rode the rest of the way. Now we are in wooden barracks in the same woods where we stayed at night coming from Toul on Sept. 22nd. There is a Y.M.C.A. about one hundred yards from our barracks.

Oct. 24. Forêt de Puvenelle. We have today off and have been running around. I have been twice to Griscourt. They have a sales commissary there and a Y.M.C.A. There are also a few French people in there. Our Captain and Lieutenant Julian came back today and seem to (be) alright. Also a fellow named Evans who we left in Toul drunk. The last I had seen of him he was staggering around looking for the Fort Lee Ferry.

Forêt de Puvenelle. We had drill for half a day today and got along very (well) considering that we have not had any for over a month. In the afternoon we were taken out to work on a road an hours hike from here. I was surprised to see that the road we were working on was only about a mile from the woods where we camped when working near Fey en Haye. We worked one hour and came back in time for supper. Wrote a letter to Cox & Co. Paris telling them to send me a check for the amount there. Also sent letters to Alice and Al Dresch.

Oct. 26. Forêt de Puvenelle. Worked all day on the road and had our dinner brought out to us. Tomorrow is Sunday and I am expecting to go for a walk and see some of the country.

Oct. 27. Forêt de Puvenelle. Charlie, Ralph, Ray and I went for a walk today as it was a fine day and we wanted to see some of the villages around here. We went to Dieulouard and it is quite a large town. There were a few French soldiers there and a lot of American soldiers were billeted in the empty houses. Also a couple of French stores and some cafes. I bought a flashlight, some ink and flints for my lighter. The other fellows had some beer and we walked around and saw the town. Then we got a ride back on a truck and Ralph and I went to Mamey to get some chocolate of the Y.M.C.A. but it was closed. After supper Ralph, Charlie and I went to Griscourt and found everything closed there. Ray went over to Dieulouard with some other fellows and I suppose will not get back to quite late.

Oct. 28. Forêt de Puvenelle. We had to walk about two hours to get to work this morning. We were collecting rolls of barbed wire that were scattered around the woods this morning and getting out rock for a short piece of road on the 301st Engineers dump. We are working with them now and were at Fey en Haye also. The artillery has been doing a lot of firing for a couple of days now near here. Some of the fellows were in Pont au Mousson this afternoon and evening. They had to go in dugouts for over two hours as the Germans shelled the place and did quite a lot of damage. The papers say Ludendorff has resigned.

Oct. 29. Forêt de Puvenelle. Worked today as usual but not very hard. We are carrying barbed wire up a steep hill for use along the second line (of) defense that the Engineers are building. We just had heavy underwear and socks issued to us also a rolling kitchen and water cart. I was down to the Y.M.C.A. listening to some fellows play the piano and sing tonight. There are reports around that Austria is asking for peace on any terms. That will leave the Huns out of luck alright.

Oct. 30. Forêt de Puvenelle. We worked on the old job today. A Hun plane made a dive from the clouds as we were coming home after the observation balloon near where we worked. He was nearly to it and the two observers had jumped with parachutes when a group of Allied planes came up and he beat it with three planes in chase. They gained on him and I heard he was forced to land some distance away. The observers landed several miles from the balloon. Our Lieutenants Julian and Richardson left for some training school early today.

Oct. 31. Forêt de Puvenelle. We worked on the wire job again today. I am afraid it is too easy to last. I was down to the Y.M.C.A. and played dominoes with Charlie and Ray tonight. The papers say that Austria is asking for peace at once.

Nov. 1. Forêt de Puvenelle. I wanted a chance to go to a couple of towns today so faked sickness and stayed in the barracks until about 11 o'clock. Then Corporal O'Hare being sick too we both went down to Dieulouard and bought some things in the stores there. We got some bread and cheese and ate it in a cafe. Then we got a ride on a truck and went to Belleville where there is a railhead and a sales commissary. There we bought candy, chocolate and smokes. Got a ride back to Dieulouard and went in a church where services were being held for the dead. The church was full of civilians and reminded me of home. We reached the barracks in time for supper and nothing was said to us about being absent. That is one way to get a day off.

Nov. 2. Forêt de Puvenelle. We worked today as usual. The papers say Turkey has surrendered and given over their forts and the Dardanelles to the Allies.

Nov. 3. Forêt de Puvenelle. Today was Sunday and a very nice day. Ray, Charlie, Wiesenberg and I went for a walk after breakfast. First we went to Jezainville and from there to a town that I think is named Mazieres (This may be Maidières, per a French correspondent, as there is no "Mazieres" in this area.). It is a quite a large town and some of the French people have came back there. We bought bread, butter, cake and grapes for dinner. Got a ride to Dieulouard on a Y.M.C.A. Ford and was there a while. Then we went by way of Jezainville back to the barracks. I wrote to the Stars and Stripes and ordered two copies of Yanks. One to be sent to Genevieve and the other to Roxy. We had to get permission to leave today and tell what time we would be back.

Nov. 5. Forêt de Puvenelle. Worked as usual today. I see by the papers that Austria has signed an armistice. The Huns got one of the American observation balloons just as we were going in from work today. We are working on the line of barbed wire near Limey now and it is still a couple of hours walk.

Nov. 7 Forêt de Puvenelle. We have been working near Limey for the past two days. It rained most of the time today but we worked just the same. Fifteen of the men went on leave to Aix-le-Bains today. They will be gone for thirteen days I think and then fifteen more will go.

Nov. 8. Forêt de Puvenelle. I am on guard detail for four o'clock today but had to go out to work just the same. We did very little and came in at one o'clock. I got a haircut and cleaned my rifle for inspection.

Nov. 9. Forêt de Puvenelle. I went on guard detail until four o'clock today. After being relieved at two o'clock in the morning we swiped a can of jam and a loaf of bread from the kitchen and our relief had a little feed. We have a good guardhouse here with a stove in it. We have an extra man on each relief and he keeps the fire going while the rest are on guard. Cornwell of Kingston was the extra on this relief. We heard last night that an armistice had been signed by Germany but last night the artillery fired more than any other night. The sky was lit by the flashes all the time. I saw by the paper today that German envoys were on the way to France to get Gen. Foch's terms for an armistice. After coming off guard we went to the gas chamber for a gas test. It was not bad although mustard gas was used but it must have been weak.

Part 9 somewhere near Thiaucourt, France to Trieux, France. November 12 to November 21, 1918

Nov. 12. Bois du Four. Near Thiaucourt. We are still in the woods and have moved in a larger tent. Last night I saw my first auto trucks with lights turned on since coming in this section of the country. Most of the cars dont even have the lights in shape to use. We expect to stay here for a couple of weeks.

Nov. 13. Near Thiaucourt. Last night was the coldest I have seen over here and we slept cold all night. I worked on a dirt road most of the day and for a couple hours on a plank road that the Engineers are building in along a railroad. The papers say the Kaiser has gone to Holland. Guess he is out of luck alright.

Nov. 14. Near Thiaucourt. I did not go out to work this morning. Charlie, Ray and I are repairing a dug out for us to live in. My platoon drilled this morning and worked this afternoon. We hear that they are going over on German territory for a while. I have seen plenty of troops and guns returning from the front. Just received some papers and magazines from Genevieve today, also a check from Cox & Co., Paris.

Nov. 15. Near Thiaucourt. We slept better in our new dug out last night. We have a stove in it and made a little extra supper before turning in. French fried potatoes, corned beef with onions, bread and coffee. I worked in the forenoon on a road and drilled in the afternoon.

Nov. 17. Susacourt. (Possibly "Suzémont".) We worked for half a day on the road and then were paid. I got 143½ francs. Right after that we rolled our packs and moved. We had to carry our full equipment in our packs. Hiked through Thiaucourt and Xammes. We slept on the ground in a field near Xammes that night. Charlie, Ray and I walked back to Thiaucourt that night and went to a Salvation Army station but could not buy anything. We were called out three o'clock next morning and had to wait until nine o'clock to start. A line of troops and wagons went up all morning and I hear we are going to follow the Germans out of Alsace Lorraine. We hiked to Chambley where I fell out to fix my shoe and got on the wrong road. Had to hike back for several kilometres and a bunch of other fellows from the 51st also. Some of them stayed in Xonville and some more in Sponville but I managed to hike here to Susacourt where the Company is. I have a bed sack full of straw to sleep on and a stove in the next room. And with some batteries, wire and a bulb we found here a fellow fixed an electric light for us. These villages were held by the Germans for four years and are in good shape. All the street names are German but there are no people to be seen anywhere.

Nov. 18. Thuneeville (Thumeréville). We started at 7 A.M. and hiked through Porcher, Brainville, Puxe and Jeandelize to Thuneeville where we are now. Reached here about noon and have had our feet inspected by the doctor. A large number of the boys have sore feet. Some of them fell out and are behind yet. The Germans left here only three days ago and the fellows are out collecting souvenirs. Some have found spiked helmets. We saw a bunch of Russian, Italian and English prisoners that the Germans had turned loose a few days ago.

Nov. 19. Thuneeville (Thumeréville). We have sheet iron barracks here with bunks made of poles and wire. Our rations gave out and the mess sergeant got some from another company. Also a few of us fellows went out and found some cabbage and beets. We were all marched to a brook today and had to wash our feet. I was to a woods near by and saw a prison camp. The Germans had made the prisoners cut down trees and burn for charcoal. One kiln was still burning. The huts or barracks where they lived were rather poor places I think.

Nov. 20. Thuneeville (Thumeréville). I was out to a large farm house today where Germans had been billeted. The(y) had built comfortable rooms in the barns for themselves. Also a bunch of small barracks. I got some buttons for souvenirs. Was over to Mouaville and some of H.Q. and M Co. boys. They all think we are going home soon. We leave here tomorrow I think. Two of our blankets are going to be carried for us on a wagon. That will make our packs a little lighter.

Nov. 21. Treiux (Trieux). We started this morning about eight o'clock. Hiked through Mouaville, Fleville, Lixieres and Anoux. The Germans had used most of the large buildings there for a base hospital. We had dinner at Mancieulles. Reached Trieux about four o'clock and are billeted here for the night. The whole company is in one row of nice deserted houses. We have a stove where I am and a carbide lamp. There are not many people in these towns but they are all glad to see us and have put up the United States and French flags and other decorations. Our Regimental band played a while tonight. We are the first American troops in this section of the country. There is a prison camp here and a few Russian prisoners were left by the Germans. They are using what was once a theater for a barracks. We are only a few miles from the German border.

Part 10 Woldereninger to Wormadange, Luxembourg. November 22 to December 2, 1918.

Nov. 22. Woldereninger. The fellows on furlough came in at Trieux last night. They reported a fine time. We left there about 8 A.M. and at 8:15 we crossed the German border. I am sleeping in the hall of a deserted hotel on the floor with Sparling. The names of the towns we passed through today were too long for me to remember. But I noticed that there were quite a number of people in them and some of the stores seemed to have plenty of things for sale.

Nov. 23. Aspelt, Luxembourg. We hiked to about two o'clock today and I am billeted with a lot of other fellows in a barn in a town named Aspelt. We have plenty of straw for a bed. Mays and I are bunking together. We are in the Grand Duchy of Luxembourg and the people seem very nice. There are plenty of cafes here and a small store. We can buy candy but it is very expensive.

Nov. 24. Aspelt, Luxembourg. We are still in Aspelt and I don't know when we move again. I was on a detail with some other fellows to wash and grease the wagons today. It was not a very nice job for the weather is cold and we had to use cold water.

Nov. 25. Aspelt, Luxembourg. Still in Aspelt and would like to get out. It has rained here all day and we have no place to go and nothing to do. We can't go in the cafes and it is cold in the barn. They have put guards on all the cafes and I am on guard detail for tonight. We are going to drill a couple hours each day.

Nov. 26. Aspelt, Luxembourg. I was on guard last night and my post was the supplies. Had plenty to eat while there and when I came off post at 2 A.M. I took a loaf of bread, two cans of jam, two cans of mock turtle soup, one can of Welsh rarebit, candles and matches with me. Might as well take enough to last a while. Was off guard detail at one o'clock and went to help Sparling shoe horses. We are shoeing all the horses for the 2nd battalion in a blacksmith shop in this village. The tools are very poor but we manage to do a little work.

Aspelt, Luxembourg. I have worked all day in the shop. It rained all day and the Company had to drill for a while just the same. I had to use old nails and it was hard work but better than drilling out in the mud.

Nov. 28. Aspelt, Luxembourg. It is Thanksgiving Day and I have not been working. Have been writing letters part of the day. We can write now where we are and what we are doing. Also wherever we have been since coming over. The Company had a goose dinner today. Ten geese was all (that) could be bought and it hardly gave us each a taste.

Nov. 29. Aspelt, Luxembourg. Last night Mays and I went through the rain to Mondorf les Bains. It was about three or four kilometres away. We were in a few stores but could not get anything we wanted until we came to a small restaurant. There we got consommé and hot waffles. The waffles were good but I did not like the consommé. Worked in the shop again today but not very hard.

Nov. 30. Aspelt, Luxembourg. Last night some of us went to a farmhouse and had our supper. It was not a fancy meal but plain good food and plenty of it. It cost us each five francs and they had fifteen or twenty fellows there tonight. Today the Company hiked down to Modorf les Bains and took a bath in the sulphur baths there. Sparling and I were not able to go as we had to work all day.

Dec. 1. Aspelt, Luxembourg. Adams and I took a walk to a small town near here named Frisance this morning. Nothing there except a battalion of M.P.s. I was detailed in the kitchen for this afternoon because of a slip I made in the manual of arms. Was excused noon time. I went to the Captain and asked for permission for Sparling and I to go to Mondorf for a bath. He said he was not allowed to let any of his men go out of town but he would not watch us to see that we did not go. We went down and bathed in the sulphur swimming pool. Afterward we visited some of the stores. I had to pay six francs for a piece of cloth for a towel. We came back and went to the farm house for supper. Their bread is made of whole wheat I think but is fairly good. They have no coffee but make a drink of roasted grain. It is very good with milk and sugar.

Dec. 2. Wormadange, Lux. Sparling and I started to shoe a horse in the shop this morning and were stopped by the Major as he said the man was charging five dollars a day for the shop and that was too much. We found a few old tools and put one shoe on before dinner. Started to shoe the horses on our kitchen and orders came to move. We started about two o'clock and hiked to eight o'clock that night. Part of the way along the Moselle River. Seven of us are billeted in a house in a large town named Wormadange. The people here are very nice and as our kitchen was not here yet we asked the woman if she could get us a supper. We had the best feed I have had since leaving the States for five francs and I am going to sleep in a room by a fire. Hope we can stay here a few days.

Part 11 Conz, Germany to Wengerohr, Germany. December 3 to December 14, 1918.

Dec. 3. Conz, Germany. I had a good sleep last night and bought a cup of warm milk before starting out. We left about 8:30 with the band playing and the colors flying. This is the first I have marched behind our regimental flag. Passed through Ahm and another small town on the left bank of the Moselle. Both sides of the valley are covered with vineyards and a railroad follows the river on the German side. We saw a train of U.S. freight cars going in the same direction we were. Also a couple of trains coming back filled with French soldiers. They were prisoners of war going home I guess. Crossed the river into Germany a few minutes after eleven at Grevenmacher and fell out near Oberbilling for dinner. Hiked through Wasserleich and Reinig to Conz where we are going to spent the night. Adams and I are billeted in a house with a German family. I don't know if we get a bed or not but think we do. I talked to an old man tonight who had spent a few years in England. He told me Conz had a population of about four thousand. There is a railroad station and yard here.

Dec. 4. Fohren, Germany. The German man came in last night and insisted on giving lots of wine. By signs and the few words we knew of each other's language we talked until after ten o'clock. Then we had a good night's sleep in a real feather bed and left about eight o'clock this morning. Hiked through Trier and Ehrang besides a couple of small villages. Trier is quite a large city. It has large stores that seemed to have a good stock and a trolley system. Women were running some of the cars. It rained a little all day and we were all tired out when we came to Fohren where we are now. I am bunking with Mays in a room in a deserted house. We have plenty of straw and I am tired enough to sleep good.

Dec. 5. Fohren, Germany. I did not sleep last night. I died and the bugle brought me to life again this morning. We stayed here all day but probably will move tomorrow. I have been sitting around and wrote a few postals. Am to(o) stiff to walk around and there is nothing to see in this village. I bought candles as they are cheaper than in Luxembourg.

Dec. 6. Wengerohr, Germany. Left Fohren about eight o'clock and hiked through several small villages and one small city named Wittlich. That is quite a nice place and Headquarters with Co E were left there. We are about four kilometres from there in a small village named Wengerohr. We are going to do guard duty on the railroad. I am billeted with Mays and McLoughlin in with a nice family. Mays and I bought supper in the next house for four francs each. It was very good. The man in the house brought us in some wine tonight. We have a nice room with a stove, table and electric lights. I don't know how long we stay here but expect a week at least.

Dec. 7. Wengerohr, Germany. I was on K.P. today and did not work very hard. The company is doing guard duty on the railroad here. Some of the posts are a long distance away and the fellows were on post a long time before being relieved today. Some who went on at seven o'clock last night did not get relieved until nine or ten o'clock this morning. The owner of this house brought in lots of straw for us to sleep on. It does not look nice in the room but we will sleep better. Mail was brought in today and I got quite a bunch.

Dec. 8. Wengerohr. I did not do much today except sit around. Maria the little girl here is teaching us German words and we are teaching her English. I was on patrol duty on the railroad from four until ten P.M. We walk to a tunnel stay there two hours and then come back. The men are getting leather jackets and shoes now. I got shoes but had to give them back as they were too small. The patrol duty is not bad. While at the tunnel we stay in a shanty and talk to the German watchman.

Dec. 9. Wengerohr. I stayed around the house most of the day and talked to Maria. Went on patrol duty at six P.M. One other man and (I) went to the shanty on further side of tunnel. He laid down in the floor and I on a bench. Two hours later our relief woke us up. We went back and stopped at the kitchen where we got some stew and coffee. This patrol is some soft job. The man's name where I am billeted is Jacob Arth.

Dec. 10. Wengerohr. Mays and I took a chance and went to Wittlich this morning. Our captain had said we could not get in without a pass but no one stopped us. We each bought a ring and some flashlight batteries. At the Y.M.C.A. we got chocolate and tobacco. I did not do anything in the afternoon and I go (on) guard from one A.M. to 7 A.M.

Dec. 11. Wengerohr. Went on guard and was not relieved until 8:30 A.M. I slept about an hour this morning and then ate a bunch of hot waffles. The sergeants say we may move any time now.

Dec. 12. Wengerohr. Went on guard from six to twelve this morning. Mays and I went to Wittlich this afternoon. The Captain said today that we would leave tomorrow at eight o'clock but tonight he changed the order. I don't know when we go now but part of the track guard has been over by some other troops.

Dec. 13. Wengerohr. Did not go on guard on guard today but was around the station for a while. The Germans are sending numbers of locomotives down the line. At night Mays, McLoughlin and I went to Wittlich for a couple of hours. The officers are not taking any mail here now.

Dec. 14. Wengerohr. I did not do anything during the day but at night Dooley, Adams and I went above the station where some U.S. cars were loaded with rations. We managed to get away with some bread and salmon. Gave some of it to Orth tonight.

Dec. 15. Wengerohr. I was supposed to go on guard on the railroad at two A.M. but the corporal said stay in bed and we went out at five thirty. We made a mistake and went on the wrong tracks but it made no difference anyway. In the forenoon I and Adams went for a walk to a small village where an old German showed us through the electric lighting plant and a grist mill. In the afternoon some other fellows and I went over again and looked the mill over. Today the sun shone and the weather was nice for the first time since we left Aspelt.

Dec. 16. Wengerohr. We had inspection of equipment today and received orders to be ready to leave at eight o'clock tomorrow. An areophane made a bad landing near here a couple days ago and was wrecked. We have had to put a guard on it ever since.

Part 12 Aldgund, Germany to Treis, Germany. December 17 to December 26, 1918.

Dec. 17. Aldgund. We left Wengerohr eight o'clock and hiked until four thirty. We are now in a small village along the Moselle named Aldgund. Coming here we walked on the railroad for about seven kilometres and the rest of the way on the road along the Moselle. Eight or nine of us are in some kind of a public building. We have straw to sleep on, electric lights and a stove. We got a boy to bring us some wood for which we gave him a pack of Bull Durham some soap, and bread. Soap and tobacco are better than money in Germany now. He brought two bottles of wine for us later. It has rained nearly all day.

Dec 18. Sehl. We left this morning at eight o'clock. It has rained all day but we did not get bad wet. Part of the hike was over a mountain. It was about (?) kilometres shorter that way than over the road but was a hard climb and very cold on top. We are now in Sehl about one kilometre from Cochem. I was in Cochem tonight and bought a cameo pin for sixty marks. We bought some food where we are billeted and was charged five marks a piece for it. It was only a little and we all think the woman over charged us for it. But this is the first time we were over charged on our trip for eats.

Dec. 19. Treis. We hiked from Sehl to Treis this forenoon and I am billeted with a lot of other fellows in a large building that I think is a dance hall. It is not a very large town but the whole second battalion is to be billeted here. There are no lights in the dance hall but we have a stove and plenty of straw. I am getting so used to sleeping on a pile of straw that I won't be able to sleep on a real bed when I get home. We are still in the Moselle Valley. There is a pontoon bridge here in charge of some engineers.

Dec. 20. Treis. We spent the day cleaning ourselves and equipment. Stood retreat tonight and we are going to drill every day while here. Lieutenant Richardson came back today. Julian and Matthews are in Coblenz I hear. Adams and nine other men were sent to Cochem today on a detail. It is some kind of carpenter work and we hear they are going to make overseas boxes. I hope it is true.

Dec. 21. Treis. We had inspection of quarters and equipment today and did not drill. My Christmas package came with some other mail today. The captain said the building was too small for the hundred men who were in there and he was right. Now a lot of the men have hired rooms of the people and we have more room in here.

Dec. 22. Treis. Today is Sunday and we did not drill. We have been issued steel helmets in place of the ones we threw away on the hike. I was to church in the morning. Chaplain White was there and he told us he had heard Gen. Pershing say he was going to send us home by way of the Rhine. Spent the afternoon writing letters and reading.

Dec. 23. Treis, We drilled on the road in the town today and as it rained we were given the afternoon off. I got mail from home and some papers. The papers were all pretty old but are interesting for me.

Dec. 24. Treis. We drilled five hours today and also got paid. I had 164 francs, my first pay as first class private. Tomorrow is Christmas Day and I don't think we drill.

Dec. 25. Treis. Last night a bunch of the boys got drunk and this building was pretty lively until twelve o'clock. Today I have been sitting and writing most of the time. Last night it snowed for a while and the ground was not fit to go for a walk. This is a Devil of a place to spend Christmas. We hear a lot about going home but I don't know how much of it is true.

Dec. 26 Treis. We drilled for half a day and this afternoon Mays and I went for a walk on some of the hills near here. The sergeant came in tonight and gave orders for us to be ready to leave at eight o'clock tomorrow morning.

Part 13 Lehmen, Germany to Guls, Germany. December 27, 1918 to April 7, 1919.

Dec 27. Lehmen. We left Treis this morning and hiked to this place. The name of it is Lehman. Had very muddy and rough roads. We wore our helmets and had to carry on shoulder and walk at attention going through towns. I am billeted in some kind of a meeting hall. There are about twenty of us and we have a stove and electric lights. I think we leave in the morning.

Dec 28. Guls. I am in Guls now. It is quite a large town only four kilometers from Coblenz. We are all billed in houses where we can have beds. Charlie Held and I are together. We have a nice room and the people treat us fine. There are three girls here I think. I(t) looks as if we had struck luck at last.

Dec. 29. Guls. It is Sunday and I have been looking the place over. I had dinner with the people where I am billeted and tonight we played games with one of the sisters and another girl. There is a small ferry here to cross the Moselle and some kind of an amusement place over there. We are not allowed to go over. There are lots of pretty girls in this place and the boys are right after them.

Dec. 30. Guls. We had orders to clean our equipment today. I took some stuff to the river and washed it. Also my feet. Orders have been issued against talking to the civilians in public and guards placed on some of the saloons. I bought an Iron Cross of a German for twenty marks tonight. Don't know if I got stuck or not. The guards say most of our officers were drunk last night. Had a good time at the house with the girls again last night and tonight.

Dec. 31. Guls. I drilled this morning for three hours and in the afternoon was put on guard. My post is a hotel along the river front and I have orders to allow only officers to go in it. Most of the other hotels are open to the men for six hours a day but two of them are reserved for officers.

Jan. 1. Guls. Was on guard until four o'clock and it was not bad. I did not have any guarding from 8 P.M. until 6 P.M. The rest of the Company have a holiday today and we have ours tomorrow. Held was drinking pretty much last night and does not feel well tonight. Mays was here to the house a couple hours trying his German on the girls.

Jan. 2. Guls. I had today off and Dooley and I went down to Metternich about three kilometers away from here. We heard there was a commissary there but was told by a guard that there was not. Also he told us there were M.P.s in town and we must be careful. We came back and in the afternoon I stayed around the house and wrote a letter and folled with the girls. Have heard since that the guard lied to us and I am going down again.

Jan. 4. Guls. Had drill all day yesterday and today the officers were around inspecting our quarters. I was to the dentist in the forenoon and had a tooth filled. It is very seldom we have a dentist around in the army. We have had some new clothes issued to us and I need shoes yet. I stayed in the house during the afternoon and had a good time.

Jan. 5. Guls. It was Sunday today and I did nothing but sit around and try to talk German most of the time. Chaplain White held services in a room we us(e) for recreation and I went there in the afternoon. Was over there and wrote a letter to Ralph tonight. Then went to bed early.

Jan. 9. Guls. Have been drilling as usual lately. We have been having some good times at the house nights and plenty of wine to drink. In fact too much of it. One of the corporals was on guard today and I had to take charge of a squad for drilling. This morning we were paid and I got 163 francs.

Jan. 10. Guls. We drilled this morning and in the afternoon the whole Company had a hot shower bath. We needed it I guess. Lena has gone away and we miss her very much. I see the officers are wearing the insignia of the Fourth Army Corps on their shoulders and hear we get them too. They look very nice.

Jan 12. Guls. We had inspection as usual yesterday morning and in the afternoon I went on guard detail. Was on until Sunday afternoon and have tomorrow off instead of today.

13 Jan. Guls. I wrote a while this morning and cleaned some clothes. In the afternoon the whole Company had another bath. Men are to be picked from the Battalion for M.P. duty in this place instead of guards.

Jan 14. Guls. We drilled all day. The M.P.s have been appointed and we are going to get gas masks in place of the ones we heaved on our trip. A Y.M.C.A. man has taken over our recreation hall and we have the latest papers and more magazines to read. He is going to have candy and smokes for sale there soon. Some of the men are building a shooting range. It looks as if we were going to stay a while.

Jan. 15. Guls. This morning those of us who want to go to night school in Coblenz made out applications and we did not drill. I(n) the afternoon all the men in the Company were given a short physical examination by the doctors. One of them said we were going home soon. I hope he is right. I am going to take a mechanical course in school if I can. Besides it will give me a chance to see Coblenz.

Jan. 16. Guls. Had drill as usual this morning and in the afternoon the band came in town and played a couple of hours for us. Some of the fellows sang. It sure sounded good especially when they played *Take Me Back to New York Town*.

Jan. 17. Guls. We drilled this morning but it is our day for using the bathhouse and in the afternoon we had time for that. The Y.M.C.A. has a small library for the boys and I am reading Heart of the Sunset by Rex Beach. We are having candy issued to us now in half pound boxes. It is very good.

Jan. 18. Guls. As it was Saturday we had the usual inspection in the morning and the afternoon off. I have been reading and writing in the Y.M.C.A. and tonight we had a lecture by an American officer from Turkey.

Jan. 19. Guls. Sunday and I was out for a walk over the hills with Mays. Had a laugh at his expense for he got caught on a barbed wire fence and tore his trousers getting loose.

Jan. 20. Guls. Drilled today as usual. We are getting practice in aiming now. Was given a pass to Coblenz for school. It is good for five hours a night for five nights a week. I went to Coblenz and could not find the school. Did not look for it very long but walked around the city. Another fellow and I bought some ice cream but it was not much good. The cream seemed to be missing.

Jan. 21. Guls. We drilled during the day and I went to school at night. I am taking a course in algebra and have an hour in school each night. Our teacher is an officer and seems very nice. The Army has taken over several large school buildings and we have plenty of room. There is a large Y.M.C.A. there and I got my French money order cashed.

Jan. 23. Guls. Was to school last night. I did not go back to Guls as soon as it was over. Went to the Y.M.(C.A.) instead and watched the masquerade they were having for the soldiers. Tonight I went to Coblenz before supper. Got a shave in a German barber shop and then bought a couple hand bags for Roxy and Vera. They cost 160 marks and while in the Y.M.C.A. after school I lost them. McLoughlin and I went to a restaurant for American soldiers and had a late supper. It was very good and cost four marks.

Jan. 24. Guls. I am on guard detail for tonight and am a supernumerary. I have to guard prisoners and don't have much to do. This morning we had a bath and were issued gas masks instead of those we heaved on our hike. Mine is too small for me but all I want it for is a souvenir and it will do for that.

Jan. 26. Guls. I came off guard Saturday at 1:30 P.M. and went to an amateur minstrel show given by some men from our battalion. It was very good and I enjoyed it as much as I have enjoyed better ones at home. Did not do so much Sunday except take a walk to a small town near here that I forgot the name of. Also put in my name for a pass to Coblenz tomorrow but don't know if I will get it as I have a pass for school in that place.

Jan. 27. Guls. Got the pass alright and spent the day in Coblenz. Fifty men from each company got a pass. When we reached Coblenz each man received a ticket for dinner and supper at the Union Restaurant. Mays and I were together and we kept on a move all the time. I bought two more handbags costing 181 marks and some other things. At night we went to a show at the Y.M.C.A. Today was my 25th birthday and it was the ex-Kaiser's birthday too. But I believe I enjoyed myself today more than he did.

Jan. 29. Guls. We have been on some new schedule of drilling this week. It is mostly new skirmish formations. The Y.M.C.A. had a show here last night but I was in Coblenz and did not see it. But this afternoon we were dismissed early so we could go to a show from headquarters. I did not think it was as good as the other one I saw.

Jan. 31. Guls. Went to school last night as usual but today was on K.P. I did not work very hard. When I got through at night it was too late to go to school. There was to be a show of some kind here tonight but it was so cold in the theater they did not have it.

Feb 1. Guls. We had inspection this morning and the afternoon I spent reading and writing. They had a lecture for us tonight but I did not attend it. I hear orders have been issued that we are not to buy anything in German stores.

Feb. 4. Guls. I did not do much except read Sunday, and Monday night was on kitchen guard so I have today off. Have been sitting around in the saloon reading. The Company is on the shooting range today. I would like to shoot but will wait until some other time. A lot of fellows have the influenza and have been sent to the hospital. We are not allowed to go to school and the Y.M.C.A. is closed.

Feb. 5. Guls. We had a sort of sham battle in the hills today and in the afternoon I was on a detail to wash wagons for the Company as they are to be painted soon. There were six of us and it did not take long. But it was a poor job this weather.

Feb. 6. Guls. We had about an inch of snow fall last night and it looked a little like winter this morning. I was on detail to take horses to Coblenz and give them an antiseptic bath. It was about five miles and I rode there and back on an old horse without a saddle. Tonight I am so sore I can hardly sit down.

Feb. 15. Guls. I was on guard last week on Friday and Saturday. One day we all went to Coblenz to see the football game between the Fourth Corps and the Fourth Division. The Division team won by the score of 3 to 0. Friday night Mays, Adams and I went to Metternich to see the Hagenbeck circus. It was very good but small.

March 1. Guls. Have been too lazy to write lately. We can get passes to Coblenz quite often now and if a person wants to take a chance he can easy get in without a pass. I was in one night that way. We are not drilling as hard as usual and I hear that next week we only drill in the morning. Three new sergeants are in the company and two of them are from Kingston. We will be allowed to go to school again in a few days I think. The weather is getting warm and it seems like spring.

March 26. Guls. Had another streak of laziness and have written nothing lately. We have been drilling as usual and I have had several passes to Coblenz besides going in nights without a pass. Had a seven days leave in Aix-les-Bains which I enjoyed very much. Today I was inoculated and suppose I will be sick tomorrow. A(n) auto just went off the bank on the other side of the river and the driver was drowned.

March 29. Guls. I had a surprise a couple days ago. Five men were made corporals and I was one of them. I was off from drill for one day on account of the inoculation and yesterday all the non-coms had an examination. I don't know if I passed or not. Today is Saturday but we did not have the usual inspection as there is a horse show near here and anyone is allowed to go. I have to go on guard detail this afternoon. Got letters from home lately that the folks are moving again. Brooks says the place they are going to is very nice and I hope he is right.

Apr. 3. Guls. I went on guard Saturday and had charge of the supernumeraries. Was on to Sunday after noon. Monday we all had to take our clothes and equipment to the Madhouse Hall for it all had to be inspected and checked up by the Major. I had charge of the overalls and it was some job. Everything was given back Tuesday but half the men did not get their own stuff. Yesterday forty men of the battalion were sent for a trip up the Rhine. I was one of them and enjoyed it although the weather was a little cold.

Apr. 6. Guls. Friday the whole Company went up in the hills to work on a new shooting range. We have to dig a deep trench in the side of the hill and it will take some time. I am leaving here for school in Brohl Monday and will be gone for three months. Saturday I was with a squad in the kitchen. The mess sergeant said the men came late and I had to have them all there again this morning but only for a few minutes. We were all paid today. I drew 174 francs as the rate of exchange is different than before.

Part 14 Brohl, Germany. April 8 to May 15, 1919.

April 8. Brohl Germany. Six of us from Co. F. left Guls Monday morning and had to spend about four hours in Coblenz. Reached Brohl about five o'clock and were put in barracks with a bunch of other fellows who just arrived. The barracks are only about half finished and this morning most of us had to move for the officers formed us into platoons and we had to have each platoon together. I am in the fourth platoon and have the second squad. Was to the Y.M.C.A. last night and today and had hot chocolate with cake. The engineers are still working on the barracks and it will be some time before we have everything arranged.

Apr. 12. Brohl. The school has started and we are having two hours lectures in morning and three hours practical work in the afternoon. I think it will be alright. The platoons were changed around a couple days ago and by a mistake I was listed as private. It is just a(s) well for I don't have to worry about a squad. This morning we had inspection of equipment and barracks and now have the rest of the time to ourselves until Monday morning.

Apr. 13. Brohl. Was for a walk to Andermach yesterday afternoon. It is a pretty nice place and O'Donnel and I found a Y.M.C.A. with ice cream and pie for sale. We came back on the train. This morning I was on a detail for a couple hours to get rations and to a movie in the afternoon. Some of the boys were back to the Company on pass and say they are working very hard and expect to move in some other town very soon. I (am) glad I am here now.

Apr. 25. Brohl. We have been getting a couple motors to work on besides the German trucks. One is a Cole Eight and the other is a Dodge. They are set up in one of the buildings and the section I am in has been working on them for a few days. They were taken down and we have them put together again. We have to put guards on the German trucks nights and I was on for one hour. Also during the rainy weather the Rhine rose so high a guard had to watch nights to see that it did not get high enough to do any damage. Have been to several shows nights lately and was down to Andernach Saturday afternoon. Sunday was Easter but we did not have any eggs. Instead they gave us plenty of ice cream and candy. The School has a baseball team and played their first game today with C. Co. 301 Engineers. The score was 34 to 8 in favor of the school.

May 1. Brohl. It has been raining a lot lately and we have a couple stoves in the barracks. Last Saturday Ingram and I went to the Third Army Carnival at Coblenz. It was good but we got disgusted because a lieutenant put us on detail for a few minutes and we left early. It seems Pioneers have to work everywhere. Today we were issued new clothing that we needed and I got a oat and trousers. They will have to made over before I can wear them. Hear a lot of stuff about going home but suppose it is same as usual.

May 6. Brohl. Tried to get a pass to Guls after inspection Saturday but did not succeed. Took a walk down to Anzig in the afternoon but only stayed a few minutes. It is quite a large town and has an American aerodrome and airplanes in it. Sunday was up to Andernach for a while. Tuesday we were paid in marks instead of francs. I drew 451 marks. We had to be very particular arranging our barracks as a General and the men who have charge of the education system came to inspect us and make a couple speeches. We all watching the papers close to see what the Germans say about the peace terms. Probably they will protest as usual and then sign. Just got a letter from home saying the paper announced the 51st Pioneers would leave Germany the last of April. We seem to be here yet however. The new Y.M.C.A. theater was opened last night for the first time and there was a good show. We have a show of some kind every night mostly movies.

May 15. Brohl. Tried to get a pass to Guls last Saturday but was out of luck. Was down to Andernach on Saturday on also Sunday night. Oppenheim was down to the Company Sunday and brought us word that the 2nd Battalion had left for Wengerohr. They have some work to do and we got orders to leave tomorrow morning at nine o'clock. We go on truck. The Engineers are getting ready to move and we had to put the trucks back together quick. They expect to go home and we hope to be not far behind them.

(page missing here?) ... and have been loafing around most of the time. I hear that we work again tomorrow. There is a report around that troops have been stopped from going home until the Germans sign peace. I don't know how much truth is in it.

Part 15 Trier, Germany to St. Naizare, France. May 25 to June 19, 1919.

May 25. Trier. We worked on the Remount up to the 23rd. That after noon orders came in to move next morning at nine o'clock. However the train was not ready until about two o'clock and we had to hang around to that time. Now we are in barracks at Trier getting rid of some of our equipment. The whole Regiment is in here I think and we will probably leave tomorrow morning. I hear our next stop is Le Mans and I suppose we will go to Brest from there. These German barracks are fine and the non-coms all have good rooms. I am in with Wienekski. Was sick all last night and have been to the doctor this morning. I guess there is no doubt we are going home now.

May 30. Malicorne France. Was to the doctor again and he first suggested the hospital but as I objected he let me off. Was very sick most of the day but was able to leave with the Company when it went to the train later that afternoon. We slept on the train that night but did not leave until the next morning at eight o'clock. We had box cars with forty men to a car. Our bed sacks were filled with excelsior but at night we were packed in like sardines. Wednesday the 28th we landed in this place. It is named Malicorne and is near Le Mans. Most of us are billeted in ga___ etm_ around here and have been kept busy with inspections. Also we have turned quite a lot of stuff in and are (our) packs are much lighter. I think we leave for port in a couple of days.

June 3. Malicorne France. Have had several inspections lately. The last one, yesterday, was by a captain from the embarkation center and I believe it was the final one. We all hope so any how. Two men from this platoon were just made sergeants. I don't think we will leave for Brest until the first of next week. Until then we will drill. Two hours in the morning and two in the afternoon. Lieut. Fields is drilling this platoon and he sure makes it snappy. There is a rumor around that we may parade in Albany when we get in the States. Most of the boys seem against it.

June 7. Malicorne. Have been drilling as usual and this morning the Regiment was assembled while our collars were decorated. We have all been given a service bar with one star on it. According to latest reports we are going to St Naizare either the 10th or 11th and will sail at once.

June 9, 1919. Malicorne France. Sunday forenoon we were all inspected for cooties by a couple of officers from Le Mans. One man in our company was found to have them. Today we were taken for a short hike during hours in the morning. At night we had regimental retreat for the first time. Afterwards our picture was taken.

June 15. Montargu France. We left Malicorne Friday the 13th in the afternoon. Hiked to Nazair. Our packs were carried on auto trucks. About 6:30 that evening we left Nazair in the usual box cars and arrived here early next morning. We are billeted in _l__ans and attics and are having plenty of inspections. Last night we had equipment inspection after ____ a l____ and were _as__ ___ ___ anything we needed now (new?). Have had cootie inspection twice. Were paid late last night after inspection and I drew 218.00 francs. As g____al a f_____sgh of fellows we d____ again. Today __ ____ ___ we have not had much to do but I think tomorrow will be a busy day. We will probably stay here about a week.

June 19. St. Naizare France. Had a little excitement Sunday night. Some soldiers and Frenchmen had a fight and the whole battalion was (confined to?) the (streets in their billets?). I heard the ____ was coming so Mays and I went for a walk along the river. When we came back a few hours later we came near getting in trouble over but everyone was allowed to go out again. Had usual drill and bathing for two days and then left Wednesday.

COMPANY G

The following is from the diary kept by CORP Harold Fuller of Company G. His diary and several papers are located at the USAHEC. The diary has been transrribed and condensed by the author. His diary does mention Company G getting gassed.

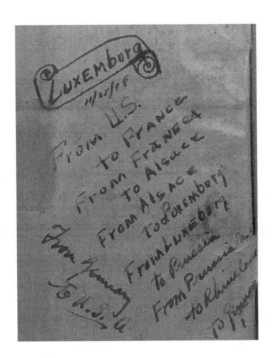

4 July 1918. Spent morning cleaning up. Went to Spartansburg. I didn't care a hell of a lot for this town.

5 July 1918. Went to rifle range all day. Took all day to shoot 30 shots. Came back and took bath. Feel fine. Buns mess.

6 July 1918. General inspection again. Drilled some more. Received mail from Otis and Mother.

7 July 1918. Washed clothes again in P.M. Joe D. hurt his hand at rifle range. Co. divided into Platoons. Some more new men just arrived.

8 July 1918. Took Exams for Corp. Drilled the rest of the day.

9 July 1918. Put on a real job in the canteen. Just the life for me. Went to work at 8 and held no R and R.

10 July 1918. Laid in bed while the rest of the students stood R. Got up at 7:30 went to mess and then to canteen. One hell of a business believe me. Ice Cream and candy galore.

11 July 1918. Day off. You know every other day off for [Filluon?] this job.

12 July 1918. S.o.S. [possibly Same Old Song, or Same Old Sh*t]

13 July 1918. Unlucky day for me. Lost 2 bucks in a poker game with Greenwald.

14 July 1918. Done some washing. Went to work. Packed some souvenirs for the women friends.

15 July 1918. Today I had to go out for Regiment inspection. The Big Boys viewed us. Saw Tonic Conklin.

16 July 1918. Expecting to leave to go across. Everything is packed.

17 July 1918. Cleaned up all my clothes and tent. The boys cleaned up the camp, ready to move.

18 July 1918. 11:30 everybody lined up for the hike to their train. Left 12:30. Reached train at 3:30 and were on our way to France I guess.

18 July 1918. Next thing I know we were pulling in Baltimore. Next Washington. Wilmington and Philadelphia nearer home every minute. Got off train and slid over to Red Cross and saw Mr. Wilson and sent a couple of cards. Saw the aeroplane mail.

19 July 1918. Detrained. Marched about 9 miles to Camp Merritt. There we were put in Barracks. Immediately telegraphed the old man.

20 July 1918. Had to get our stuff out for inspection, in the meantime the old gent came down. Some glad to see him.

21 July 1918. Everybody came down. I was sure some glad boys to see them.'

22 July 1918. Ma brought me a lemon pie. My favorite. Stayed all day with the folks. Had dinner a M Hall with Pop.

23 July 1918. Issued overseas uniform. Very glad to know we were going over. Worked all night get materials for my squad. Kind of tired out.

24 July 1918. Received my furlough. The old gent came down. Went home with me. The folks were very glad to see me. Made a trip around to see the family. Also hit Jack's lunch about 1:30 o'clock that night. Got filled up.

25 July 1918. Got up from my bunk on the floor. Went to the station to take the 8:45 to Merritt. All the folks were there. Aunt Minine cooked me a chicken. Joe Crawford, Frank and I ate it in Merritt. Some fine feed. All flusterated. Lay down for 2 hours and slept. Woke up and was told to pack everything for the boat. Gave Earl Budd a note that I was going.

26 July 1918. Stayed up all night waiting for orders. We left at 3 Bells. Hiked up the Palisades for 4 or 5 miles. Oh, what a hike. Never will I forget it. Several hundred dropped out from exhaustion. We got on a ferry at Alpine Landing and then for Hoboken. Boarded the Kroonland and set sail about 3:30 in the P. M.

27 July 1918. Sailed and sailed escorted by 6 sub chasers. 1 dirigible, 2 airplanes and a cruiser. We sailed along and picked up 3 more transports from Newport News. We went south all day and still sailing south.

28 July 1918. We looked over the boats and found that we have 6 more transports with us. 2 torpedo destroyers, 1 cruiser. We get up at 4 A.M. every day for raft drill and stay on deck all day some long day. We have 39 on our raft. In the afternoon we all have to strip and have the ocean water turned on us.

29 July 1918. I guess they must have seen a sub or some damn thing as we are sailing at full speed in all directions. Saw lots of flying fish and strange sea animals. Had hose on us again today.

30 July 1918. Oh, the sea is rough. Lots throwing up their meals. But I feel fair that's all. Boy oh boy how it rocks.

31 July 1918. We are still moving about 18 knots an hour going zig zag. No place to go. It's hell to be here with 4000 others. All together I guess there is 45,000 on the ships of our fleet.

1 Aug 1918. We are in the sub danger zone. We were the same as usual. Looking for subs.

2 Aug 1918. Wrote a letter home. Saw lots of large fish jumping out the water. Finland hanging behind. Engine trouble. A sub was sighted. We rode East North and West zig zagging for an hour. Everything was smooth.

3 Aug 1918. Nothing very exciting.

4 Aug 1918. Met our convoy on the European side. Captain read the over sea orders for us. Some crap.

5 Aug 1918. Thinking of seeing land but not yet. Given orders to roll pack. Ship rocking like hell.

6 Aug 1918. Man fell overboard. We tied a red lantern on a raft and threw it over board hoping that he might get on it. The raft was left behind. Kind of cold. At last land was sighted. We pulled in the harbor at Brest about 4 bells. All night unloading.

7 Aug 1918. We marched through the outskirts of Brest to some damn nice wet, swarming lot. We pitched tents and has some bacon for mess.

8 Aug 1918. Some morning. Cold and rain. Only allowed 1 canteen water per man per day. We had some more bacon. and bread today. Roads rotten and filthy. It looks rotten for a start to me.

9 Aug 1918. Nothing real exciting. 3 meals today equal to 2.

10 Aug 1918. Had charge of water detail. Got lots of wine. Spent 7 bucks in the first day. It's unsweetened. Can you imagine 1 canteen water to drink, shave and wash with.

11 Aug 1918. Had my leggings and shoes off for the first time since we left the boat. We had a shower bath at the Napoleon's Barracks. The first in two weeks or more.

12 Aug 1918. I found out where I could by walnuts. I bought 8 qts and F.H. and I ate them. Hungry as hell.

13 Aug 1918. Packed up and left at 8 o'clock. We boarded a train at Brest.

14 Aug 1918. We pulled through St, Nueizen - Gambelle - Reines.

15 Aug 1918. Passed through Touls. Saw lots of Hun prisoners. Passed through Bourgas.

16 Aug 1918. Passed through Dejou where we had eats then we pulled into Isutille and had gas masks issued us. Some was sure going to happen then. Bo Co Hospitals.

17 Aug 1918. Sexey-Aux-Forges. Pulled out of Isutille in the night and hit Toul in the morning. Near Maron where we detrained and marched to Sexey-Aux-Forges where we are quartered in Billets and cow barns. Plenty of wine but little food. Can't buy any either.

18 Aug 1918. Went to Nancey and damn near got court martialed. But I had a hard line of - - -.

19 Aug 1918. Drilled this afternoon. Wrote several letters home. Ha ha. The first sign of war. An airplane battle and a bombing party just raise hell. Some air fight. The Anti air craft put the Kibosh on those damn Huns.

20 Aug 1918. Another raid on Nancey. The bombs killed 30 and hurt 27. Had gas masks drill today putting on in six seconds. A raid overhead. You can hear the tap tap tit tit of the machine guns on the planes. Anti-aircraft had search lights on them.

21 Aug 1918. Drilled all day in gas mask and Skirmish - Extended order. Went in for a bath in Kiel Canal.

22 Aug 1918. Drill all day. Same as usual. Wrote several letters.

23 Aug 1918. Drilled all morning and had some battle in P.M.

24 Aug 1918. Rained in A.M. Went to Pont St. Vincent in the afternoon, also hailed while I was there. I looked the bomb barded buildings over. Some night.

25 Aug 1918. Expecting to move at any moment.

26 Aug 1918. Had another [?] battle and went wandering in the mountains.

27 Aug 1918. Drilled in the morning. Went for a hike in the afternoon down one side of the Canal and up the other side. Then we went down to the river and took a bath and Brockway got drowned. [Brockway, Roy F, PVT, Co. H 51st PIR.] I swam and tried to find him when went down but they didn't find him until late in the evening.

28 Aug 1918. Drilled all day. Held funeral service. We went to Moran in the evening. Came back and went to bed.

29 Aug 1918. Drilled all day until 3 o'clock when we packed up ready to move. At 4 o'clock we strarted to hike. Hiked all night until 4 in the morning when we pulled into a lot and rolled up in the blankets and slept until 8 o'clock. We had N.T. and coffee which we made ourselves. We packed up and hiked until 2 o'clock when we pulled into Troussey.

and found billets in barns. We passed through a tunnel about 1 1/2 miles and it was dark. We could see flashes of the big guns far away.

1 Sep 1918. Getting cool and feels like fall. We cleaned up the village streets.

2 + 3 Sep 1918. Cold and foggy. Walked to Pagney. Met some Salvation Army women. Bought candy. We had orders to pack up again and left at 7 and hiked ten miles. We landed into barrack near Toul. I also left the Co. and roamed to Toul. Had air raid last night, shelled hell out of our barracks, just like hailing in a thunder storm. But the Auto Craft brought one of the German planes down ass over head. Killed the 2 men.

4 SEP 1918. They split the Co. up, some on K.P. some ammunition dump and etc.

5 SEP 1918. I am one of the few left behind at Toul.

6 Sep 1918. Charge of K.P. today. Just got barracks bag. Another detail just left to move ammunition.

7 Sep 1918. I went to the R[ed] Cross where I had some cocoa, donuts. Gas mask drill. Went over to Y.M.C.A. (French) (Made today.).

8 Sep 1918. Roamed until I was tired.

9 Sep 1918. Had gas mask drill for one hour. We loose our bags today. 51st had entertainment at the French Y.M.C.A. also Mrs. and Mr. Rutherford from Denver gave us a good time. After everything was over I went to bed.

10 Sep 1918. Orders to pack up and give our beds to Frogs. We stayed out in the rain. Hell of a night.

11 – 12 Sep 1918. We hiked through Toul on way to the front. We stopped about a mile from the German trenches. In mud up to our ass. At 1 o'clock the artillery started to open up for the St. Mihiel drive. We went direction back of the Infantry - Rain Bow Div. and followed them and built the road for the artillery to advance. We filled in the Von Hindenburg trenches with dirt and trees and everything. Advanced. Then I went burying the dead - Searching dugouts and watching the tanks advance. Also, the infantry. Great sight. Oh, what a drive. 17 kilometers. Only part of the Co. were here. At night we lay under fire. I got 16 picks and laid them close together and laid on them so as not to lay on the wet ground. Start to cut stakes for barb wire and Geo Yeager and I was between the

13 - 14 Sep 1918. 1 + 2 lines piling stakes. The Huns were only on the kill but they didn't do much firing just then. It was a great sight to see the French women and children that the Americans made the Huns relieve in their drive. They were very happy.

14 Sep 1918. We hiked from St. Mihiel to another New Front. We had to dig in. We used a captured German Balloon shed for a kitchen. We had fine eats with the 117 Engr's.

15 Sep 1918. Slept in a truck with my blanket around me. We took stakes to the lines her also. While shells were bursting all around. The second wave where I was I lost everything except what I had in my pockets in this drive.

16 Sep 1918. Still sleeping in trenches unconcerned as hell. Heavy fire in action. Hear things of all kinds going through the air over our head.

17 Sep 1918. Still in trenches sleeping evenings. Shells and planes going over head all the time. In the night we were hiked back to Paunes and Bery where we were loaded in trucks. Slept in dugout under house.

18 Sep 1918. Arrived in Toul Barracks again and home never looked sweeter. Wrote home my experience in the drive.

The 51 Band gave us a reception and were glad to see us back safe. Not all of us, but most of us.

19 Sep 1918. Roamed to Toul at the Red Cross and got clean underwear and socks and cocoa and sandwich and also a bath. A great treat. Received a letter from home.

20 Sep 1918. Received my first pay in this land 115 Francs. Then all hell couldn't find me. I celebrated my good luck. We packed up and hiked 20 miles. Night half shot to boot.

21 Sep 1918. Stayed in field until 2 bells and 5:30 pulled in woods and pitched tents. Packed up and passed through Griscourt and landed in Fey En Hey.

22 Sep 1918. Packed up and hiked toward the front. Saw A. Kiener, had a talk, then we went to a lot and picked tents the other side of shrapnel corner.

23 Sep 1918. At S. Corner the Red + [Cross] had a place in a building and I had hot cocoa. While talking with F.G.,A.K., G.Y. and some others, a shell landed very close nearby hitting G. Yeager Bro. It shot the mud all over him. The shell came around S. Corner all the time but we still get our hot cocoa.

24 Sep 1918. Worked on road. A Keenes came along on his truck. I stopped him and he had a canteen of beer. Of course I didn't take any. While the men were picking, one of them hit a grenade and it wounded three of them. They were sent to the hospital in ambulance from the front. Only over the hill.

25 Sep 1918. Worked on Fey En Hay road. Saw 7 Hun planes bring down 1 English plane right over our head. The pilot was shot 7 times but bought the machine down safe. The mechanic was dead. A letter from home today.

26 Sep 1918. Worked on road- ambulances bringing wounded in by the hundreds quite a battle on tonight.

27 Sep 1918. Continued work on road. Shells still coming over.

28 Sep 1918. Worked on road. Issued chocolate, 5 cigs and a package of chewing gum at mess tonight.

29 Sep 1918. Rained all day. Worked on road. No artillery could advance. Rain all the time and work of Pozaner all night. Good cause. We should worry.

30 Sep 1918. Rather cold - road work all day. Wrote home by candle light.

1 Oct 1918. Went near the line with 20 men to fill in shell holes that were made during the night by shells. They had the range on the road and as fast as we filled them in, they would drop one somewhere else. Got orders to have every man in dugouts. Drive coming off. **Huns sent over gas.** For 2 hours. All had our masks on. No one hurt this time.

2 Oct 1918. We came out of the dugout and thought we would sleep in the tent about 10 o'clock. F.H. and I were the only 2 left in tents. But we had to get in a dugout. For the shells came all around us one after the other, you should of seen us haul ass. We lost everything. We heard Bulgaria has laid down arms and Turkey is all in.

3 Oct 1918. Worked on road. British reported to have taken Lt. Quinten and are on way to Cambria. All kinds of bets on Peace just now. We are working union hours.

4 Oct 1918. Three more men hurt today from reckless ways. Pulling the string on a Hun grenade. Lots of Hun planes cause over today I was in Death Valley.

5 Oct 1918. Worked on road. No shells coming over but lots going over. That means it is time us to advance nearer the infantry.

6 Oct 1918. We moved our watch back 1 hour. Had today off to rest up in. Well we were driven out of our tents again and they ripped tents up. Blankets and all. Damn good thing we got out when we did for a shell hit the tree at which my tent was at the bottom.

7 Oct 1918. Rain all day. Worked on the road. Found a fine dugout for Joe Yaeger, Frank and I. Had a great time singing. We had some chocolate also.

8 Oct 1918. We packed up in the rain and hiked to a wood and found a fine officer's dugout. Concrete - stove and a Barracks in it. It's great. No shell came come in unless it comes in the door which faces the Hun lines. The shells go over and come in front but they don't bother the dugout.

9 Oct 1918. Started a new road to the front. We heated some water in the dugout and washed at night. Just like home. But no place to go. But to bed.

10 Oct 1918. Had a great sleep last night. We went on the road with the men. Saw a great air battle in which the Huns brought down 1 French plane. Our plane had photos of different tours. I hooked them from the wreckage.

12 Oct 1918. Two Coast Artillery guns 10 + 12" are just outside our dugout and when they shoot- good night. We worked on road to Thiacourt. We got hold of a can of jam and it was great.

13 Oct 1918. Day off. Sent home slip for Xmas Box. A rumor that Germany is withdrawing. Fuzzy gave us some of his talent and a few songs and we passed the night away smoking and signing.

14 Oct 1918. Worked all night and day on road last night. The gas alarm was sounded but didn't get any of the gas. But we all

put our masks on and left Joe sleeping. We forgot him and never awoke him. Received word that Germany will withdraw his troops.

15 Oct 1918. Played duce poker every night. The boys got me for 50 last night. Worked on the road again.

16 Oct 1918. Rained all day and night. We worked on road all day. Played poker all again until 2 o'clock in the evening.

17 Oct 1918. Worked on stone quarry. Lots of Hun planes flying around too high to shot at. Played some more poker. Wrote home. Had fine sleep.

18 Oct 1918. Worked on road. Saw 30 of our planes in a bunch. God help the Kaiser when they drop their load. German shells drove us from work for 4 hours. We are using a can of bacon grease with a shoe string for a wick. That's our lamp.

19 Oct 1918. Worked on road. Rumor Allies have captured Ostend and Lilli and Huns are evacuating Bourges.

20 Oct 1918. Rained all day. Stayed in. Played cards and wrote home. Rousted to a walk and dug up 5 bottles of Wine. We had a comedy.

21 Oct 1918. Worked on road between Rennyville and Limey about 9 o'clock. All the guns along the front opened up. They are giving Huns hell.

22 Oct 1918. Nothing new. Worked on road.

23 Oct 1918. Started a new plank road. Some road.

24 Oct 1918. S.o.S. Played poker.

25 Oct 1918. Worked on road and saw lots of air battles all day. Had underwear issued. Ho Ray.

26 Oct 1918. Worked on road and roamed woods for souvenirs. Saw some trench mortars.

27 Oct 1918. Sick as hell - cold - lost my hearing for two weeks. Played cards and hung around camp. Went to Noveont and got some cigars.

28 Oct 1918. Worked on road. We sent over quite a barrage.

29 Oct 1918. On road. Heard Austria laid down arms. Hun planes still coming over.

30 Oct 1918. Worked on road. Hun planes thick as hell. The looks of things. Germany has us outnumbered in planes as they come over when they darn please. They brought down one of ours today and forced another to land.

31 Oct 1918. Still on road Air filled with all kinds of planes. H. Craw came over and we played poker, took him over the top for about 50 Francs.

Lt. Gilbert shell shocked came to sleep in our dugout as it the safest in the woods.

1 Nov 1918. Heavy fog - one could cut it with a knife. No planes today - at ease. Cox came over and we played poker. Gilbert taken back to the rest camp. Ho Ray.

2 Nov 1918. Worked on road. Gave 25 France for a cake of chocolate. Heard Turkey surrendered. Peace looks near.

3 Nov 1918. Over slept. Got hell from Captain. Played cards. Saw lots of planes. Sgt. Slatin shell shocked. Gone to a rest camp. A cootie bit hell out of me.

4 Nov 1918. Worked on road. Paper stated Kaiser had advocated [abducated?]. Received mail from home. Feeling fine. Fuzzy is got the itch.

5 Nov 1918. Election day. Vote for Smith. That's who I am betting on him.

Lots of Huns shells flying around just now. They shot down 3 of our balloons today.

6 Nov 1918. Worked on road. Had more has alarms. Plenty of amusements in the shell line.

7 Nov 1918. Heavy fog. No planes. Went to Vieville. Saw some old Krupp guns. Austrian armistice terms were signed.

8 Nov 1918. On road again. We fired on Hun planes which were in range but they kept on moving.

9 Nov 1918. German spy arrested - dressed as an officer. Three other planes disguised as allies were around here and got away with murder. The bastards. Heard Germany was given 72 hours to sign armistice. Went in shelled church at Vieville. -Remyville completely ruined. Not a building left. Looks like hell hit it.

10 Nov 1918. Called a 4 o'clock in the morning with rifle and belt and pulled in back of the line in case of a drive or counter attack. We laid there most of the day and then came back so were sure that Germany had signed the Armistice. Sent out patrols 12 kilometers and the Germans had evacuated - Ho Ray.

11 Nov 1918. Ordered to stick around in case the Huns should start something. Heavy barrage until 11 o'clock. We sent over a million $ [to] one Kaiser gets kicked out.

12 Nov 1918. Ordered to police the woods, then went out and worked on the plank road again. No shells or planes. Everything quiet.

13 Nov 1918. No noise - don't seem natural. Ground frozen. Every troop had a fire. you could see lights all over the land. The first fire we ever saw outside of the dugout. The Huns had a machine gun in the church steeple at Beville also observation port.

14 Nov 1918. Worked on road and blowing up German mines. And getting organized again.

15 Nov 1918. Cold and windy. Drilled in morning. Worked on road in afternoon. Going to move into German lands. We are in the Provauell Woods and Euvizene Woods.

16 Nov 1918. Drilled all morning. Got orders to move at noon. We hiked forward Germany through Thiacourt, Xammes. I stayed up all night by a fire too cold to sleep. Awful wind blowing.

17 Nov 1918. Every body up and on the move at 5. Hiked all say throguh the Chambly- St. Julian Sponville and stayed in Suzemont. Had to break ice in canteen to get a drink of water.

18 Nov 1918. Started to hike at 7 and hiked 18 kilometers through Jeandelize, Branville to Thumereville where we pulled in German barracks and stayed the rest of the day conditions in Barracks filthy and rotten.

19 Nov 1918. Snowed a little for the first. On guard at . Thumereville. Got paid again. Ho Ray.

20 Nov 1918. Still on guard. Nothing very exciting. Went through German saw mill. The rest of Regiment joins us. Sleeping in pup tent with Joe Durland.

21 Nov 1918. Started Hiking 7:30. Hiked all day going through villages decorated with French and American flags. Mouaville Fleville - Auaux. Ate mess at Meuceiselles - Tucquegnieux and billeted in Trieux.

22 Nov 1918. Mostly missing towns that we passed through. Started hiking at 8 and crossing German at Lorine Luie going through Lommerauge and Feutsch. Not inhabited. Billeted in Wollermeringin where beer was plenty and we kept hiking. I had a fine time there and got a German watch here also.

23 Nov 1918. Left at 8 o'clock hiking until 1 o'clock landing in Aspelt which is in Luxembourg. I was to Luxembourg the 24th and had a fine time.

24 - 25 – 26 - 27 Nov 1918. Still in Aspelt. Drilling five hours a day and we got lots of wine. Just signed the pay roll. While writing this book I was asked to have supper with the boys. It was fine. Frank and I are in a hay loft. Tomorrow Thanksgiving. Good night.

28 Nov 1918. Thanksgiving - Roast Beef. Misty day. No place like home.

[The days in between are filled with issues with billeting and playing cards. From here on, only selected items are included.]

3 Dec 1918. Started from Wormelding En Anuitt.

4 Dec 1918. Started to hike and hiked all day until 6 o'clock until we struck Fohren. Passed through Mivralich, Waldtung, Frixes, across river to Trier [?] and passed Belliview and passing through [ ] , then Ehranf and Briset and then to Fohren. Some hike 29 kilometers. Rain all day. Some mud. Billeted in cow barn. Had 4 meals in 3 days.

5 Dec 1918. Lazed around all morning in the damn rain. Got a fine cold. Oh, hell. We packed up and hiked 14 kilometers and now with a German family. They gave me coffee and bread. This town is Salmrohr. I am off to bed (floor). So long.

6 Dec 1918. Still in Salmrohr on guard. Done lots of writing home. Fair weather. Slept fine.

7 Dec 1918. On guard all night - feel shaggy today. I needed all day sleeping 2 hours all night. This is the end of a perfect day. Tired out. Received 12 letters from home town. stayed up all night answering them.

8 Dec 1918. On guard again. First time in history they put corporals on guard duty. 1 meal all day again. The food is rotten.

9 Dec 1918. Nothing very interesting. On guard duty again. Guarding R.R. for U.S. troops to ride to Coblenz from Luxembourg. I am thinking of going around world as I am this far. This is not the army of occupation, it is the army of starvation. Enough said.

10 Dec 1918. Came off guard duty 8 bells. Family stuck a pig. Rain this P.M. Ran out of rations. Wrote 14 letters.

13 + 14 Dec 1918. Hiked all morning. Taken to Cochem in trucks. All most had a fit. Cochem to Guls by Isenbaum. Given beds with the German family. They seem to be fine.

25 Dec 1918. Xmas. No use putting down in book. Should never forget it.

26 Dec 1918. Attack acute indigestion. In bed 3 days.

30 Dec 1918. Getting ready for 31 – Sylvester's Day. Every day is Sunday. Had pictures taken in Guls.

4 Jan 1919. Not much news only a Revolution in Berlin. Let them revolt as long they keep quiet in Guls.

8 Jan 1919. We had an issue of new uniforms and it looks like homeward bound. but I don't think so. S.O.S.

9 Jan 1919. Wrote a letter to Rose Cox on the Orange County Herald. Heard [Theodore] Roosevelt is dead.

COMPANY H

Frank E. Weeks, was a sergeant in Company H of the 51st Pioneer Infantry. A letter that he wrote to Col Moses Thisted was published in "Pershing's Pioneers."

Weeks did not remember the exact date, but it was probably in January 1918 that most of the old New York National Guard 10th Infantry was transferred to regiments of the 27th Division, leaving only a skeleton of the NYNG 10th Infantry with the non-commissioned and commanding officers. Drafted men were used to form the 51st Pioneer Infantry. These draftees had to be made into soldiers.

In his letter, he talked about the action that he saw in the Woerve Section, the St. Mihiel Offensive, Meuse Argonne and later on the Moselle and Rhine Rivers with the 51st Pioneers were part of the Army of Occupation of Germany. He wrote:

"In the St. Mihiel drive I was one of the sergeants in charge of a platoon that was assigned to action in the trenches. We were to crawl over the top and blow up the barb wire for our infantry to advance. We then went over with the advancing infantry. The sergeant with me remarked, 'Frank, some of us are not coming back.' Well, he was right. As we were advancing the Huns machine gunned us. I yelled to him, 'Bill, duck.' You know what he said. I ducked into a shell hole. He was hit and killed right next to me. His last words were "Look out". Then as we advanced one of the privates stepped on the German barbed wire and was electrocuted. I was lucky. I stepped on the same wire but apparently did not cause a circuit."

He went on to describe how he was gassed during the St. Mihiel Offensive:

"We reached a patch of woods where there was a West Point captain in command of a detachment of the 89th Division. I requested to join them to which he agreed. I had my men dig small entrenchments in zig zag lines for protection from exploding shells. The captain notified us that the Germans were about to attack us and to hold our ground no matter what happens. I had a picture of my mother on me and I looked at it and said this may be good bye. Well we managed to send some machine gunners to the end of the woods and they sent a number of machine gun blasts which apparently changed the Germans minds about attacking. It was here that I received a dose of gas. After over a week of living on raw bacon, hard tack and chewing coffee beans, the captain gave us permission to work our way back to our outfit in the rear of us. One at a time we worked our way back and forth and landed in a barn full of hay where they bombed hell out of us."

When he and his men rejoined their outfit, he decided to stay with his buddies, rather than go to the hospital. He refused to go to the hospital in spite of his commanding officer's wishes.

They continued constructing roads to the front lines, etc., and then went on to the Argonne.

After the war, he regretted this decision when he experienced trouble with his throat and chest. Without hospital records to document his injuries from the gas, he had trouble with getting medical services from the Veterans Bureau. He had to track down his former commanding officer, who was able to confirm his story that he had been gassed. He had a throat operation and also some bones removed from his nose to improve his breathing, and received a 10% disability rating.

COMPANY K

These photos are labeled "Company K" and are both from April 1919. The 51st Pioneer Infantry newspaper on 19 April 1919 gave a listing of the Company K players. In the first inter-company baseball game in the Third Battalion series played at Guls, Company I defeated Company K by a score of 9-1. Company K had the following players: 3rd Base: Pratt; Short Stop: Robinson; Left Field: McIntosh; Center Field: Loffin [Laffin]; 1st Base: Hinds; 2nd Base: O'Shea; Right Field: Troy; Center: Vitzer [Yetzer]; Pitcher: Parfitt.

Company K 51st Pioneer Infantry, April 1919, Courtesy of James and Eric Waxman.

Company K 51st Pioneer Infantry, April 1919, Courtesy of James and Eric Waxman.

THE PIONEERS

We read about the doughboys and their valor, which is true,
And of the gallant part they played for the old Red, White, And Blue:
We read about the H.F. A. and their ever-roaring guns,
Also the heavy part they played in blowing up the Huns;
The Infantry, the Cavalry, the hardy Engineers,
But we never read a single word about "The Pioneers".

They slept in pup tents in the cold and worked in mud and mire,
They filled up shell holes in the roads, 'most always under fire;
Far o'er the lines the scout plane goes, directing the barrage,
Just as zero hour draws nigh, or just before the charge.
As o'er the top the doughboy goes, to put the Hun to tears,
But who went out and cut the wire? "The Husky Pioneers."

They buried beaucoup horses and carried beaucoup shells.
From every dump on every front, the kind of work that tells.
A heavy pack on every back, on every track in France,
They never wore the "Croix de Guerre"- They never had a chance.
And as the heavy trucks rolled by, they worked to calm their fears.
Who made the rocky roads so smooth? "The same old Pioneers."

Each branch deserves much credit, and I like to read their praise,
We helped them all, both great and small, in many different ways;
The Shock Troops and brave Marines, the Ammunition Train,
The Signal Corps, the Tank Corps, and the Observation Plane.
The War is won, the work is done, so here's three hearty cheers,
For the outfit that I soldiered with, "The Good Old PIONEERS."

(By One of Them)

From "Philadelphia in the World War, 1914-1919", Philadelphia War History Committee, Wynkoop, Hollenback and Crawford, New York, 1922, Page 773.

Final Thoughts

As I sit to write these final thoughts, I am filled with gratitude to all the people I have met along this journey. A shout out goes to all those who contributed pictures, stories, knowledge and encouragement during this project. You may never know how energizing it was to connect with you, especially through social media.

It has been challenging to seek out all the sources and places where information about the 51st Pioneers has been tucked away. It is certainly rewarding to be able to combine what I have learned and share it with other descendants of these men and all others who are interested in their role in "The Great War For Civilization".

As this project progressed, it felt more and more like time travel. Through their diaries, letters and newspaper articles, the soldiers' words reached me across the century that has passed, sharing what it was to be a soldier in the Great War, as well as a 51st Pioneer Infantryman. I followed them through a monumental year of their lives.

My goal with this book is for it to also be useful as a reference in my further studies of the 51st Pioneer Infantry Regiment. Hopefully, the future holds more places where additional pieces of their story are saved. My sincerest hope is that more finds come my way and yours.

The 51st Pioneer Infantry can be found at:

On the web at: http://51stPioneers.com

On Facebook at: https://www.facebook.com/51stPioneerInfantry

On Twitter at: @51stPioneerInf

To learn more about Dr. McMahon's books, https://www.amazon.com/author/margaret.m.mcmahon

FIFTY-SEVENTH ANNUAL

R E U N I O N

★ 51st ★
Pioneer Infantry Association

KINGSTON, NEW YORK

Saturday and Sunday, September 13, 14, 1980

Proceedings of the FIFTY-SEVENTH ANNUAL REUNION
HELD AT
THE HOLIDAY INN, Kingston, New York

With the centennial of the United States' involvement in the War to End All Wars (World War I), our thoughts turn to those ancestors who defended our freedom. This book will show you how to learn about the military service of your U.S. Army ancestors using archives, online resources, social networking and other resources. Learn ways to share what you learn to with others.

This book covers seven days of genealogical research activities. The book includes things to do before and after the week. The book includes hints, web sites, and search terms useful for all the activities. Topics in the book complement Dr. McMahon's popular classes and lectures. The web is always her starting place to look for information about her ancestors and their lives. Web pages may contain records, data or the indexes that help locate records at a repository. Margaret M. McMahon is known as the hockey-playing genealogist. She has a PhD in Computer Science and Engineering. She has amassed over thirty years of engineering experience, including being a college and graduate school professor. She is an experienced presenter at national and international technical conferences. With the advent of parenthood, she turned her technical talents to researching her family's genealogy. She researches, lectures and writes about genealogy. Dr. McMahon has been an invited speaker at many genealogical societies and conferences in the Washington D.C.-Baltimore area, as well as several branches of her local Public Library.

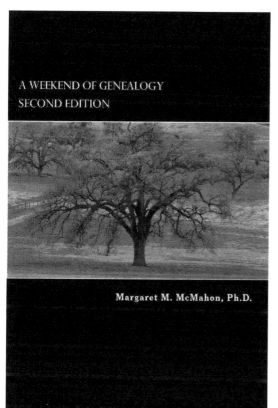

This book focuses on a weekend of genealogical research activities centered on the U.S. Federal Census and Internet searching. Activities for before and after the weekend are also included. "A Weekend of Genealogy" has been written to complement Dr. McMahon's popular classes and lectures. The book includes hints, websites, and search terms that will be useful for your research. Get ready to spend a weekend hunting for your ancestors using the records and techniques described in the book!

Made in the USA
Middletown, DE
20 September 2019